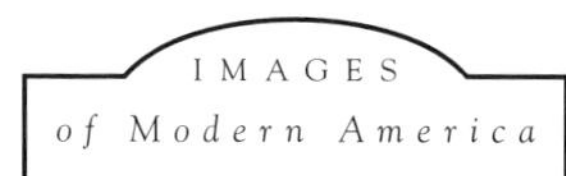

OREGON SURFING
NORTH COAST

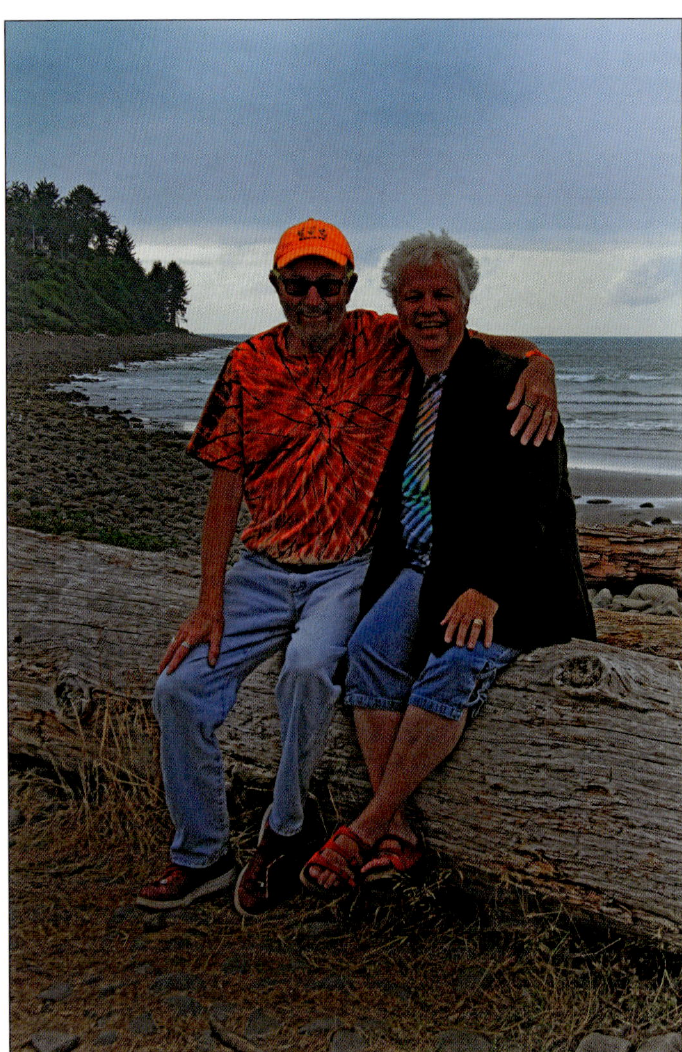

Scott Blackman began surfing the summer of 1964 at Agate Beach and was the first surfer along the central Oregon coast. He helped found the Agate Beach Surf Club and discovered his passion for photography. He has been visually documenting the Oregon coast and surfing for over five decades. Sandy Blackman was a teacher and counselor for the Lincoln County School District for 32 years. Sandy, who enjoys writing, is a successful writer and storyteller. After retiring, she and Scott started an art business together in 2005, selling their art in galleries, gift shops, and craft shows. Scott's images are featured in magazines, calendars, books, posters, and various print media. The Blackmans were inspired to tell the story of Oregon's North Coast after working with surfers on their first book, *Oregon Surfing: Central Coast.*

On the Front Cover:
Clockwise from top left: Perry Shoemake, the Point (photograph by Tim Mack); Mark Hansen, Tibby Utter, and Jerry Alto at Seaside (courtesy of Mark Hansen); 1960s and 1970s vintage surfboards (courtesy of Josh Gizdavich and Cleanline Surf Shop); Knox Swanson, kneeboarding at the Point (photograph by Tim Mack); Ron Hill and Randy Barna at Pacific City (courtesy of Randy Barna)

On the Back Cover:
Clockwise from top left: Pacific City surfers Glenn Kellow, Gerry Day, John Benson, and Kani Rowlands (photograph by Gerry Day); Jack Brown at the Cove (photograph by Lexie Hallahan); Bill Barnfield at Seaside (photograph by Dan Matthews)

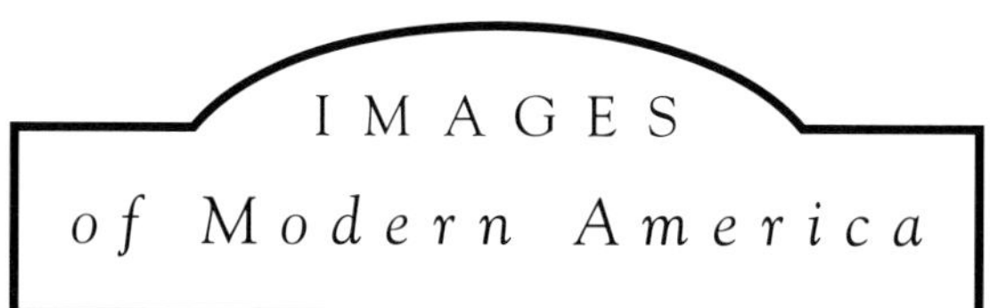

OREGON SURFING NORTH COAST

Scott and Sandy Blackman

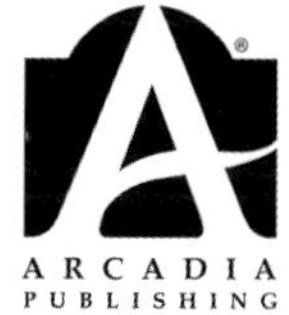

ISBN 978-1-4671-1532-2

Published by Arcadia Publishing
Charleston, South Carolina

Printed in the United States of America

Library of Congress Control Number: 2015946012

For all general information, please contact Arcadia Publishing:
Telephone 843-853-2070
Fax 843-853-0044
E-mail sales@arcadiapublishing.com
For customer service and orders:
Toll-Free 1-888-313-2665

Visit us on the Internet at www.arcadiapublishing.com

To Dana Williams, Dick Wald, and the pioneer surfers who followed their passion and surfed the cold waters of Oregon.

Contents

ACKNOWLEDGMENTS

Our research started three years ago. Two individuals helped kick start this project: Tim Mack, who donated 200 images from the early days of surfing, and Perry Shoemake, who networked with surfers, recommending us and the project. Their support was invaluable to us. Three individuals gave technology support. Our daughter-in-law Valerie Lemmon set up our Facebook page, which enabled us to share stories and images and communicate with the surfing community. Sherry Vachio, Dana Williams's wife, helped answer questions and did online research, making information more accurate. Debie Howe, our computer specialist, kept us up and running, supporting us with her skills. The surfing community has embraced us and contributed in so many ways that it is difficult to single out everyone. We have listened, laughed, and videotaped close to 50 north-coast surfers. Some of them are featured at the end of chapter three. We have received thousands of images, articles, and memorabilia over three years. We regret that only a portion will be in the book. All the other images and stories will eventually be found on Facebook at Oregon Surfing: Past and Present. Recognition must be given to a few special individuals, including George Daggatt, who collected and compiled early surfing images into a photo album. Five decades later, the album is an irreplaceable resource preserving surfing history. Many of those images are in our book. Knox Swanson has been a true collector of surfing memorabilia since the 1970s. Dick Wald videotaped surfing with an eight-millimeter camera and shared his footage over the years. Dellanne McGregor and David Matthews provided accommodations during our research visits. Jeff Hull, Perry Shoemake, and Mike Burger were our historians and fact checkers. We are grateful to the entire surfing community for sharing and being a part of our lives. It has been an enjoyable, educational, and life-affirming ride for us. We appreciate everyone's support, be it large or small. Your amusing stories and refreshing comments have enriched our book and helped us to historically document a small wave of Oregon's surfing along the North Coast.

Introduction

Oregon surfing began in 1962 at Indian Beach within the Ecola State Park, north of Cannon Beach. Seaside and Cannon Beach had laws prohibiting the use of floatable devices at the beaches within the city limits. This law prevented surfing until Dana Williams sought permission from the Seaside City Council to allow surfing from Avenue U to the Tillamook Headlands. Cannon Beach lifted its restrictions in 1967. Once the laws were changed, surfing began in earnest, first at Seaside's Cove in 1963 and at the Point in 1964. Seaside became the hotbed of surfing starting in the 1960s and continues today. Producing a world-class left along the West Coast, it attracted many surfers who have stayed and spread out along the northern coast.

Credit must be given to the various surfers, board makers, and surf shops who helped advance the sport of surfing in Oregon during the early days. Dana Williams, more than any other individual, was in the right place at the right time. Williams, a San Diego surfer finishing his last hitch in the military, was assigned to Tongue Point, near Astoria, in the early 1960s. He discovered young Seaside teenagers who wanted to learn how to surf. He mentored and influenced many over the years, organizing the Seaside Surfing Association (SSA) in 1963.

From Portland, Dick Wald, a self-proclaimed adrenaline junkie who was married with two small children, left skin diving and started surfing. In January 1964, Dana and Dick recognized the Point wave. Dick returned and is credited with being the first to surf the Point in October 1964. The Point was a high quality wave that broke to the rider's left. Dick encouraged others to surf the Point, and many were soundly thrashed or damaged their boards on the rocky beach. Leashes on boards were not invented until the early 1970s. Gary Hansen, a Seaside High School student, surfed with Wald and is credited with being the first local to surf the Point. Other locals began to surf it, and the word spread about the Point. Soon surfers from around Oregon, Washington, California, and Hawaii came to surf the challenging left.

As surf clubs began to form, surf contests became popular in the mid-1960s. Seaside's first contest was held at the Cove on February 20, 1966. It was sponsored by OSD Sea Lions, a local skin-diving club. The Seaside riots during Labor Day weekend in 1963–1965 inadvertently contributed to surf contests. The city fathers, wanting to offer alternatives to rioting, worked with the SSA members to sponsor surf contests during Labor Day weekend for several years starting in 1966. Soon, other surf contests were being held at Seaside's Cove, Indian Beach, Short Sands, and Pacific City that were sponsored by surf clubs, surf shops, and organizations along the North Coast. Surf contests faded after the early 1970s in the Seaside area. Yearly surf contests in Pacific City started up again with Bob Ledbetter in 1998 and continue today with Moment Surf Company co-owners Jeff Mollencop and Ben Johnson.

Board makers began to gravitate to Seaside. The first two notable ones in the early 1960s were Jim Sagawa and Bob Jensen. Sagawa moved to Oregon from Hawaii to attend dental school at Oregon Health and Science University and made boards in Portland. His boards were called SAG, an abbreviation of his last name. Sagawa was a Point rider with Dick Wald in the early days. Bob

Jensen, a board maker for Morey-Pope and Gordon and Smith, brought his two young sons and wife from Southern California. Living up a remote logging road outside Seaside, Jensen made boards and glassed them in his home. A 1960s Jensen board won at a raffle by the Ter Har family has been on display for five decades at their Seaside clothing store. It has never been used.

Many surf shops along the North Coast have come and gone over the last 50 years, but three of them are worth noting. The very first surf shop in Seaside was owned and operated by brothers Jim and Bill Theiring of Coos Bay. The shop, located on Broadway Street, was open from Memorial Day weekend to Labor Day weekend for three summers between 1964 and 1966. Bill would close the Seaside Surf Shop and reopen it in Coos Bay the rest of the year using the same name. As early entrepreneurs of surfing, the Theiring brothers owned surf shops in Coos Bay, Seaside, Portland, and Santa Cruz, California, in the 1960s. Jim lived in and ran the Santa Cruz surf shop, sending boards to Bill, who ran the shops in Oregon. The Theirings were among of the first to sponsor surf movies. They financed Bruce Brown's visit to Oregon to show his movie *Endless Summer* at Portland's Benson High School and at Oregon's first surf contest in Coos Bay, in June 1965.

Santa Cruz surfer Art Spence, Seasider Jerry Harrington, and Portlanders Dan Matthews and Tim Foley became known as the Tillamook Head crew. Beginning in the late 1960s, the crew lived together and ran their surfing business intermittently in Nehalem Valley and Seaside. California surfer Bill Barnfield joined them before moving to Hawaii to become a well-known board maker. Lanny Shuler joined the group in 1971. The surfers who came together under this logo made boards that were experimental at a time when the surfing industry was moving from longboards to much shorter and more maneuverable boards. That they were locals who lived and made boards in Seaside was also part of the allure. There was a great pulling away from big-name, mass-produced boards. Boards built in backyards and garages became very popular during this era.

The last surf shop of note was Cleanline Surf Shops in Seaside and Cannon Beach, for their longevity. Cleanline in Seaside was started by Josh Gizdavich and his business partner of two years, Jack Molan. Gizdavich was a local boy who started surfing in the 1960s. Seaside's Cleanline shop opened in August 1980 and celebrated its 35th year in business with Gizdavich in 2015. Many North Coast surf shops were open as a way to purchase surfing equipment at a discount, experiment with board making, or support surfers' passion for surfing. Many shops disappeared as fast as they arrived. Today's surf shops are run with good business sense and have more staying power. Cleanline is unusual for its expansion of two shops, in Cannon Beach and Seaside, and for its longevity in what is now a crowded and competitive field.

Two other individuals must be given credit for their tenacity and presence in North Coast surfing. Bruce Prator came to Seaside to follow his passion of surfing big waves around 1970. For over three decades, he dominated the Point and discovered Second Point. Jack Brown passed away in February 2015 in his 90s. He surfed almost daily from his 50s until his late 80s, role modeling his love of surfing and becoming a living legend along the North Coast.

Surfing has become so popular that the favorite surf spots of Seaside, Cannon Beach, Indian Beach, Short Sands, and Pacific City swell with crowds during certain periods. But the world-class wave of the Point is the most dominant wave, making Seaside the center of surfing along the North Coast of Oregon.

One

Seaside's Pioneer Surfers

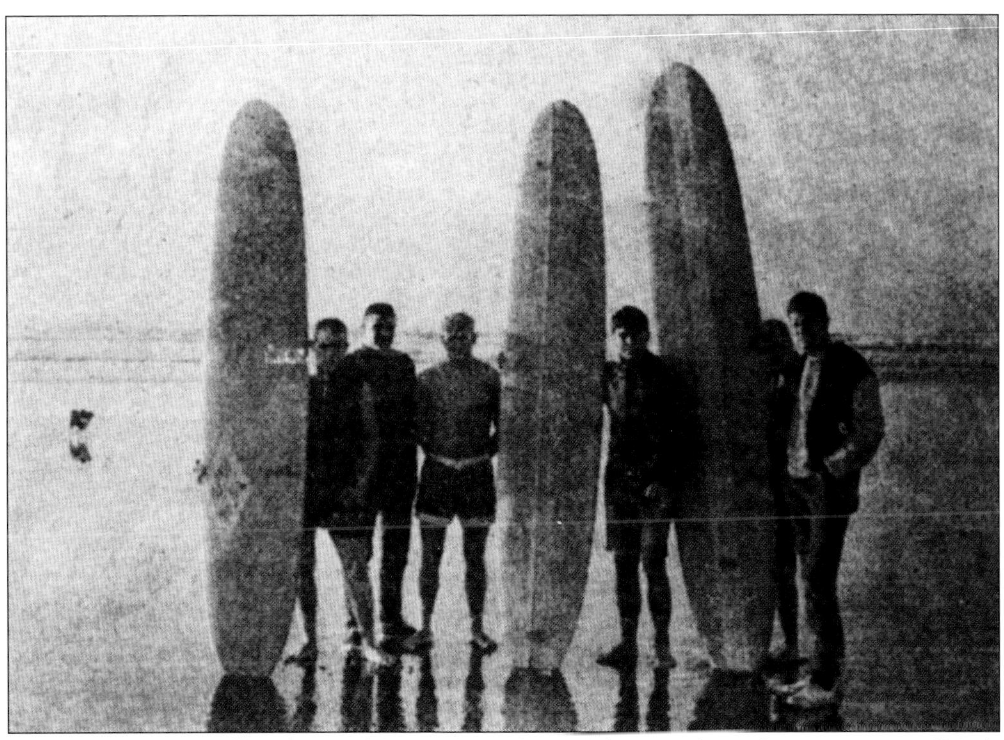

A 1963 article in the *Seaside Signal* featured members of the Seaside Surfing Association (SSA). From left to right are Jerry Alto, Dana Williams (president), John Alto, George Nelson, Tibby Utter, and Mark Hansen. Charter members not pictured are Joe Camberg, Mike Zalk, Ed Hendrickson, Norm Wilcox, John Spence, and Bill Forness. Seaside teens discovered surfing in the summer of 1962 when they met San Diego surfer Dana Williams, who was stationed with the Navy at Tongue Point near Astoria. Williams recalls, "In 1961, I was surfing Fort Stevens, South Jetty, both sides and sandbars. In 1963, we were part of Hoppy Swartz's USSA [United States Surfing Association] and the third club to form." Tibby Utter remembers, "We spent time at Dana's Seaside house talking about surfing, girls, looking at surf magazines and drinking wine." More locals joined the SSA throughout the decade until the club disbanded in the late 1960s. (Courtesy of Jerry Alto.)

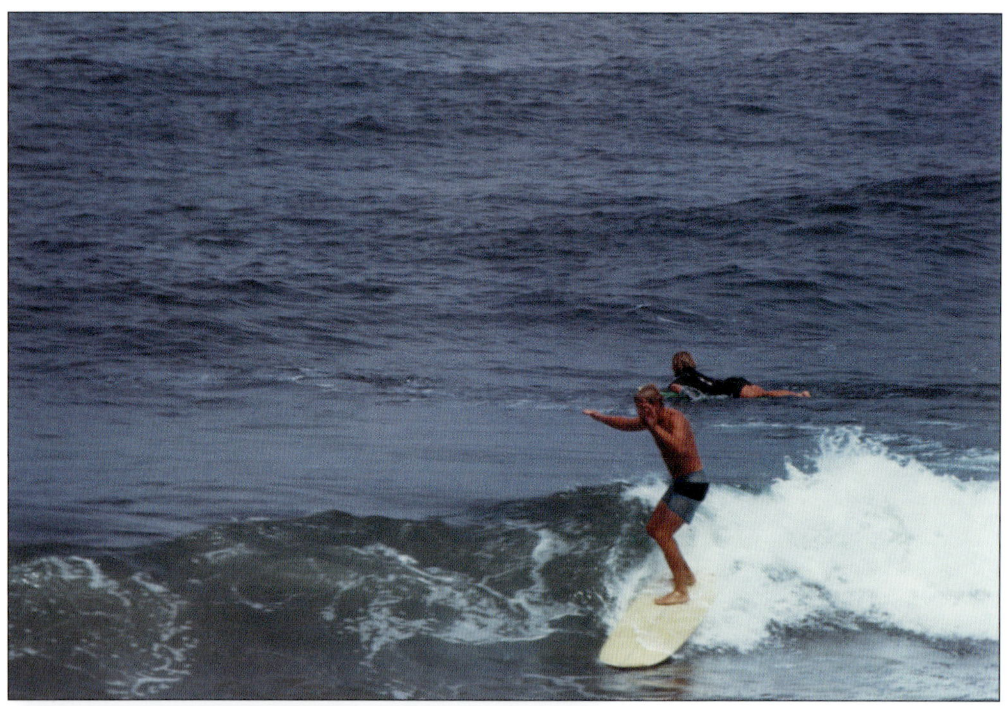

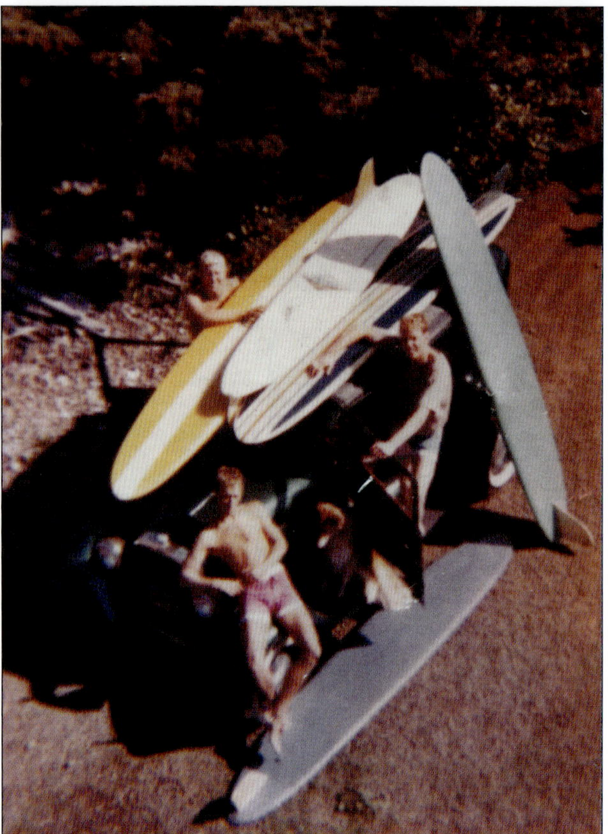

John Alto is catching a wave at the Cove in 1963. Alto remembers, "In 1961, I was dressed in huarache sandals and Dewey-Weber tee-shirt at Sunset Drive-in. Dana asked if I was a surfer. I said, 'No, but I'd like to be.' He said, 'We can fix that.' He took me to Indian Beach and taught me how to surf." In 1965, Alto spent three months surfing with Williams and his wife, Gail, on Oahu, Hawaii. (Courtesy of John Alto.)

From left to right, SSA members John Alto, Mike "Ziggy" Zalk, and Mark Hansen are pictured here with Hansen's Model A in the summer of 1962. John Alto remembers, "Joe Camberg took this picture of us from his second-story roof. I was working as a Seaside beach lifeguard and Zalk was an entrepreneur and had surfed in California. Zalk was a couple years older than me and he could afford a full wetsuit." (Courtesy of Mark Hansen.)

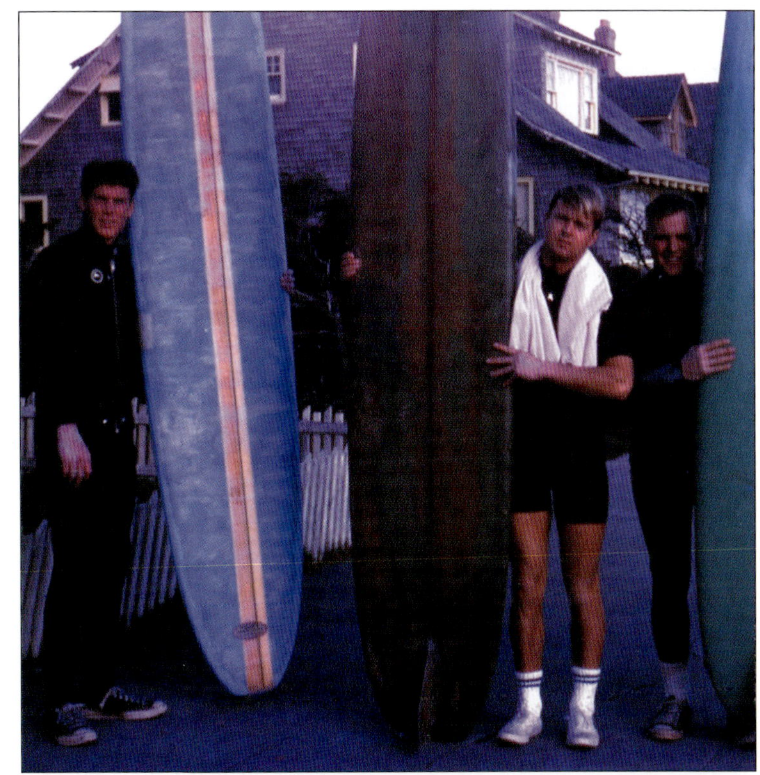

Pictured here are 1963 Seaside High School classmates and SSA members (from left to right) Mark Hansen, Tibby Utter, and Jerry Alto. All three credit Dana Williams with starting surfing around Seaside. Hansen remembers, "I saw him with an old beat up car with boards. Dana, great leader and got us going." Alto states, "Dana was the key, he had a surfboard and was from San Diego." Utter says, "I like hanging at Dana's house." (Courtesy of Mark Hansen.)

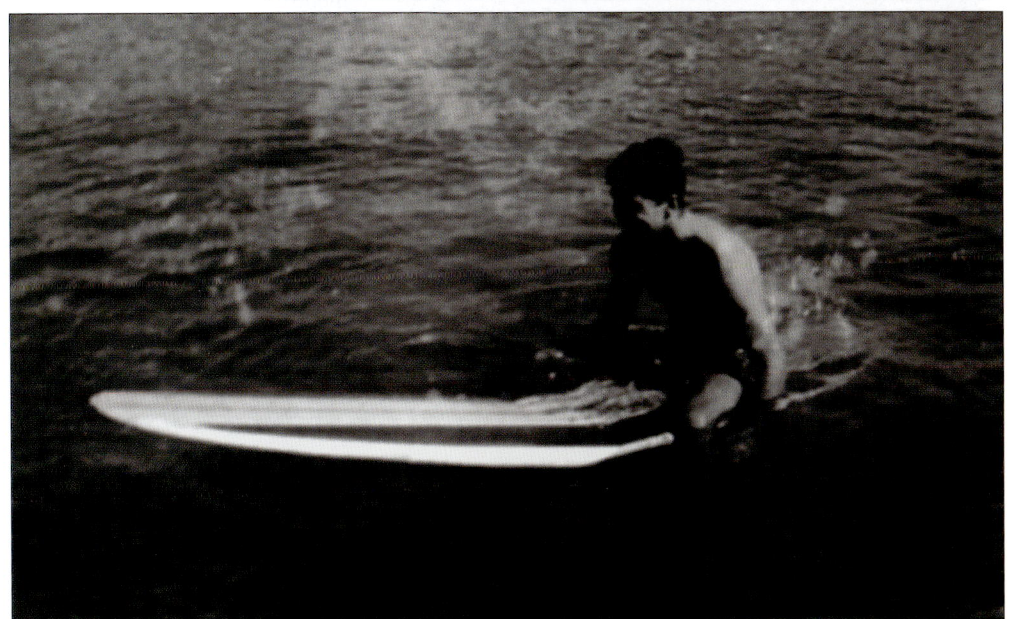

George Nelson is waiting for a wave at the Cove around 1963 during a warm Indian summer. Nelson recalls, "As kids we would hang around the beach's life guard towers. Everyone wanted to be a life guard. We skipped a lot of things to do surfing. We mostly surfed the Cove during the weekdays and Indian Beach on the weekends. There was a handful of us in the beginning. It wasn't crowded and we knew everyone." (Courtesy of George Nelson.)

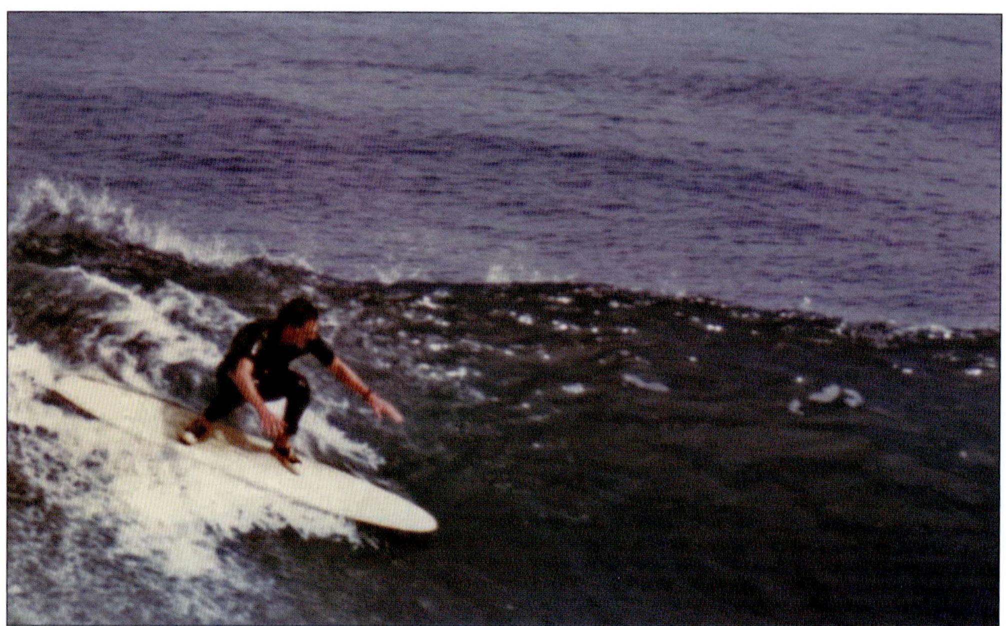

Dick Wald, seen here wearing tennis shoes and glasses, is credited with surfing the Point first. Wald remembers, "Dana and I started to see the Point in January 1964. I worked out, returning in October 1964 to ride it until my surfboard nose broke." Dana Williams recalls, "I didn't surf the Point until 1970 after I returned from Hawaii. First to surf the Point were Dick Wald, Jimmy Sagawa, then the Hansens, Bill Fackerell." (Courtesy of Dick Wald.)

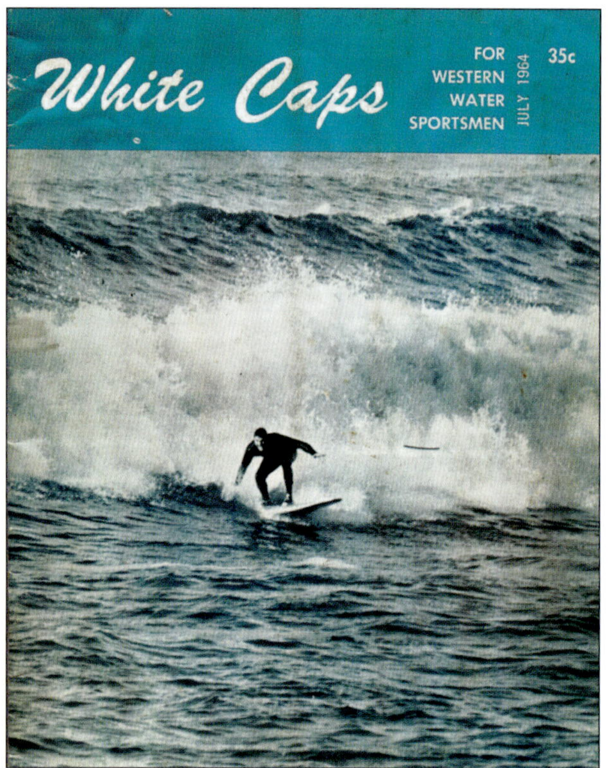

Dana Williams is featured here on the cover of *White Caps* magazine in July 1964. Williams is credited with starting surfing at Seaside. He recalls, "Surfing wasn't allowed at Seaside's beaches. Around 1962, I was arrested and fined $26 for standing on my board while lifeguarding. I requested Seaside's city council to allow surfing from Avenue U to the headlands of Tillamook Head. It was approved and surfing became legal within the city limits." (Courtesy of Mike Jipp.)

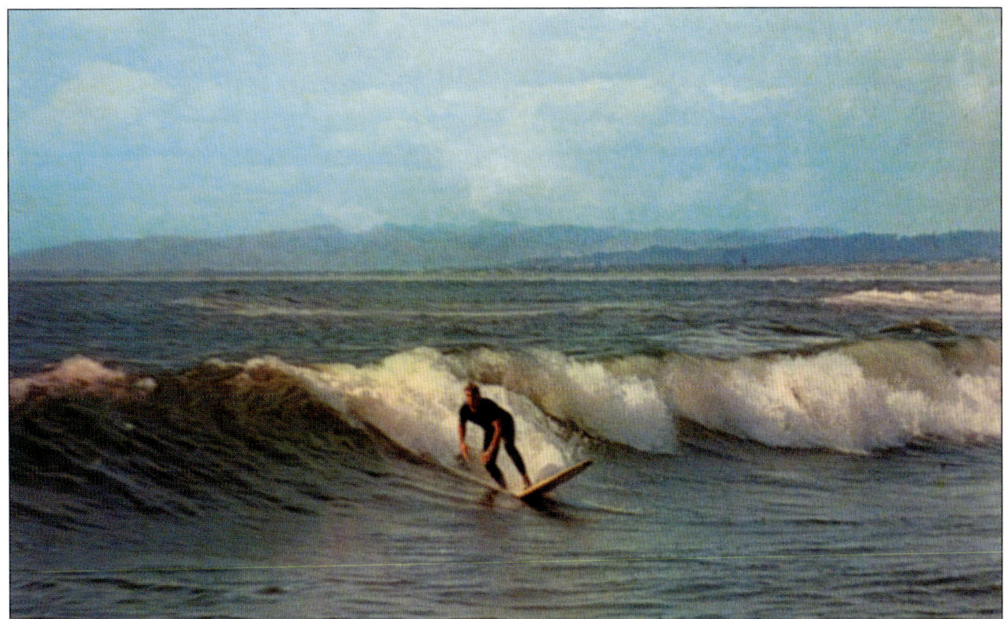

Dallas Cook is featured on this Seaside postcard, surfing the Cove. Cook recalls, "I was living in Gearhart when I borrowed a Hawaiian Olo board from the Gearhart Hotel. I used it for a summer until Wally Pashal took it out and broke it. I was 16 in 1963 when George Daggatt, Needham Ward, and myself ordered longboards that were delivered by train. They were too big for the truck freight." (Courtesy of Dennis Smith.)

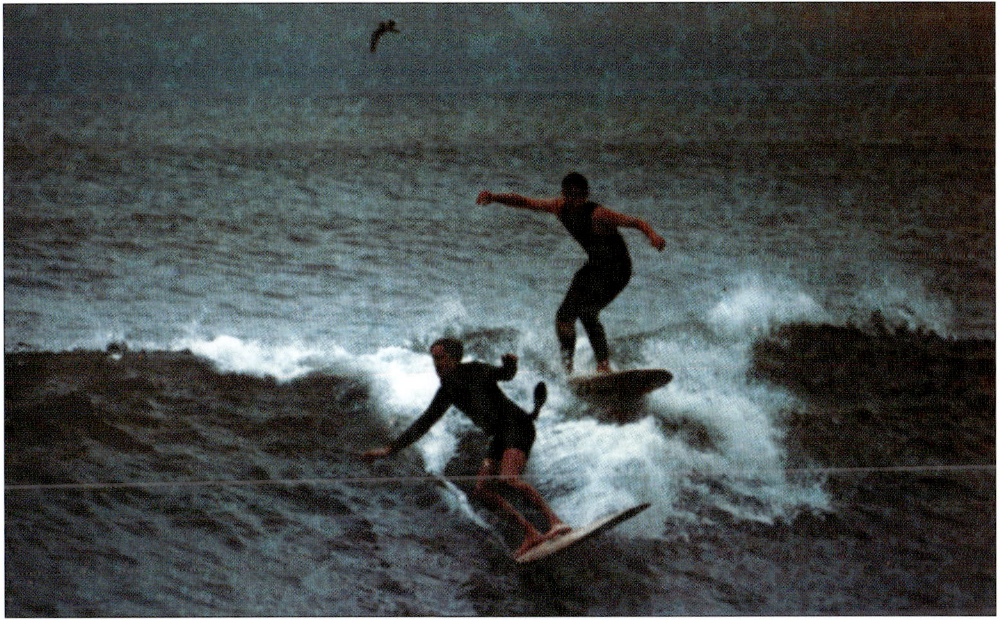

Seaside teens George Daggatt (left) and Brand Dichter are sharing a wave at the Cove around 1964. After Dana Williams, Daggatt became the SSA president. Daggatt recalls, "As a club we organized spaghetti feeds and sponsored surf contests." Living above the Lanai, Dichter recalls, "I surfed boogie boards in the early 1960s. I saw surfing in the ninth grade. It was something I needed to do. Surfing was fun. Competition wasn't me." (Courtesy of George Daggatt.)

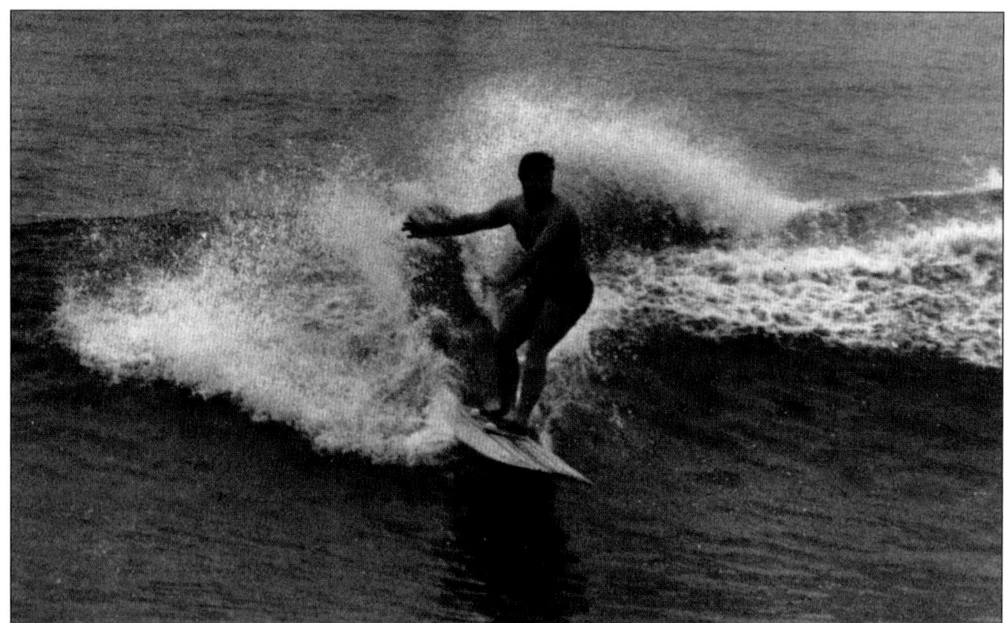

Pierre Marchand, pictured here surfing the Cove in 1966, was infamous for wearing no wetsuit and surfing in tennis shoes and trunks. Marchand graduated in 1967 and was a member of the SSA. Jerry Harrington recalls, "Pierre and I drove to Disneyland with his mom in 1963. We bought an old Hansen surfboard for $70 and brought it home in their old station wagon." (Courtesy of George Daggatt.)

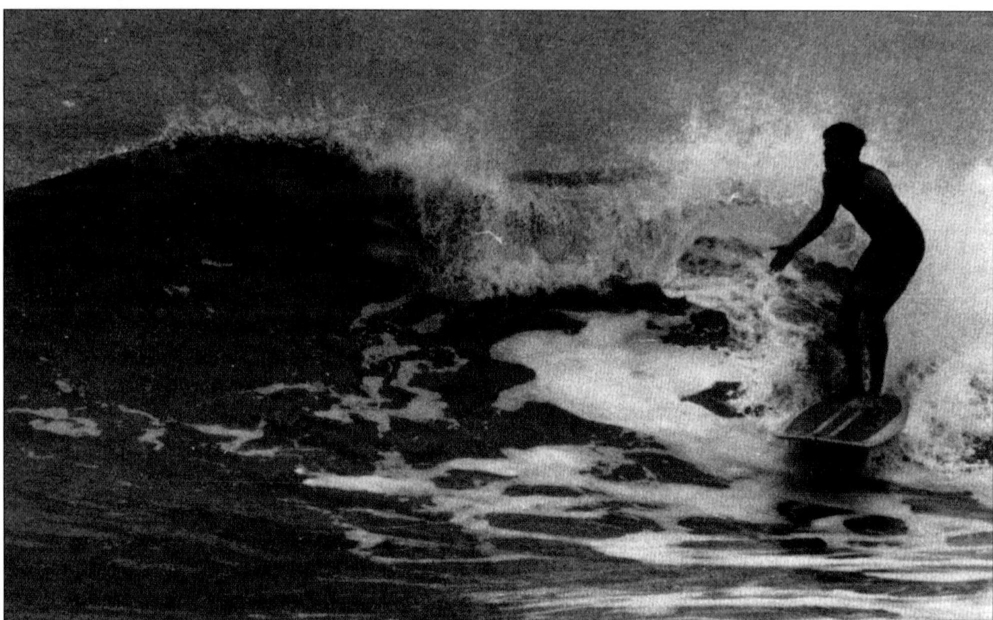

Mark Collins is pictured here at the Cove in 1965. Collins graduated from Seaside High School in 1965 and passed away in 2004. Brand Dichter recalls, "Mark was a character with a good sense of humor. We called him 'Bird' because of his stance on the board." Collins was a dory fisherman and carpenter, and before his death, he spent much of his time hanging out at the Cove, enjoying surfing and the company of other surfers. (Courtesy of George Daggatt.)

Paxton Hoag is entering the Cove in 1966. Hoag was from Astoria and took surfing photographs. Dallas Cook remembers, "I saw a box full of 8-by-10 photo prints of Paxton's pictures. He was an exceptional photographer and did more shooting than surfing." Former SSA president George Daggatt has compiled surfing images from 50 years ago in an old photo album, and fortunately, this image of Hoag was among them. (Courtesy of George Daggatt.)

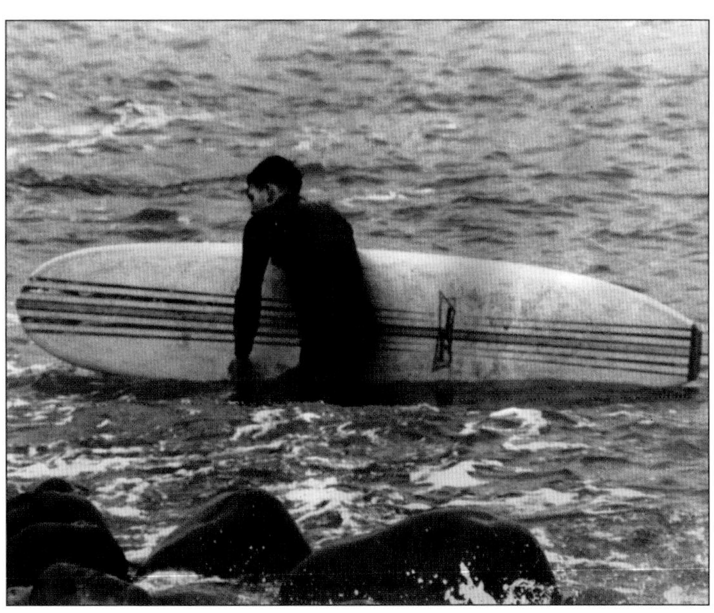

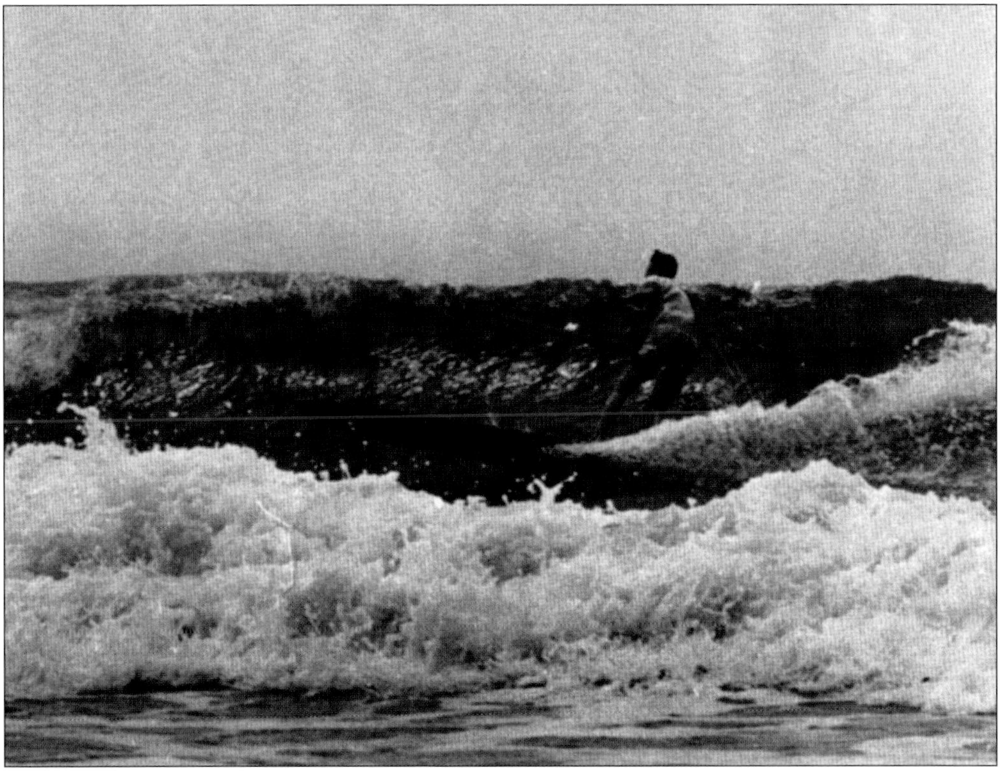

Gary Hansen is seen here participating in Seaside's 1966 surf contest at the Cove. Gary and his older brother Mark were SSA members. While in high school, Gary was credited with being the first local surfer to surf the Point with Dick Wald. Hansen recalls, "Dick did all the thinking. He said 'Let's go ride the wave out there.' So we paddled from the Cove to the Point." (Photograph by Bonnie Hansen.)

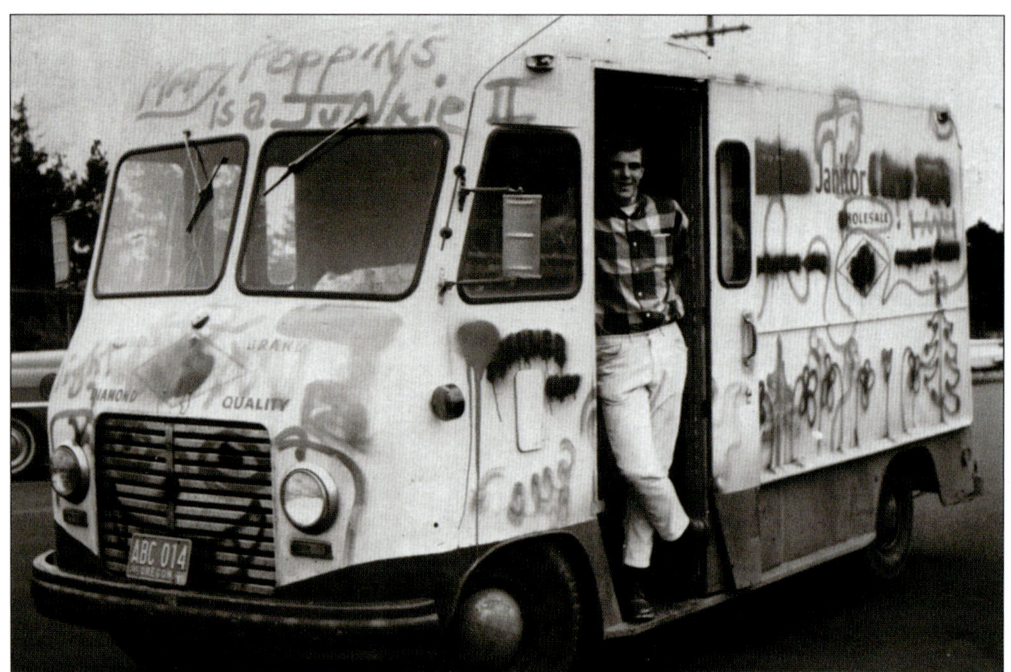

Bill Fackerell, a Seaside High School junior, poses inside a spray-painted van in 1966. Fackerell started surfing early. He was a member of the SSA and was considered a good athlete. Peter Blyth relates, "Bill and Sandy Barrett were my favorite North Coast longboarders. Both friends. Bill surfed for Jensen Surfboards of Seaside-Astoria." Brand Dichter recalls, "When Fackerell opened up the Raven Surf Shop he had a connection with Jensen and got boards from California." (Courtesy of Brand Dichter.)

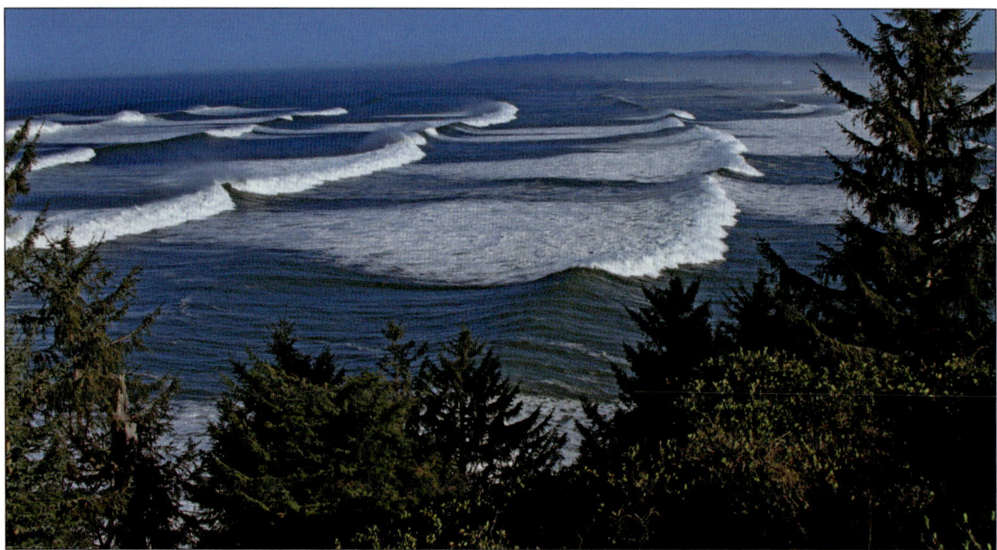

Bruce Zumbuhl, a Seaside High School sophomore, drowned while surfing in February 1966. "It was stormy, conditions were bad at the Cove," as John Brewer recalls. "A group of us watched two guys out 'surfing' in front of the Lanai. One made it in. The other got caught in the rip, carried out to the open ocean." They watched helplessly and called for help. Sadly, Zumbuhl disappeared before the helicopter arrived. (Photograph by Scott Blackman.)

Steve Johnson poses in red trunks in his Portland backyard in July 1966. Johnson recalls, "I first tried surfing with my father and his friend at Fogarty Creek in 1957 when I was seven years old. I thought I was going to die, it was so cold. I had fun and it was my first start. I bought red trunks from Mrs. Abbott's Surf Shop. Art Spence and the Tillamook Head gang gave me the surf name Red Trunks because of them." (Courtesy of Steve Johnson.)

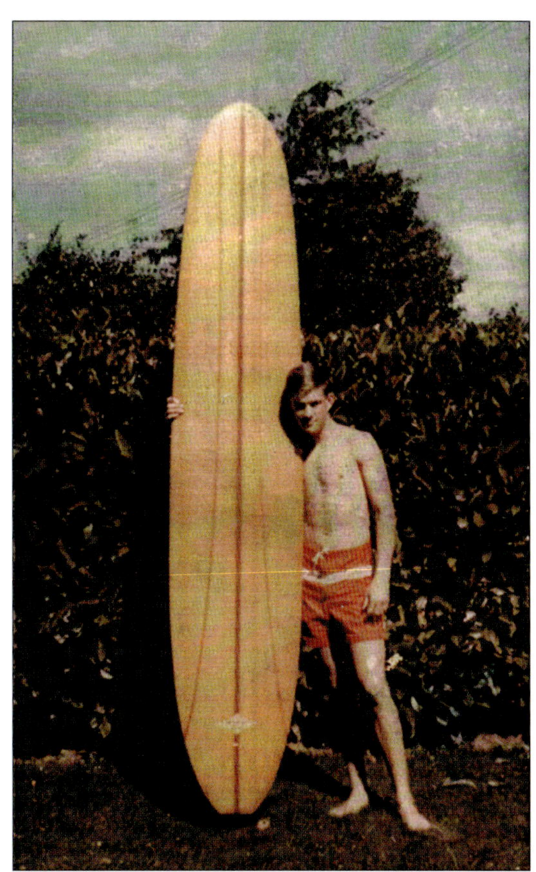

Peter de Turk is pictured here at the Point in 1966. "At age 15 I started surfing in California in 1959," he remembers. "I was in the military in Whidbey Island and heard about Oregon waves. The Point was pumping my first session, November 1966. I borrowed a Jensen board and was hooked. I am a goofy foot and it's one of the better lefts between here and the equator. It's an attractive wave to me." (Courtesy of Peter de Turk.)

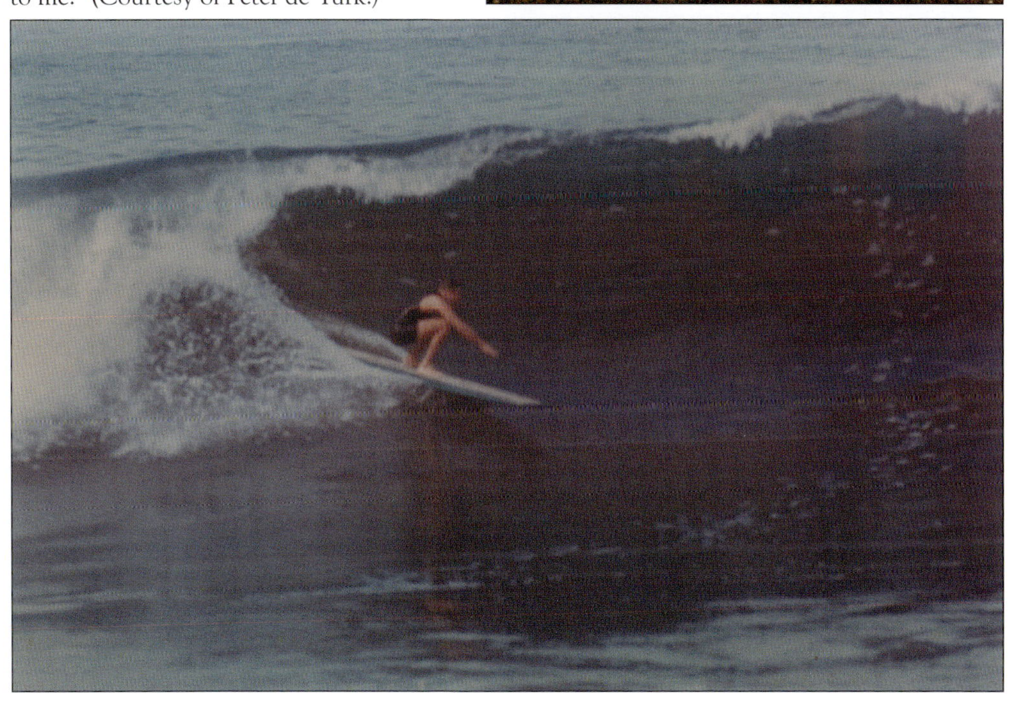

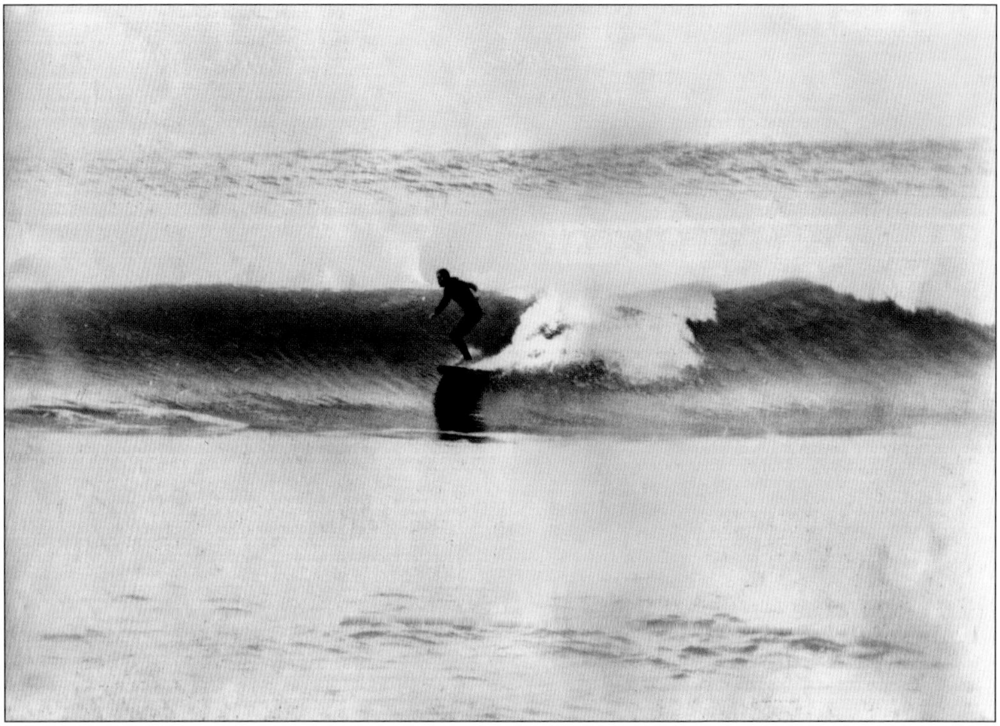

Dalton Hobbs captured this photograph of Dan Matthews surfing the Cove in 1968. Matthews recalls, "My older brother David and I would drive down from Portland on weekends while in high school. My mother thought if we came together we would be okay. We would sleep in our car overnight and then go surfing the next day." Eventually, Dan became a co-owner of Tillamook Head Surf Shop. (Courtesy of Knox Swanson.)

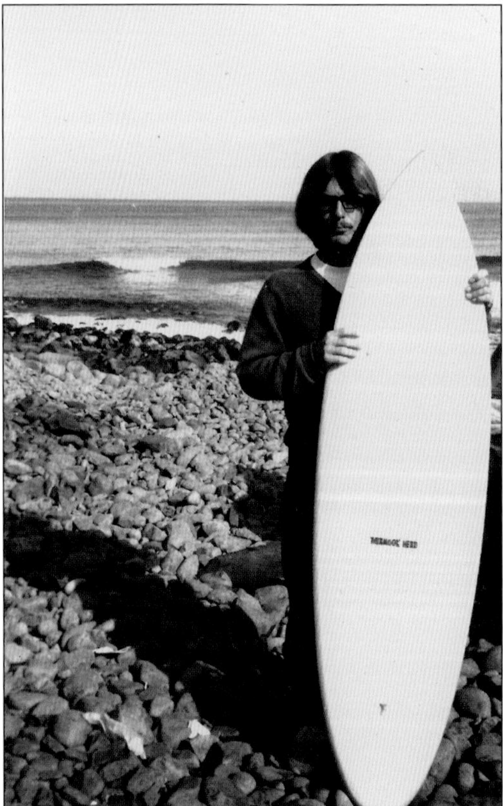

Dick Borovicka poses with his board at the Cove in 1969. "I graduated from Jefferson High School in 1964," Borovicka remembers. "Listening to the Beach Boys, I gravitated towards surfing. I borrowed a board and first surfed at Short Sands, wearing cut offs, no wetsuit. I floundered around. Later, in 1968, I visited Barbara Garratt down at Captain Johnson's cottages in Cannon Beach. I met Max Justice, Peter Adamson, and Bill Smith there." He decided to stay. (Photograph by Barbara Garratt Castillo.)

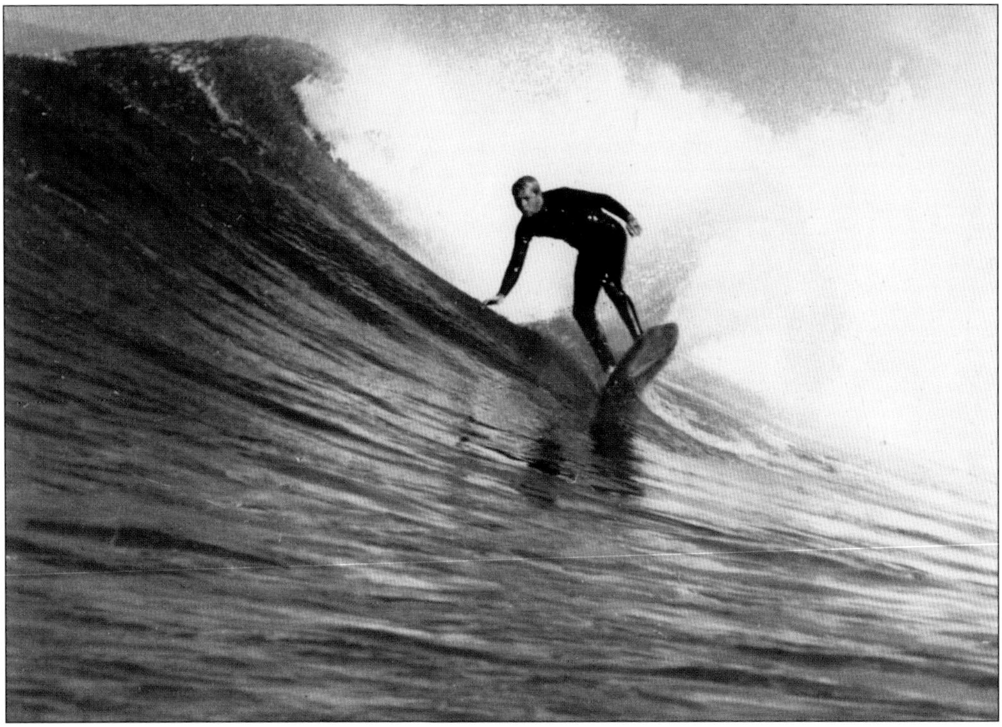

Canadian Al "Surfin" Bird captured this photograph of Bob Malo surfing the Cove in November 1969. Malo explains, "I started surfing in 1964. After graduation from Tigard High School, my family moved to Cannon Beach in 1967. Surfing means freedom. You can start out with a bad day and everything is forgotten. Any time I could get away from work, I would go surf. Sometimes when I should have been working, I was surfing." (Courtesy of Bob Malo.)

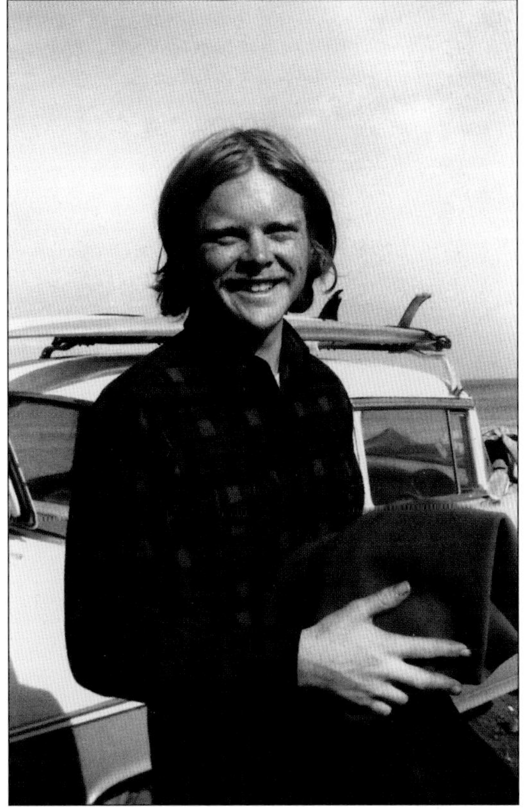

Greg "Sunny Jim" Gosser is seen here at the Cove in the late 1960s. Gosser recalls, "I was 13 years old when my dad rented a board in Portland, strapped it on our car. It took two of us to carry it down to Short Sands. I was mostly in the soup all day, then caught my first green wave. I was addicted! I eventually discovered there is a community in surfing." He has been surfing ever since. (Photograph by Barbara Garratt Castillo.)

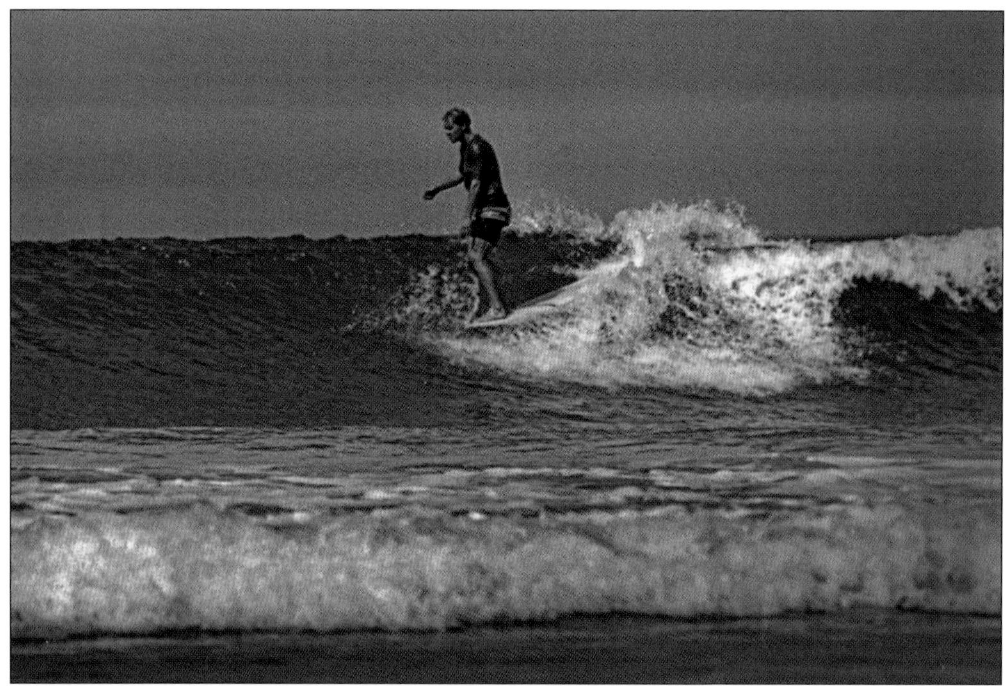

California transplant Sandy Barrett is pictured here surfing the Cove in the late 1960s. Barrett competed in and usually won the local surf contests in the 1960s. According to Greg Gosser, "Sandy Barrett surfed and looked like a California surfer. He had the biggest knobs on his knees from surfing. Such a stud. Sandy did bottom turns! He wore white canvas trunks by Katin, was on a Hansen, and wore a vest with suntanned arms and legs." (Photograph by Scott Blackman.)

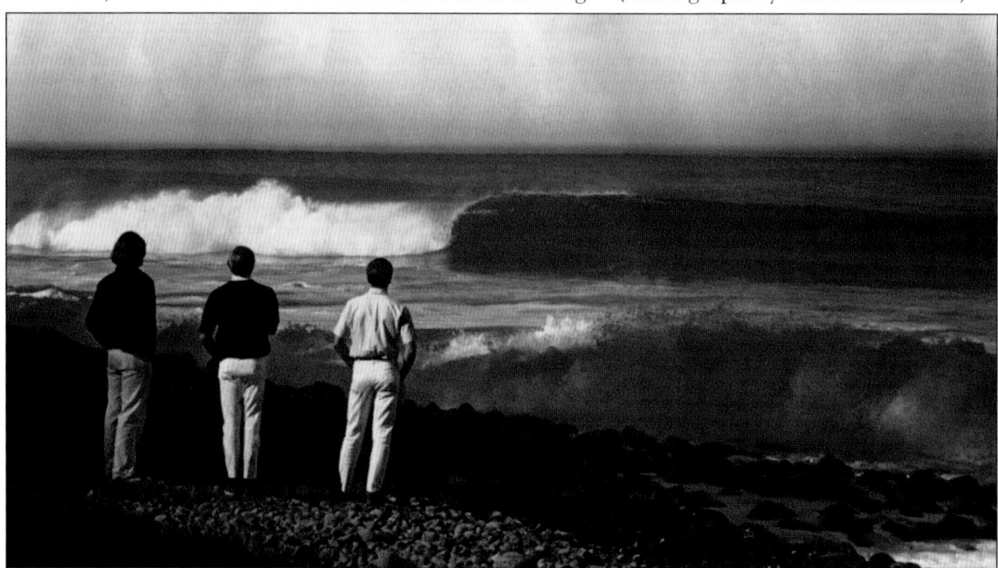

Checking out the surf at the Point in 1969 are, from left to right, Scott Blyth, John Brewer, and Mike Nitsch. Brewer, who was a skiier before he started surfing, says, "The first time I surfed I was hooked. Those first years are still etched in my dome, never to be unseated by time, age, dimming memory, or any other experience. Nothing compares to surfing when it comes to creating never-to-be-forgotten happenings." (Courtesy of Knox Swanson.)

Knox Swanson, looking like the typical 1970s surfer, is seen here putting on his wetsuit in 1971. Knox recalls, "I heard about surfing through Beach Boys music, *Beach Blanket Bingo*, and Gidget movies. I came down here in my childhood and played in the waves. Got ahold of *Surfing* magazines and started coming with my high school buddies to Indian Beach and Short Sands. My first kneeboards were made by Jeff Hull." Knox graduated from Portland's Wilson high School in 1970. (Photograph by Dan Matthews.)

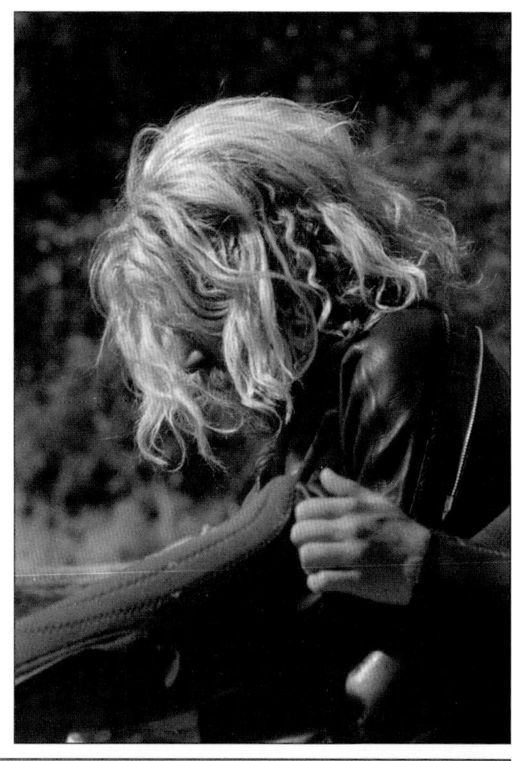

Greg Gosser, pictured here surfing the Point with a nose leash around 1970–1971, recalls, "I bought a Lanny Shuler board right after he started Evergreen surfboards. Lanny's boards were made with hard, down rails and were made for the Point. Not as good to use his boards at other shore breaks." Surfboards had no leashes until the early 1970s. At first, leashes were attached to the board's nose, but eventually they were attached to the tail. (Courtesy of Greg Gosser.)

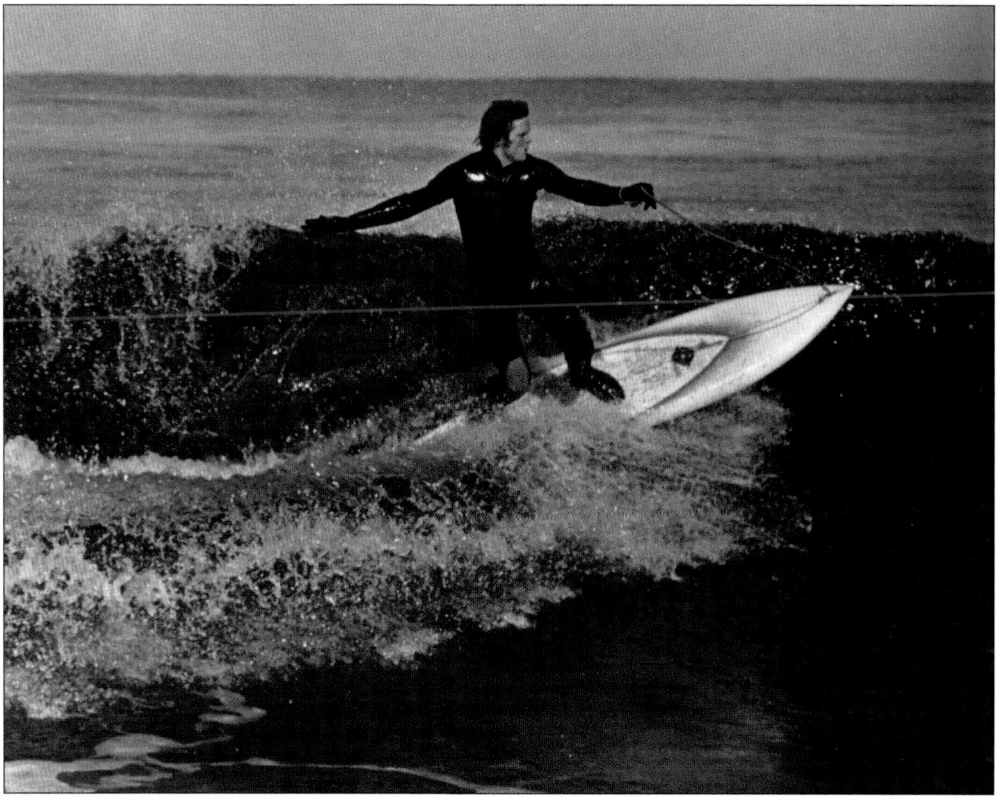

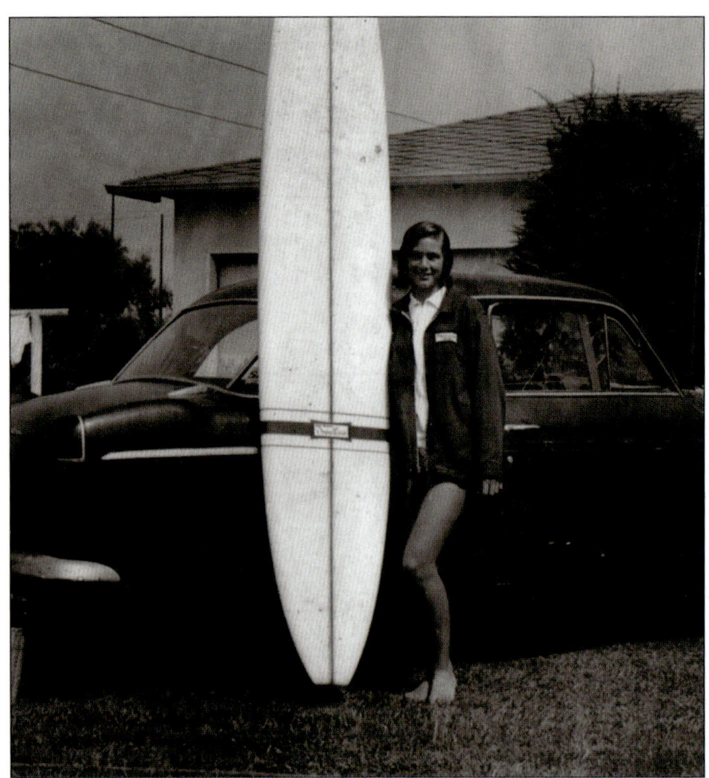

Gail Yarborough, pictured here in the late 1950s, married Dana Williams and moved to Nehalem Valley. A talented California surfer, some surfers called her "First Lady of the Point." Tim Foley called Gail "a hell of a rider, a champ." John Alto remembers, "I saw Gail surfing in Hawaii when she was nearly nine months pregnant." (Courtesy of Dana Williams.)

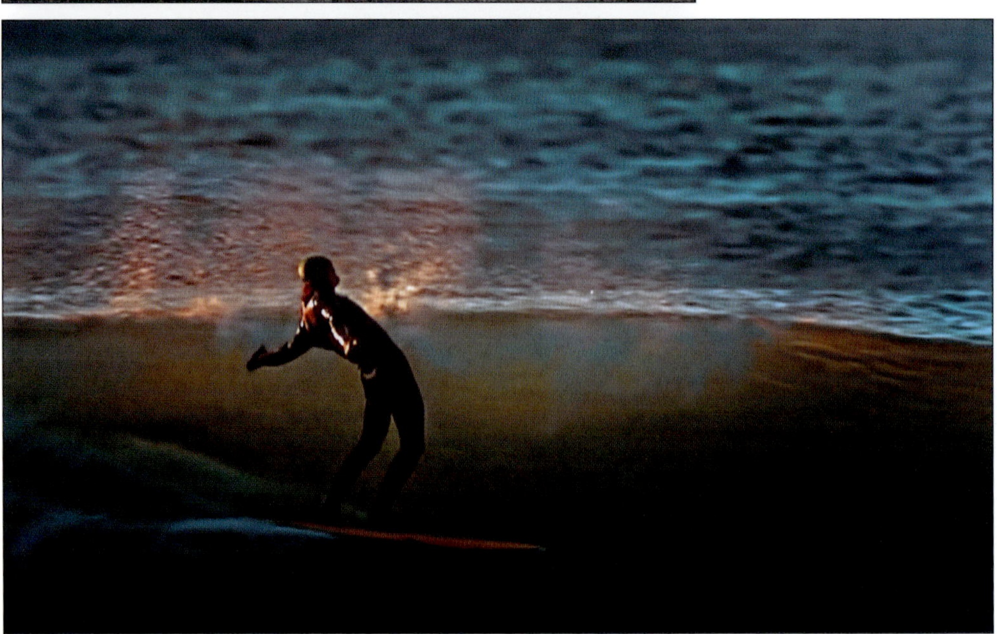

Art Spence is showing his unique "soul arch" at the Point in the early 1970s. According to Scott Blackman, "Art was something of a whiz kid, coming from the hot bed of Santa Cruz surfing. He was able to surf so well, many were in awe of his talents. Art managed to bring it all together for a brief time around Seaside. His style was his own." Dave Kopra called Spence the "Archer" because of his stance. (Photograph by Scott Blackman.)

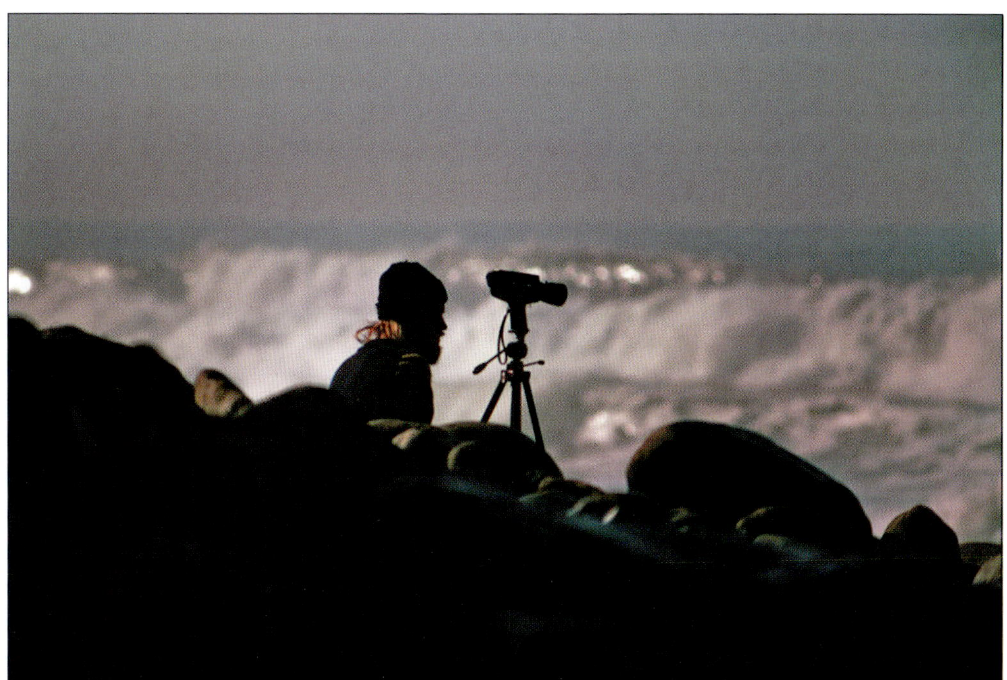

Art Spence, seen here at the Point in the early 1970s, was an exceptional surfer also known for his other talents. Scott Blackman recalls, "Everybody knew Art as an extremely talented and creative person. His artistry showed in his surfing video of the Point. He was a painter and a photographer. His creativeness and inventiveness showed in the boards he made as a partner in Tillamook Head." (Photograph by Dan Matthews.)

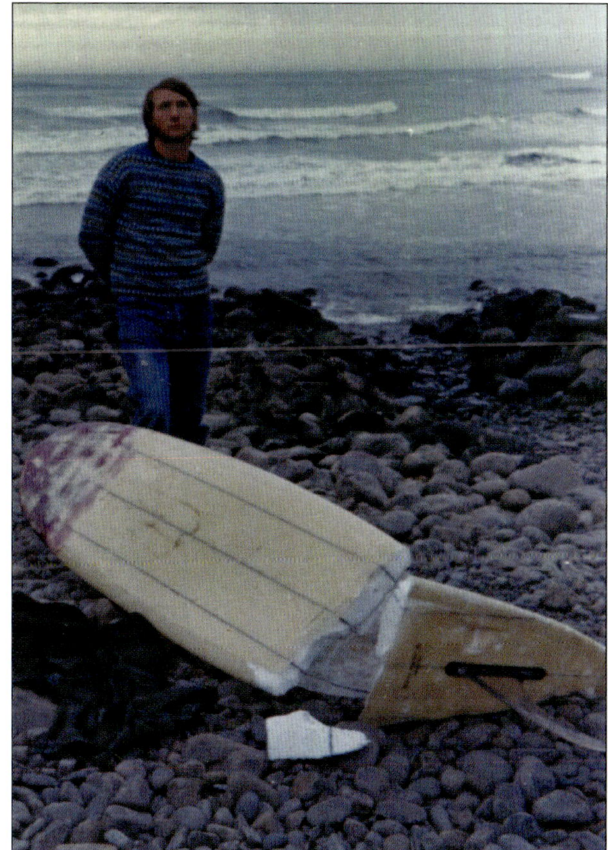

Jeff Trenary laments a broken board at the Point in the fall of 1970. Trenary graduated in 1968 from Madison High School in Portland. "I worked two years patching wetsuits and board repair at Surf & Dive in Portland's Hollywood district and met Dana Williams there. I glassed my first board in my parents' basement. My mom thought we were doing drugs or something. The entire house smelled." (Photograph by Dick Borovicka.)

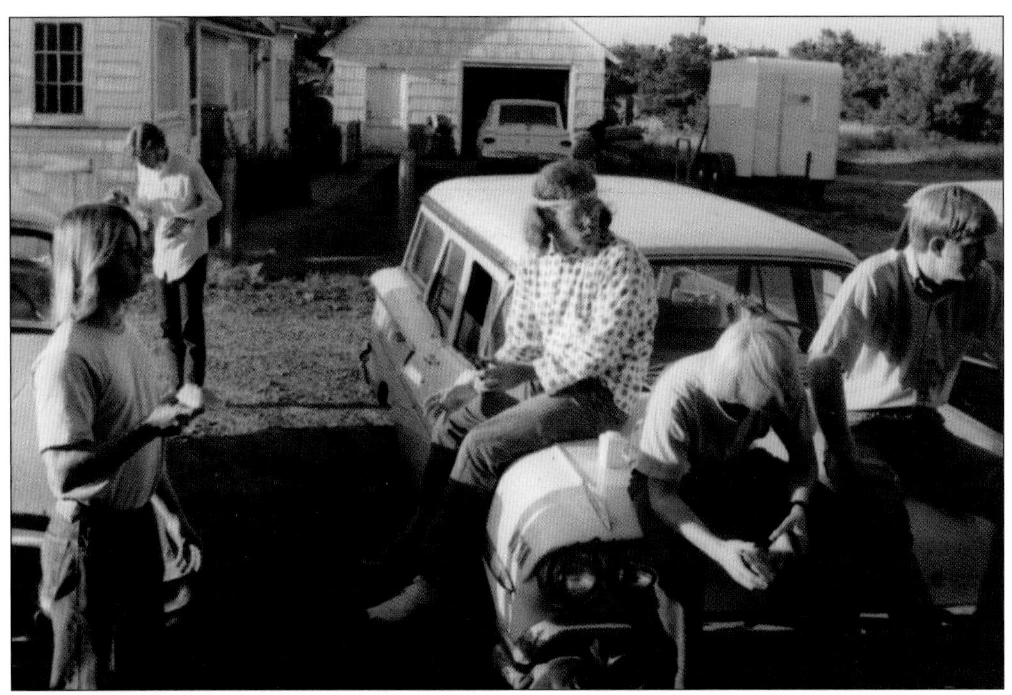

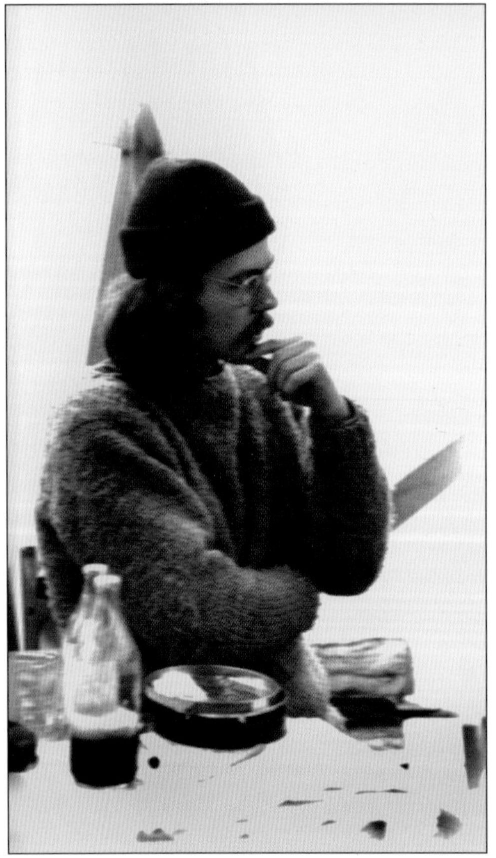

During the late 1960s and early 1970s, some surfers lived together in old houses on the north side of Seaside, which they called the "ghetto." Hanging out at Bill Smith's house are Bill Barnfield at far left, and sitting on Smith's 1958 Chevy Nomad are, from left to right, Mike Carroll from Seattle, Bill Smith from Portland, and unidentified. Smith recalls, "Barnfield and Kent Wienker who lived across the street would cook at our house." (Photograph by Dan Matthews.)

David Matthews, pictured in 1972, fondly recalls, "My brother Dan and I were influenced by surf music and movies. Together we bought a Shark board from Foster's Sporting Good Store for $45 in 1964. Our parents weren't too excited about surfing, but they supported us. They took movies of us surfing at Short Sands and Indian Beach in 1967." David lives in Manzanita now and does SUP (stand-up paddle) surfing. (Courtesy of David Matthews.)

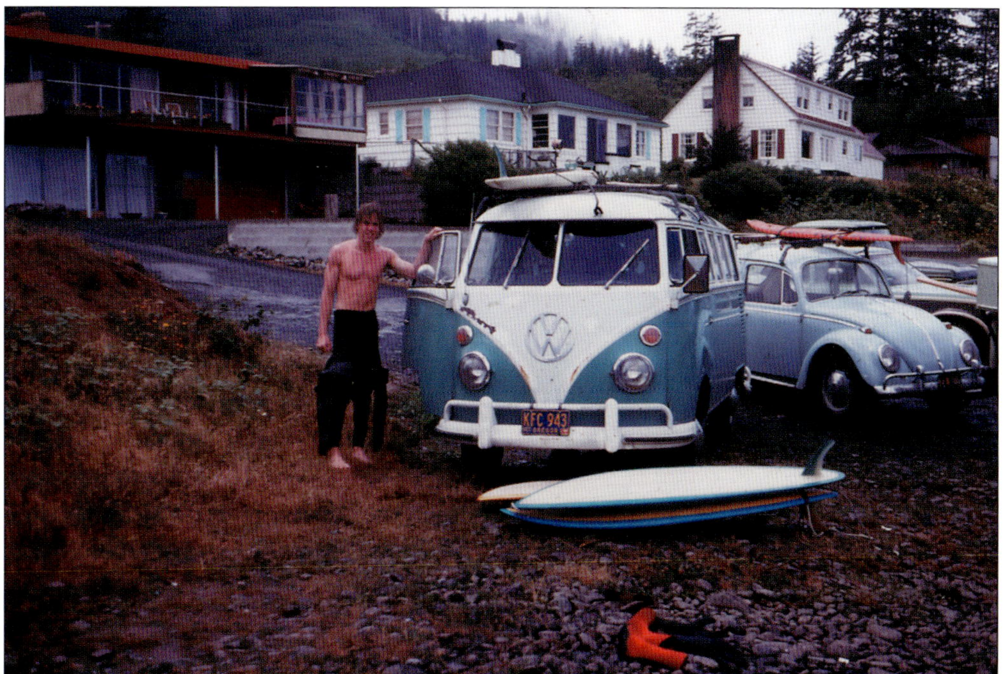

Ric Wiedmaier poses half out of his wetsuit behind the Lanai Motel in May 1972. Point surfers often parked around the Lanai, transporting their boards with Volkswagen buses and Bugs. Board shaper Jeff Hull reminisces, "Bill Barnfield had just returned from Hawaii with two Gerry Lopez boards and I rode them for hours at the Point making waves with ease. I found I preferred Lopez and Barnfield boards over my own which impacted my trajectory as a shaper." (Photograph by Jeff Hull.)

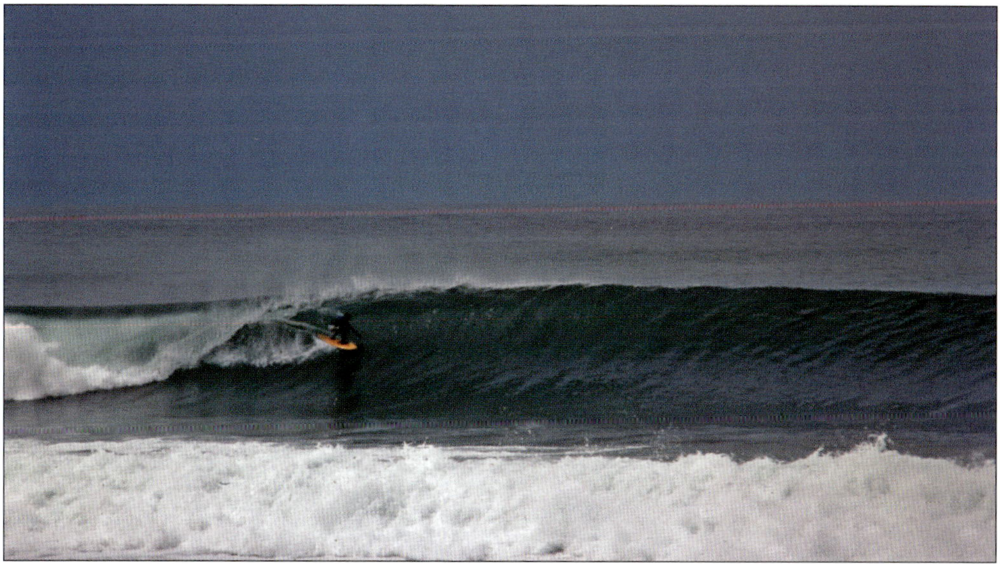

Rolf Aurness, who won the 1970 World Surfing Championships, is pictured here skillfully riding the Point in 1981. Phil Kennedy recalls seeing a surfer with a full suit, board shorts, and knee pads and thinking, "He's killing it out there, going backside and frontside for five hours. We wonder who's the guy? Later he returns to his Trans Am and stores his four boards inside. All the seats were torn out except for the driver's seat." (Photograph by Phil Kennedy.)

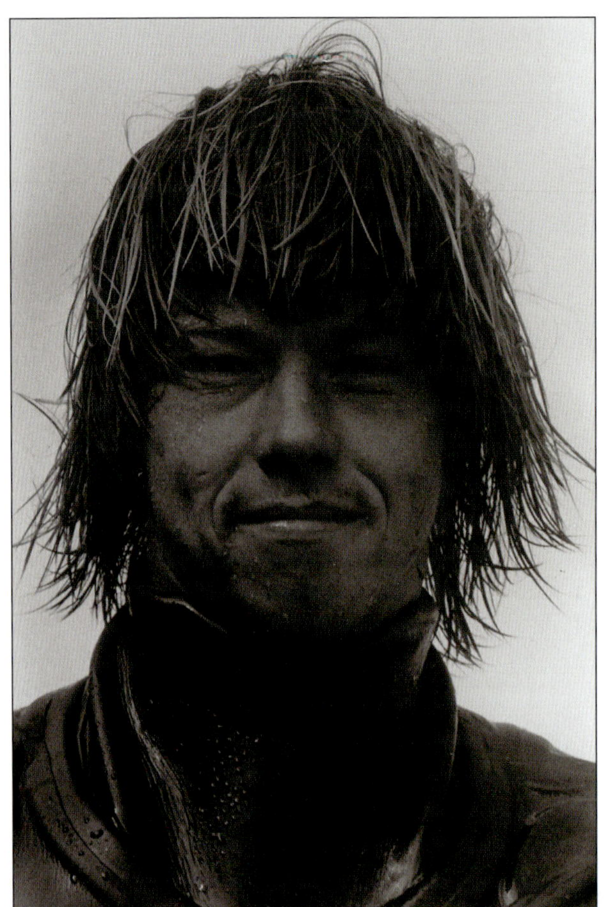

Bill Barnfield, shown here in the early 1970s, remembers, "I arrived with Kent Wienker the summer of 1969 and we lived together in Seaside on 16th Street. I had always been able to glass and shape, and regularly did so. Though at Tillamook Head surfboards, Dan Mathews usually shaped my personal boards and Art glassed them. In the winter of 1971–72, I began sanding for Gerry Lopez and Lightning Bolt Surfboards in Hawaii." (Photograph by Dan Matthews.)

Bill Barnfield, seen here, regularly surfed the Point in the early 1970s. Randy Barna admiringly explains, "Bill is instantly recognizable. Bill has a stance and style that stands out and really raised the bar on what could be done out there. On top of that, he's super generous with advice and pointers to help the kooks. Bill encouraged many on their first times out at the Point, creating lasting memories and gratitude." (Photograph by Randy Barna.)

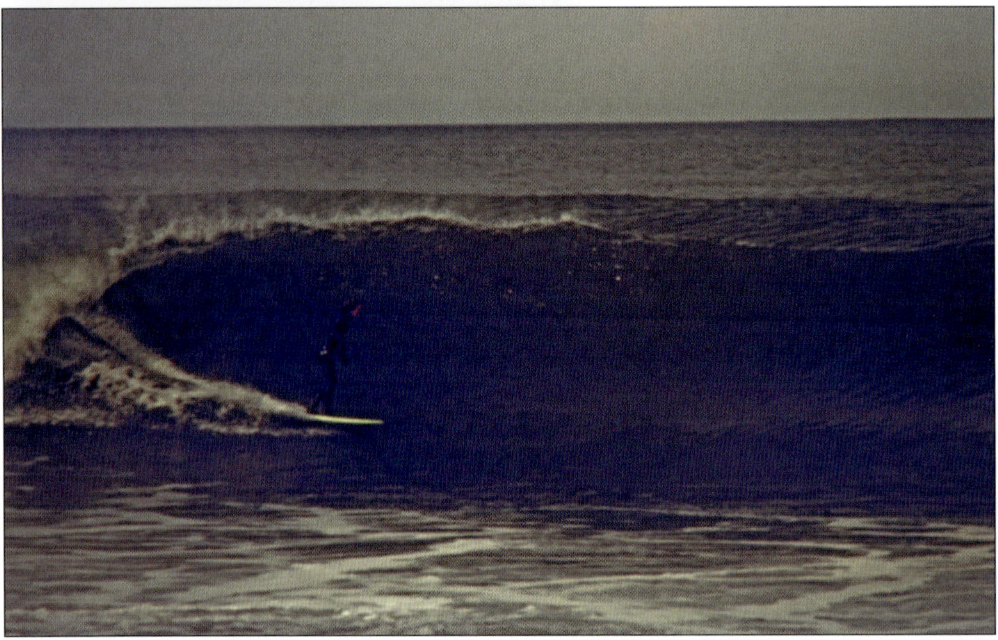

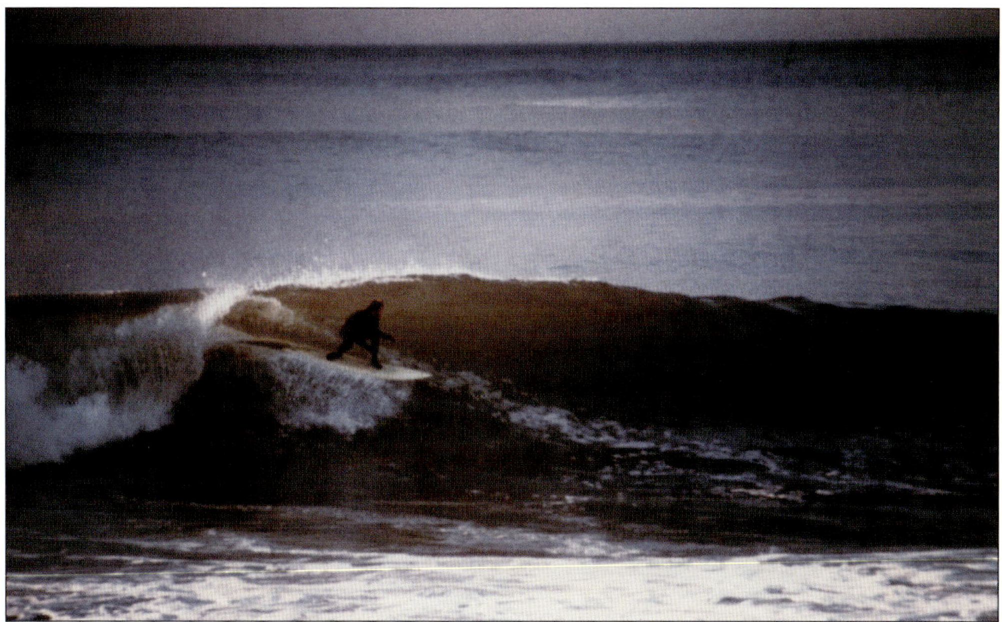

Randy Barna crouches on his board at the Point around 1972. Barna moved to Manzanita right after high school. "I spent several summer-fall seasons learning surfing skills at Short Sands and Seaside's Cove. The next two summer-falls I moved to Seaside and surfed the Point. I'd spend winters in Bend, skiing, but my best life lessons came from surfing. All my best friends are surfers . . . a bunch of characters!" Barna still surfs on a SUP. (Courtesy of Randy Barna.)

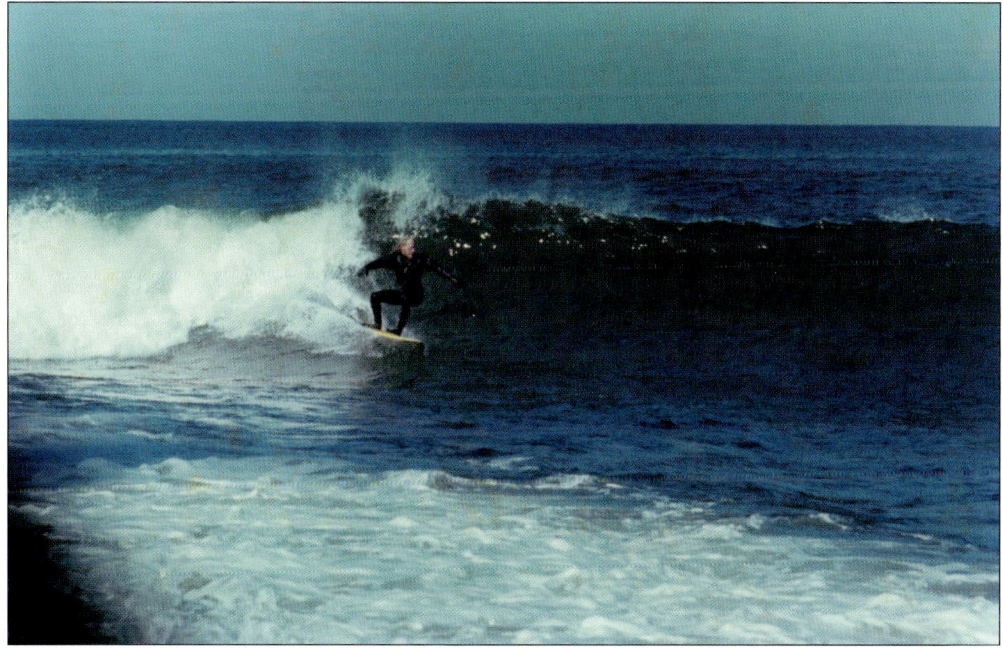

Jeff Hull is pictured here surfing the Shore Break on his orange six-foot-four board *Pumpkin*. Hull remembers, "Bill Barnfield was a good photographer and took this image of me at Seaside's Shore Break in the fall of 1972. It looks like there was a little wind on it but this photo shows how shallow that place truly is as the water drains off the boulders." (Courtesy of Jeff Hull.)

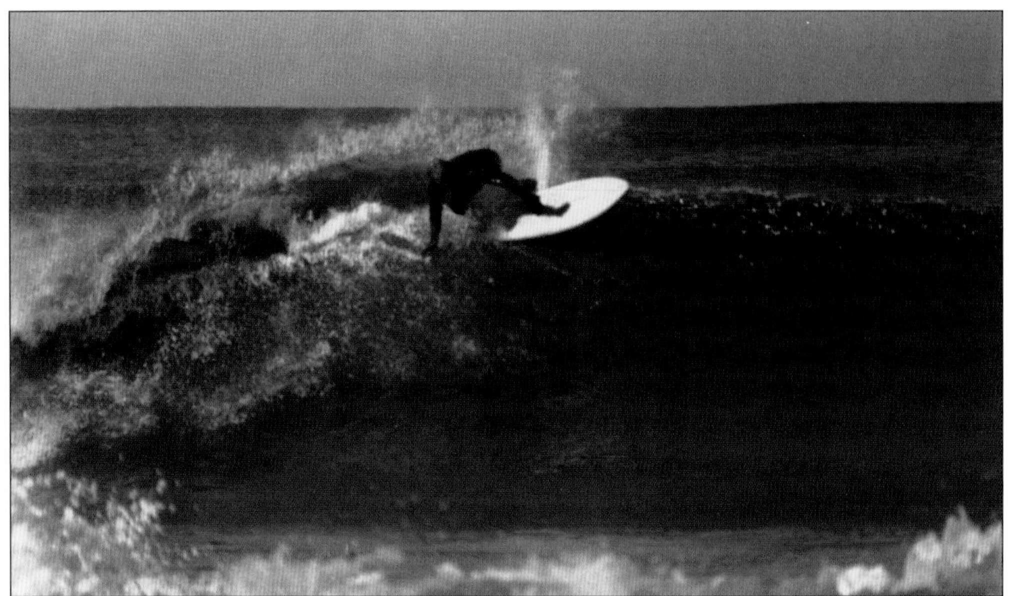

Bill Smith is seen here turning off the top at the Point in November 1973. Bill Smith and Max Justice have been friends since the third grade in Portland. Smith remembers, "Max started surfing and took me to Pacific City the summer of 1965 and to Short Sands and Seaside's Cove in 1966." After graduating in 1967, Smith and Justice moved to Seaside, eventually building homes by each other. They affectionately called north Seaside along the beach "the ghetto." (Photograph by Tim Mack.)

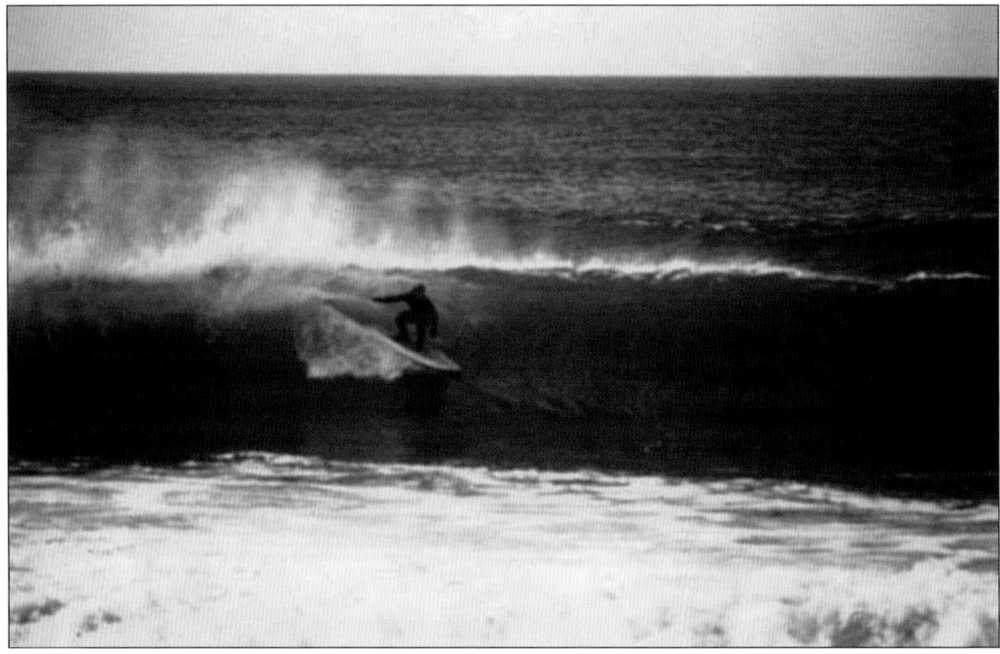

Max Justice is surfing the Point in 1973 on the Bonzer Board that he made with Art Spence. According to Justice, "Surfing is a tribe you belong to, especially back in the beginning. It was a special time that will never happen again. The new kids surfing today ask me if I wish I was out there and I just say no—I had it much better than this!" (Courtesy of Max Justice.)

Jeff Hull is ready to paddle out to the Point in 1973. Hull comments, "One of the jokes we used to play on each other in the early days was to try to get the other guy to paddle out first on questionable days. If someone with a camera was involved in the conversation, it would eventually end with 'If you go out I'll take your picture.' It worked every time." (Photograph by Knox Swanson.)

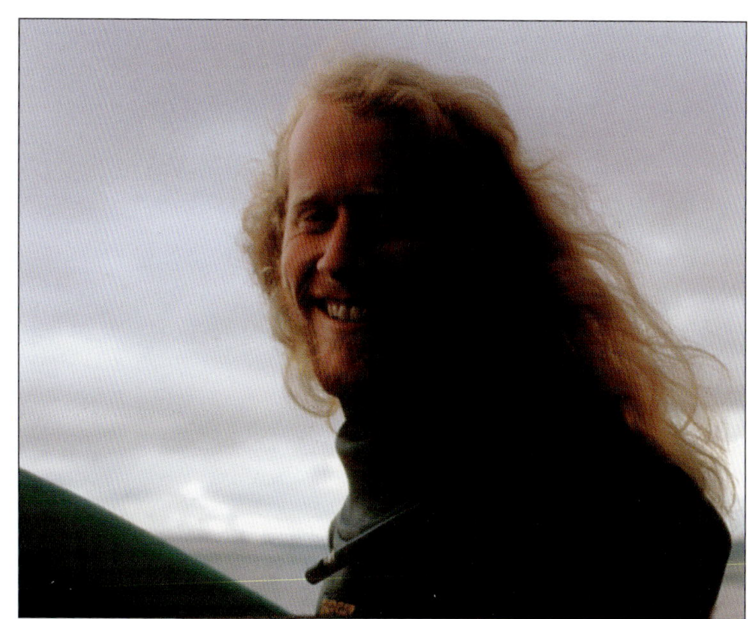

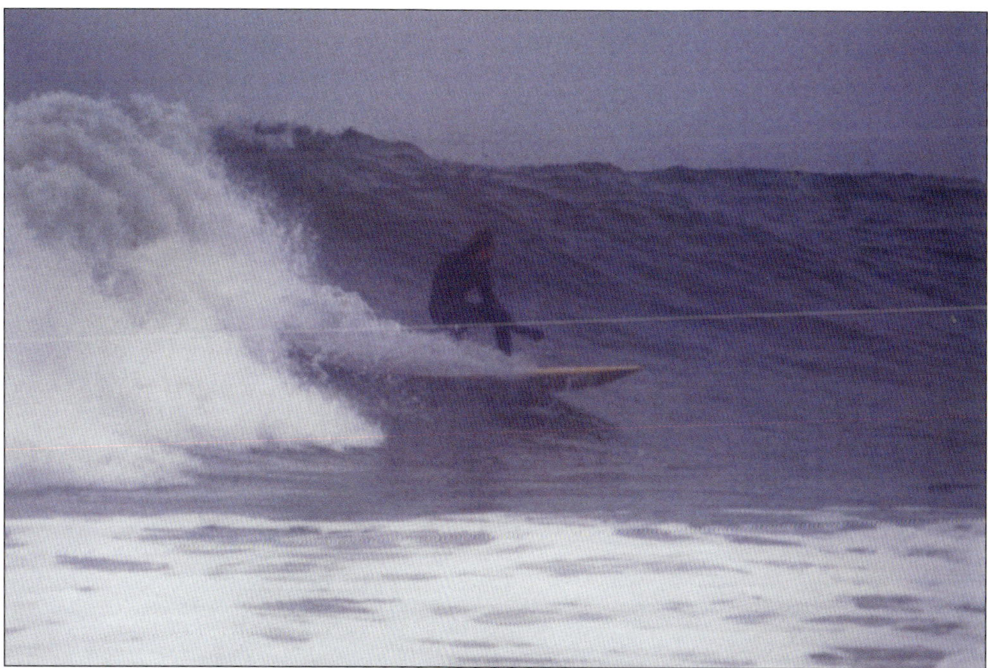

Peter Blyth is riding on a Haut surfboard at the Point in the mid-1970s. Blyth attended Lake Oswego schools, graduating in 1968. He would visit Hawaii and had an uncle stationed in the Air Force there. Blyth recalls, "I learned to surf in Oregon. My dad read about surfing and said 'Let's do it.' Some of us from Troop 12 Explorer Scouts made wetsuits and surfboards." (Courtesy of Dellanne McGregor.)

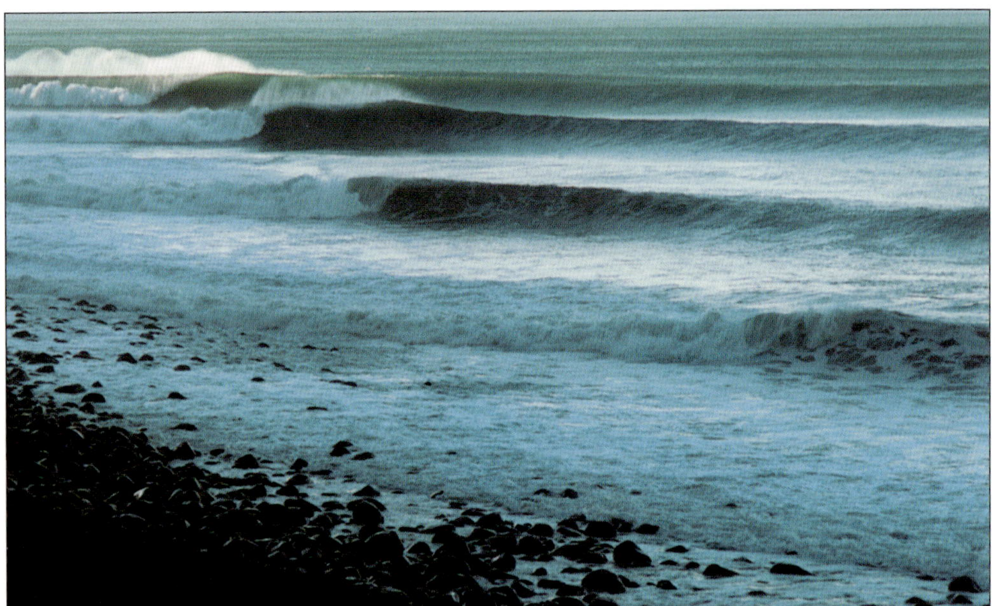

Seaside's Second Point sits out past First Point. Perry Shoemake explains, "Second Point is like First Point on steroids! An air drop followed by a full rail bottom turn, then a 400-yard wide-open stand-up barrel, then kick out just outside of First Point. Exponentially more powerful, Second Point is a 400-yard-long top-to-bottom barrel held in reserve for seasoned veterans." (Photograph by Scott Blackman.)

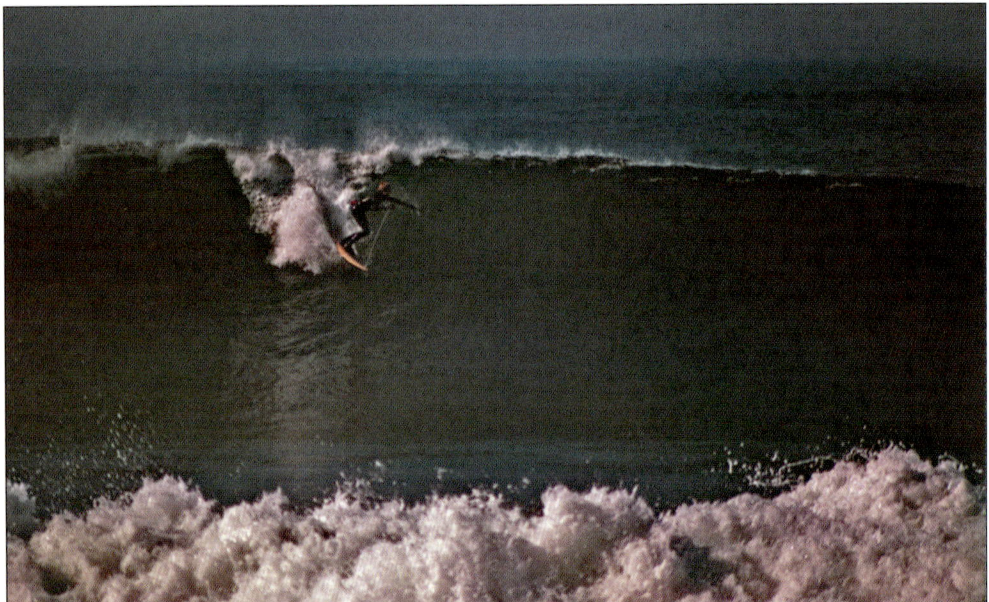

Perry Shoemake is pictured here surfing Second Point in the fall of 1972 with a nose leash. He reports, "The first time I surfed it was with Bruce Prator in 1970–1971. I am riding my seven-foot-four 'keel fin' that Art Spence shaped and I glassed with boat resin. The nose leash was dangerous: a bungee that snapped back and nailed me multiple times. Before that, there were no leashes, which guaranteed dings on our boards." Nose leashes quickly became obsolete. (Photograph by Tim Mack.)

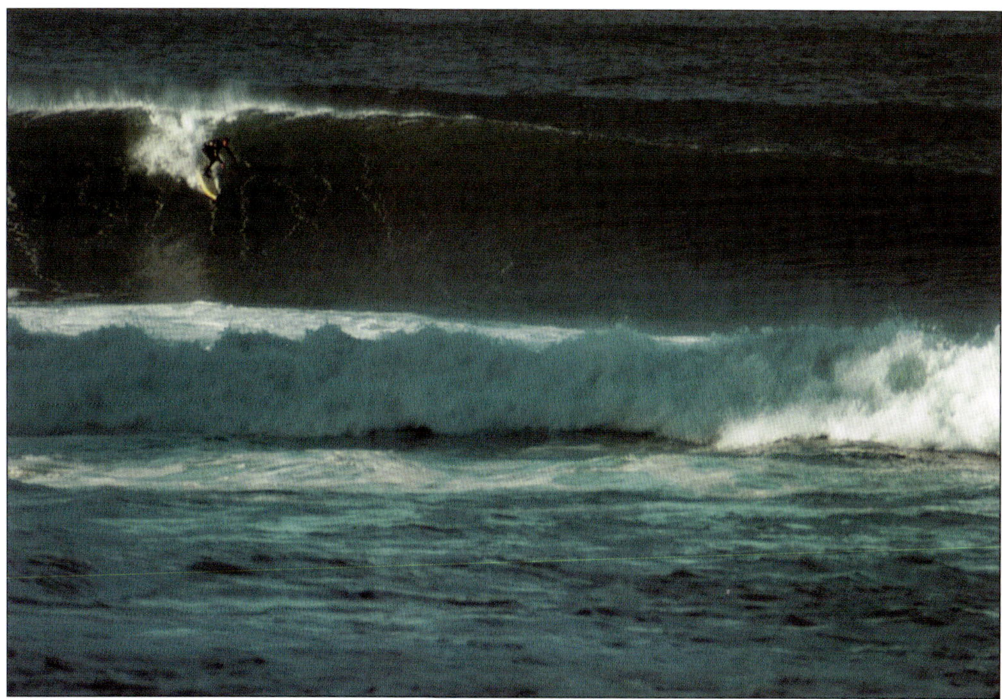

Bruce Prator is charging Second Point in the early 1970s. Shoemake recalls, "Bruce was in the Navy, stationed on Oahu, surfing the North Shore in the sixties before moving here." Prator was known as a charger. Tim Foley called him "B.B. Prator, King of the Surf" and recalls he did not like crowds at First Point. "Too many guys out and Prator would go to Second Point. He looked like an ant when Second Point was big." (Photograph by Scott Blackman.)

Bruce Prator is seen hanging out at the Point in the early 1970s. Perry Shoemake recalls, "Prator was a burly character, big mustache and glasses. He was known as Snoose for his propensity for chewing tobacco. He was the kind of guy you would want on your side in a bar room brawl. Prator acquired the nickname the 'Predator' from decades of charging First and Second Point by himself. He is a living legend whose powerful style merited the respect of generations." (Courtesy of Bill Smith.)

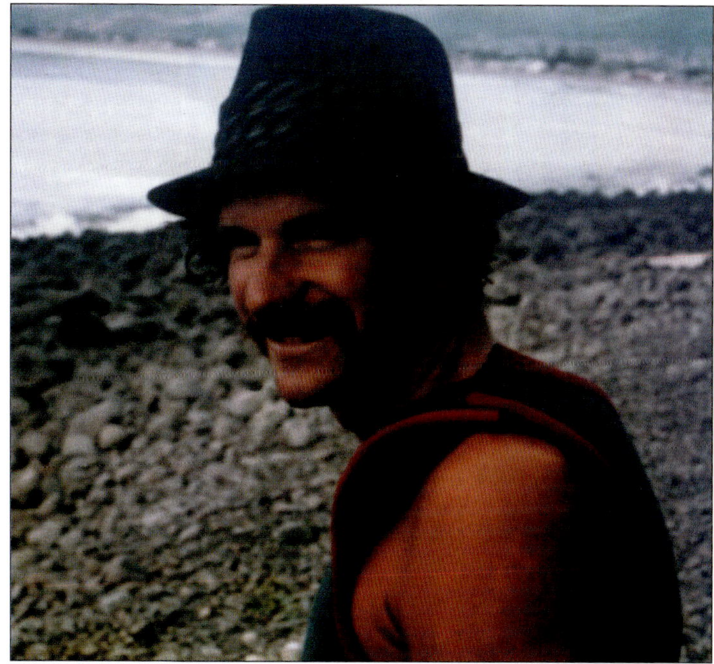

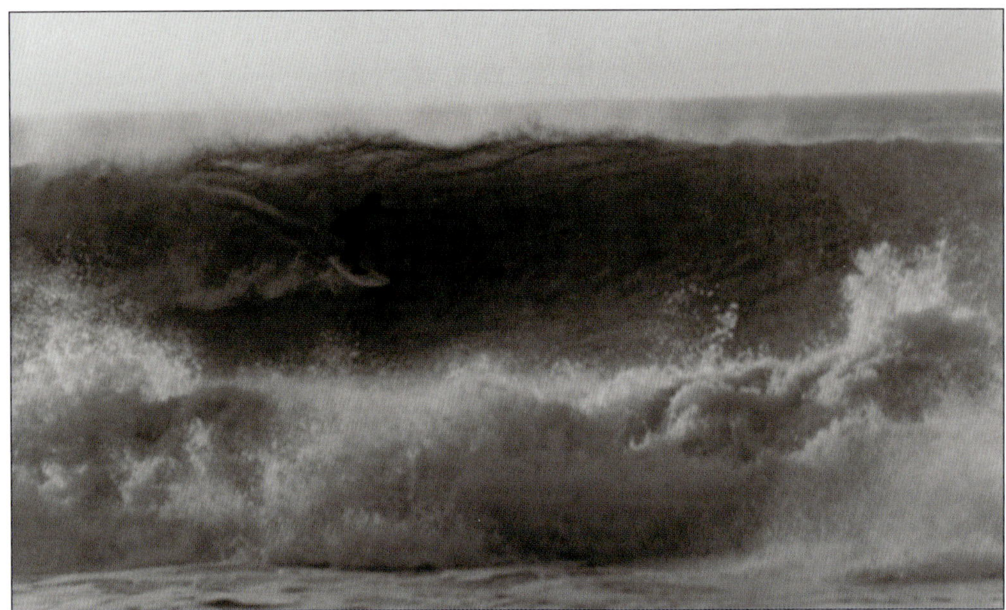

Jerry Harrington, who appears "locked in" at the Point in 1976, recalls, "We lived close to the beach and I saw Dana Williams surf the Cove. I bought my first board together with Pierre Marchand. I mostly rode soup in the Cove. By 1968, there were more people, different board shapes and sizes arriving here. I started making boards. It was sure fun at the time. Surfing went along with lots of societal changes." (Photograph by Dan Matthews.)

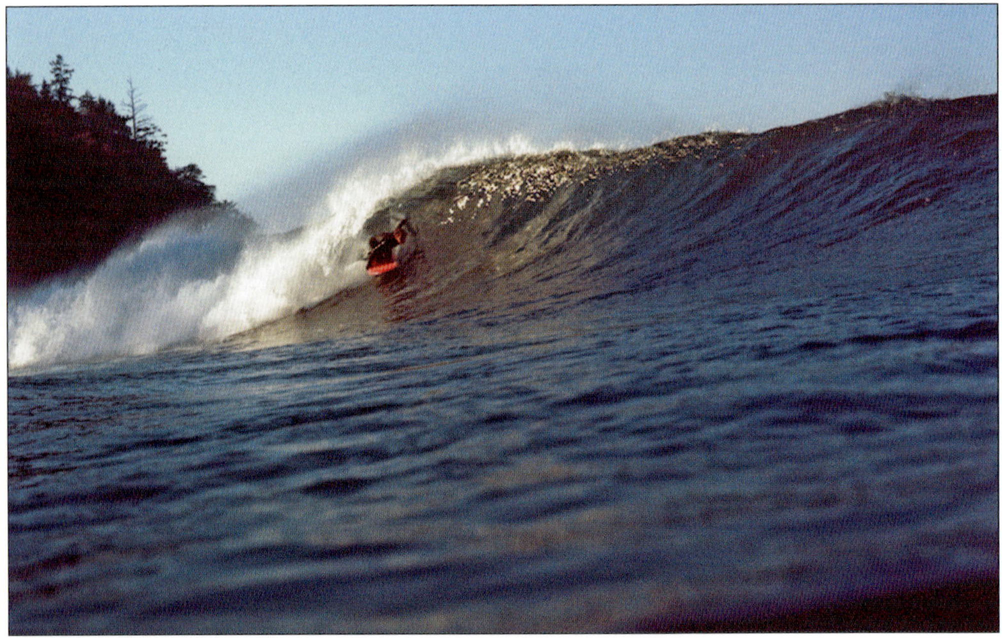

It just doesn't get any better than this. Mike Burger, pictured kneeboarding his way through the Point in 1976, remembers, "About age 13, my father would drop me off at Indian Beach to surf. It's there I met Sandy Barrett, Wally Parcels, and others. Couple of years later, Sandy and Wally took me out to the Cove for my first time. I got flogged. I was hooked and stoked! A year after graduating from Renton High School, Washington, I moved to Seaside." (Photograph by Tim Mack.)

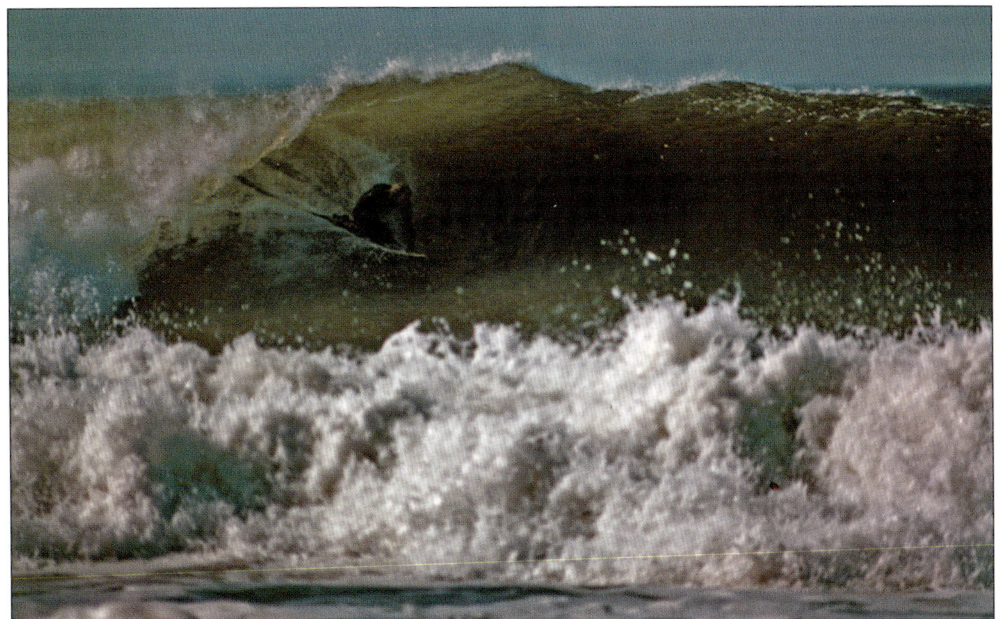

Knox Swanson, out running a nice section at the Point in 1976, recalls, "I rode straight in until I saw Sandy Barrett going right and left. My first kneeboards were made by Jeff Hull. Mike Burger and I did dawn patrol with Prator, the 'King' at the Point. We were the court jesters with him on our kneeboards. Burger credits Knox Swanson with getting him into kneeboarding. (Photograph by Tim Mack.)

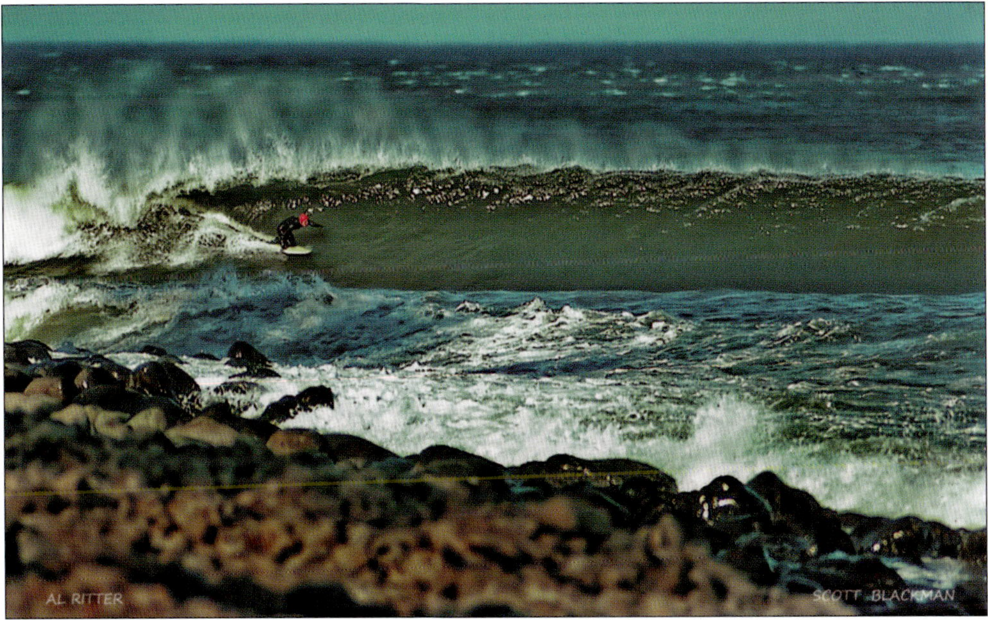

Al Ritter, who moved from Renton, Washington, after high school in 1969, is seen racing across a Point wave in 1976. Mike Burger states, "Ritter, Mike Brown, and myself all migrated to the Seaside/Gearhart/Cannon Beach area from Seattle at various times, within months of each other. The three of us, including Knox Swanson and Jerry Lampert, were the core group of kneeboarders back then. Al was a good Point surfer." (Photograph by Scott Blackman.)

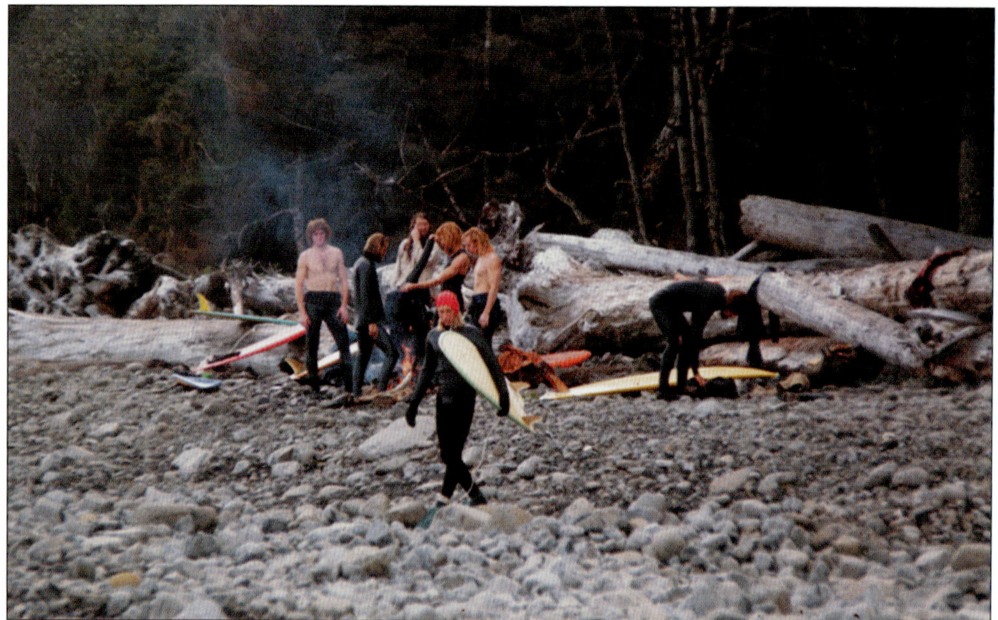

Agate and Seaside surfers are clustered together at the rocky beach in front of the Point in the early 1970s. From left to right are Agate surfer Perry Shoemake, Seaside surfers Art Spence and Jeff Trenary, Agate surfers and brothers Tim and Jerry Holbrook, with Al Ritter (front) wearing the red aqua lid. Knox Swanson comments, "at the time, surfers from California and around Oregon were welcomed at the Point in the early days of surfing." (Photograph by Tim Mack.)

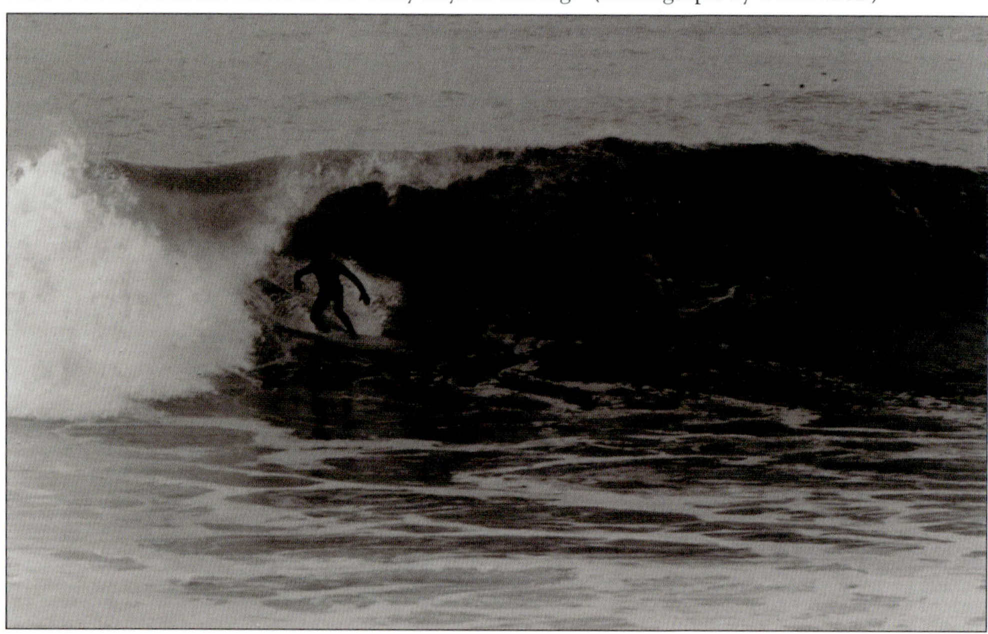

David Kopra, seen here surfing the Point in 1978, bought three acres above the Point in 1976 and calls it "God's Pocket." Jeff Hull recalls, "A hot shower often followed a surf session and something to eat or drink as we warmed up by the wood stove. We knew we had it really good being David's friend, but in hindsight it is a debt I will never be able to fully repay." (Courtesy of David Kopra.)

An unidentified surfer descends the wooden stairs through the thick brush and forest to the Point in December 1975. "The stairs were located on a landing above the Lanai Motel and below Kopra's property above the Point," Greg Gosser reminisces. Unfortunately, the aged stairway has now disappeared. Kopra has owned the land above the Point since 1976, and surfers have been welcomed for decades. (Photograph by Scott Blackman.)

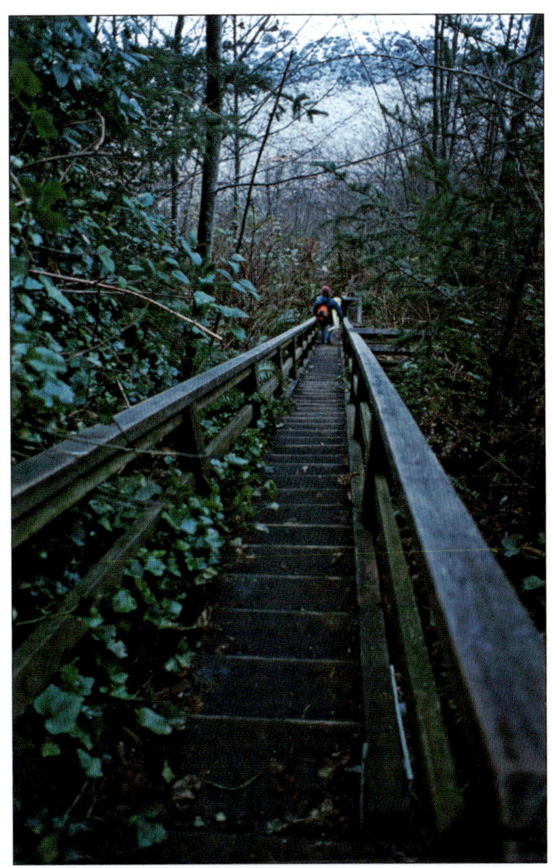

Josh Gizdavich, pictured here in 1976, became a skilled Point rider in his youth. Note the tree line in the background. "I was young and with my parents when I saw surfers run out of a van, over the rocks to the Point in the snow," Gizdavich says. "I was 13 years old in 1969 when I began to surf seriously. I started renting boards and went to the Cove. As a ninth grader I would get rides with seniors to surf at Short Sands." (Photograph by Tim Mack.)

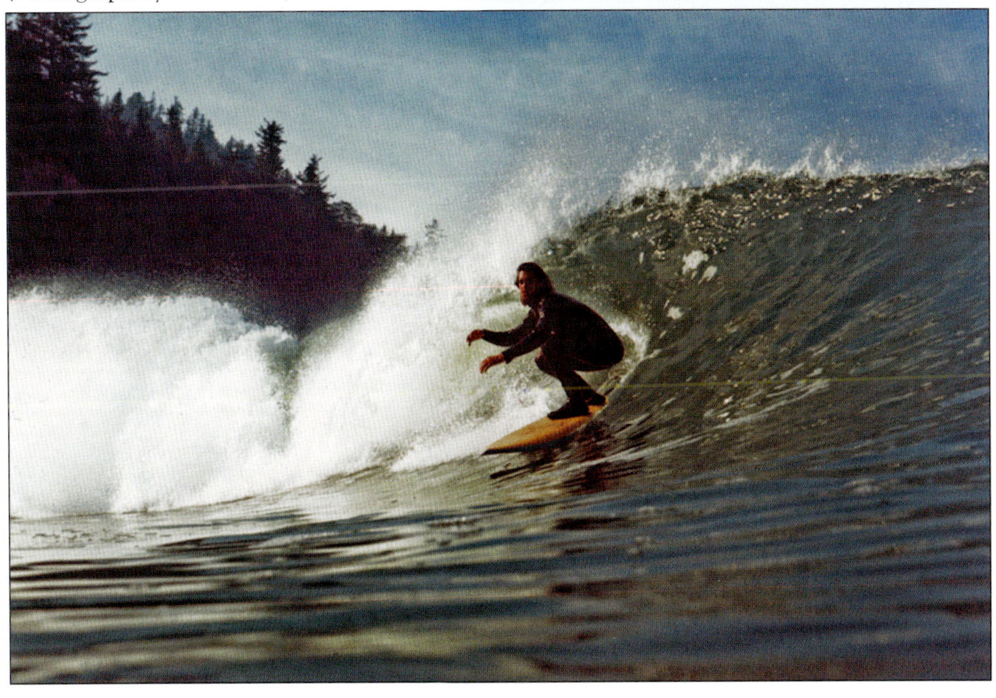

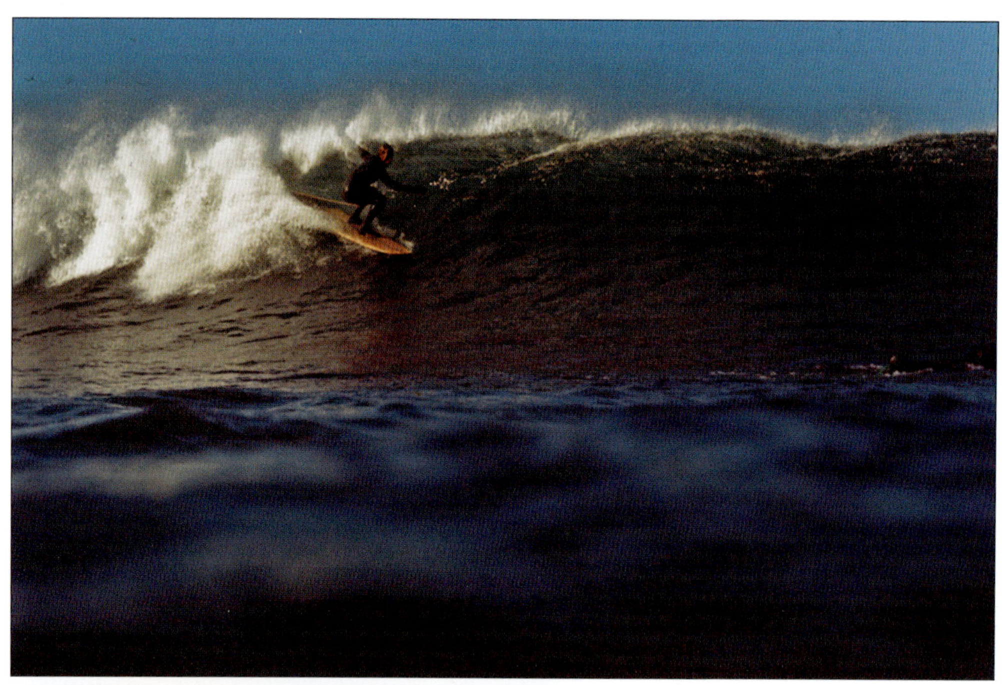

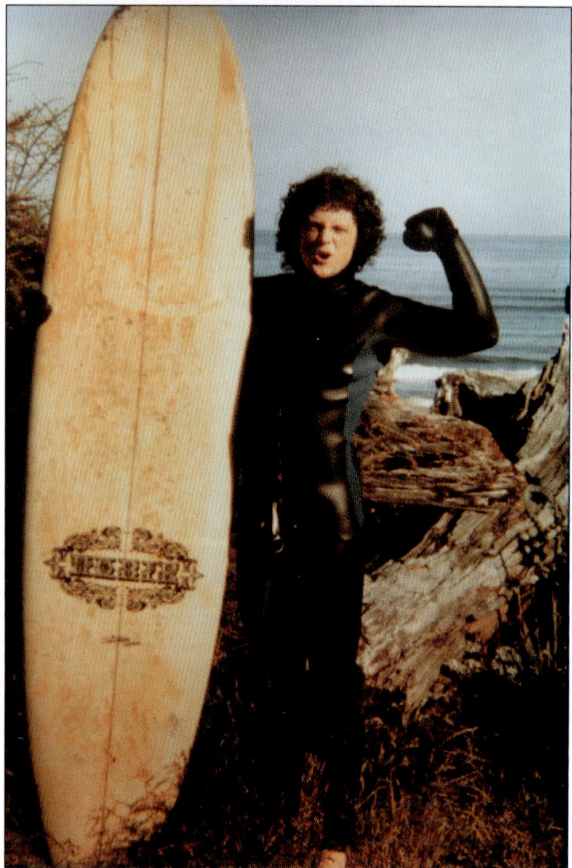

Phil Mancill, a Marine who served in the Vietnam War, is pictured here surfing the Point in the 1970s. Perry Shoemake recalls, "Phil drove his '53 Chevy coupe named *Cannabis* across the United States from Florida, where he had learned to surf. The backseat was torn out and a plywood bed stretched into the trunk. Phil was a good surfer and artist who now lives in Seaside." (Photograph by Tim Mack.)

Jack Molan strikes a pose with his surfboard in the summer of 1973. Molan was raised in Bend and graduated from high school in 1973. His parents grew up in Seaside, and he came to Seaside to surf as a teenager. Jack recalls, "Josh's brother Marco took this photo. I was given this old Hobie, and I reglassed the bottom and put a plywood fin on it. It was a long board back then, as no one rode long boards." (Courtesy of Josh Gizdavich.)

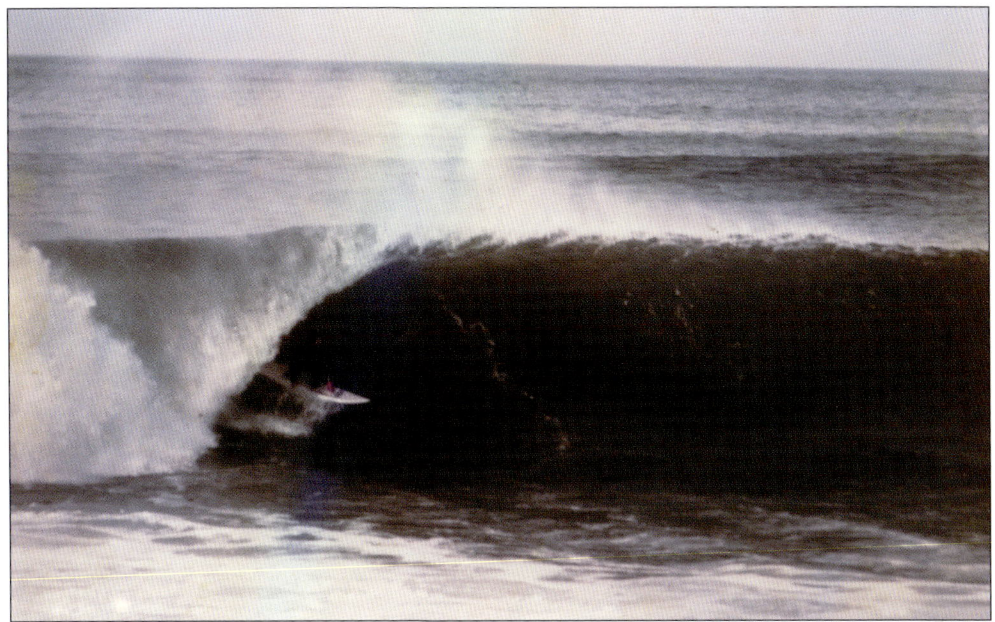

Jack Molan gets barreled at the Point on his seven-foot-ten Barnfield Lightning Bolt round-pin single fin in the fall of 1979. Jack comments, "What we had was a world class surf spot, and as surfers we knew we had it good. David Kopra had huge influence on my life. He'd come down from Alaska with new Bill Barnfield surfboards. His home was a pivot point for so many incredible Point surf days." (Photograph by Knox Swanson.)

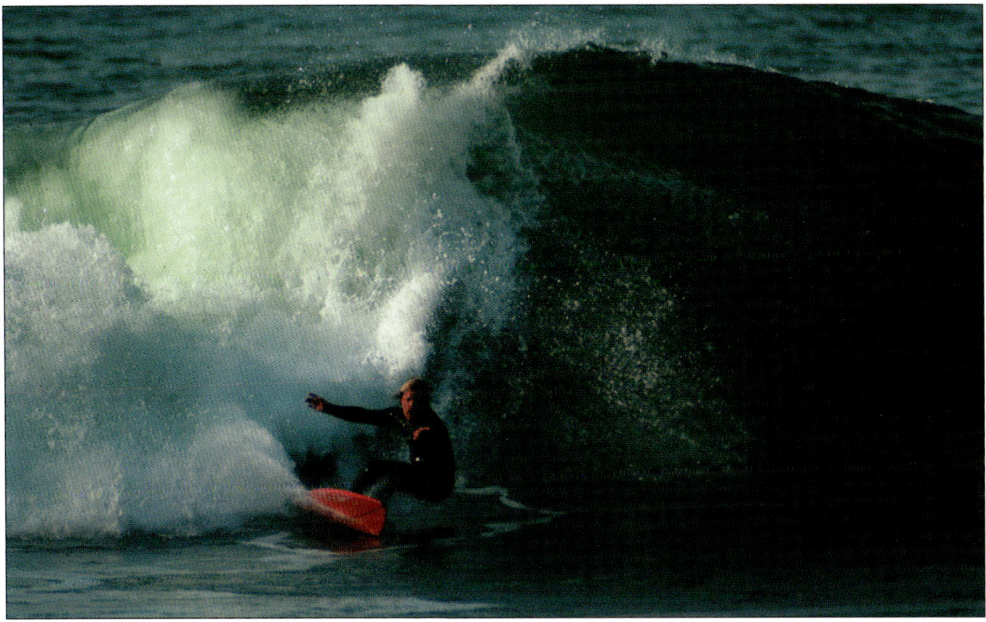

Pictured here is Jerry Holbrook in a powerful turn off the bottom of a wave at the Point. Perry Shoemake explains, "Jerry was considered one of the most powerful surfers at the Point." Surfing lore has it that Holbrook hung out with Shoemake in a treehouse above Second Point in the fall of 1972. They would leave their boards by the creek and surf like crazy, until Bruce Prator took their boards as a practical joke. (Photograph by Scott Blackman.)

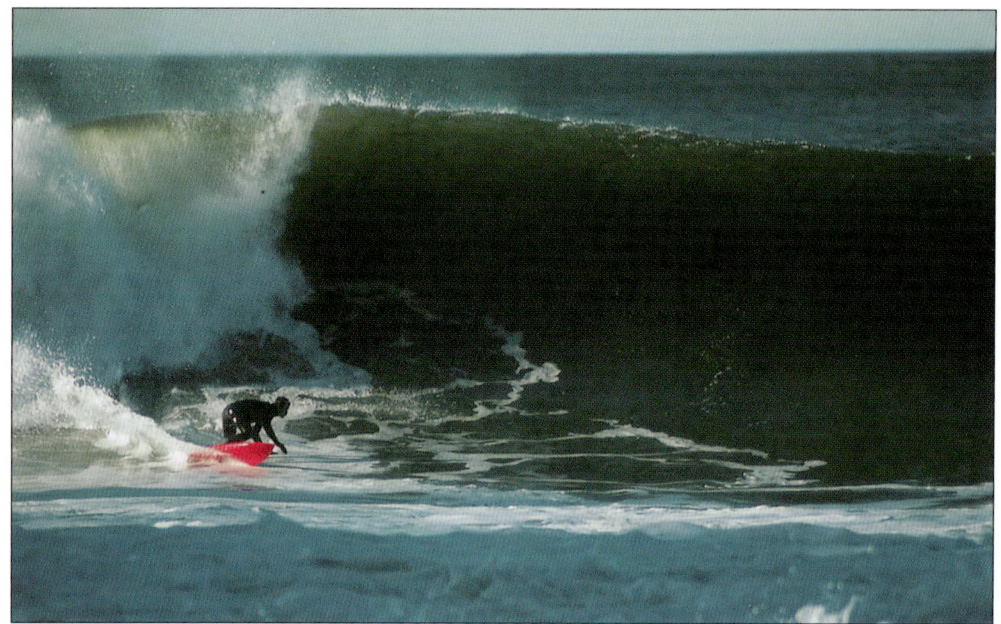

Marty Skriver is seen here jamming a hard bottom turn at the Point. According to Perry Shoemake, "Marty was by far the best surfer around. He had a fluid and powerful style that was a step above the rest. His reputation held as North Coast surfers all moved through the short-board revolution in the late 1960s and early 1970s. He lived in Seaside for a while in the seventies." Tim Foley recalls, "Marty's style was absolute smooth, total board control." (Photograph by Scott Blackman.)

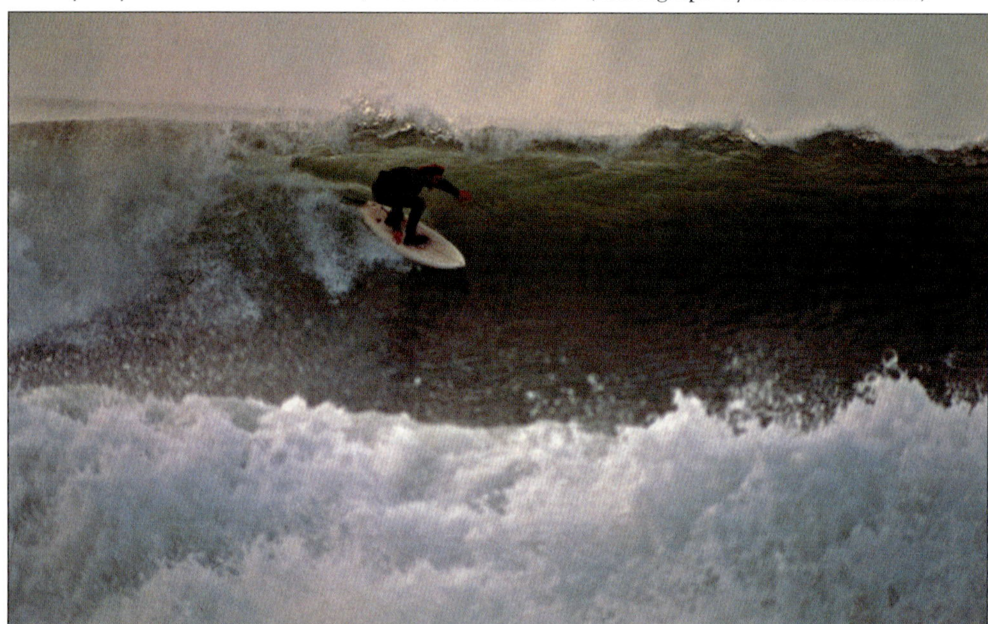

Perry Shoemake, seen here riding the Point in 1978, recalls, "I'm riding one of several six-foot-four twin-fins that I made from old longboards. I stripped all the glass off the foam and made new short boards out of them. I had to glue with resin a chunk of foam on the decks of the nose sections to get enough rocker for the new boards. I loved twin-fins (quads now!) So loose and fast!" (Photograph by Tim Mack.)

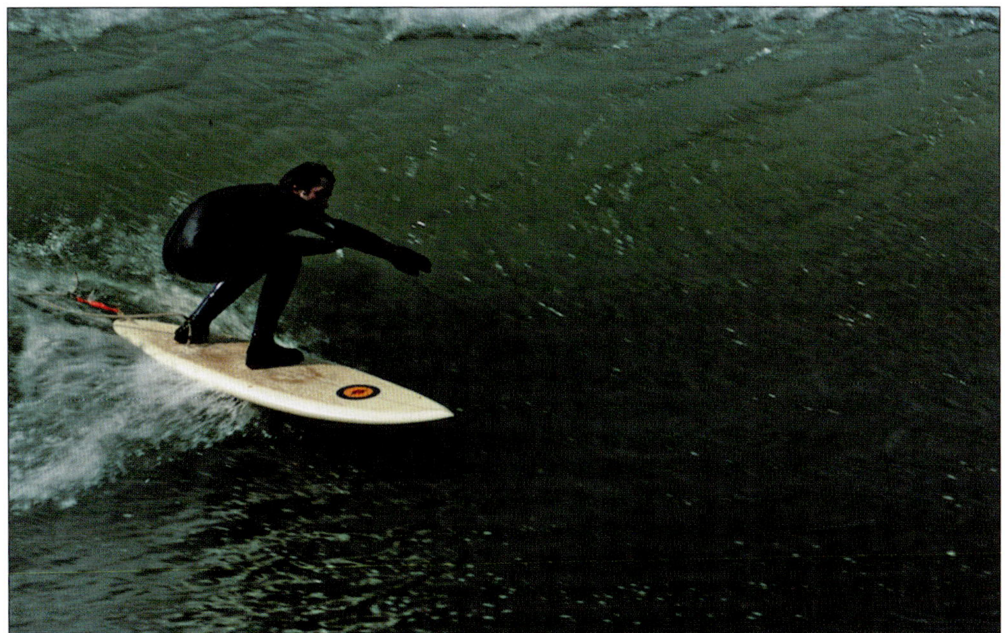

Growing up in Seaside, Marc Ward, pictured at the Point in 1980, learned to surf along with his brothers Needham Ward and Josh Gizdavich. In 1979, while working at the Crab Broiler, Marc's board was stolen off his Volkswagen van. Then, 24 years later, it was discovered at a surf contest and returned to him by Mike Jipp. The board is on display at his brother's Seaside shop, Cleanline Surf Shop. (Photograph by Tim Mack.)

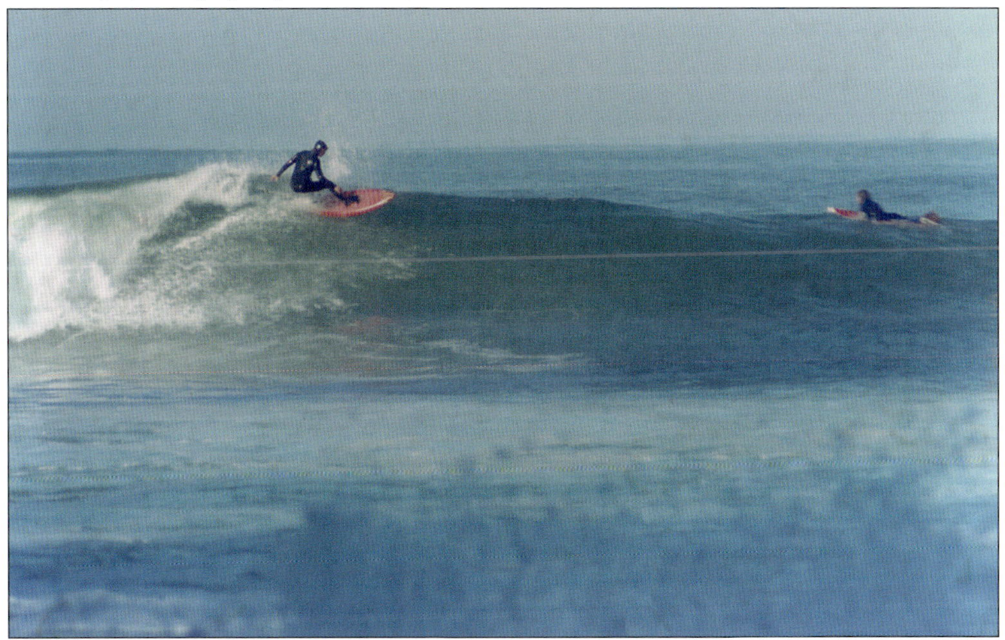

Phil Kennedy is pictured here surfing the Point in 1979. Phil recalls, "I heard about Seaside and begged my dad to take me there when I was in the seventh grade. Saw the most amazing wave ever at the Point. I moved to Seaside two days after I graduated from high school. No job, knew no one, but I had to ride that wave. I continued to surf there for 15 years." (Courtesy of Phil Kennedy.)

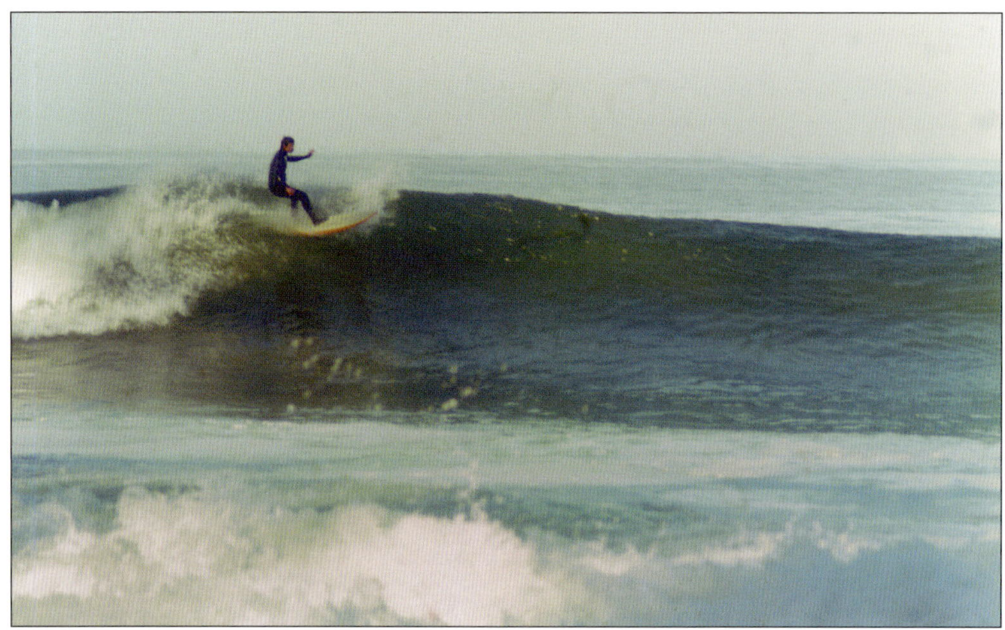

Tim Mack, an accomplished photographer and surfer, is seen here surfing at the Point in 1979. Tim remembers, "I learned how to surf in Hawaii starting when I was in middle school. I would go over there every year with my father, Forbes Mack, and surf." Mack graduated from Sunset High School in 1968 and spent time surfing various locations from Pacific City to Seaside over the years. (Photograph by Rik Cederstrom.)

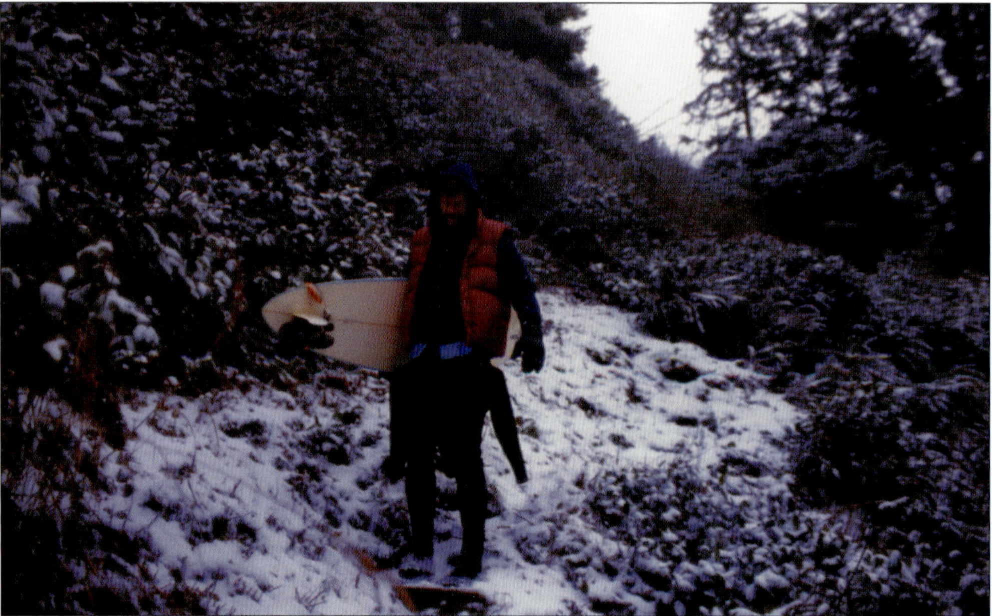

Dave Seely nears the bottom of David Kopra's trail at the Point in December 1985. Jeff Hull comments, "When it's freezing cold the ocean temperature is warmer than the beach, which seems really strange as you paddle out. We always layered up pretty well on these cold days. I often wore a short john under a full suit with hood. Snow on the ground always kept the crowds down substantially." (Photograph by Jeff Hull.)

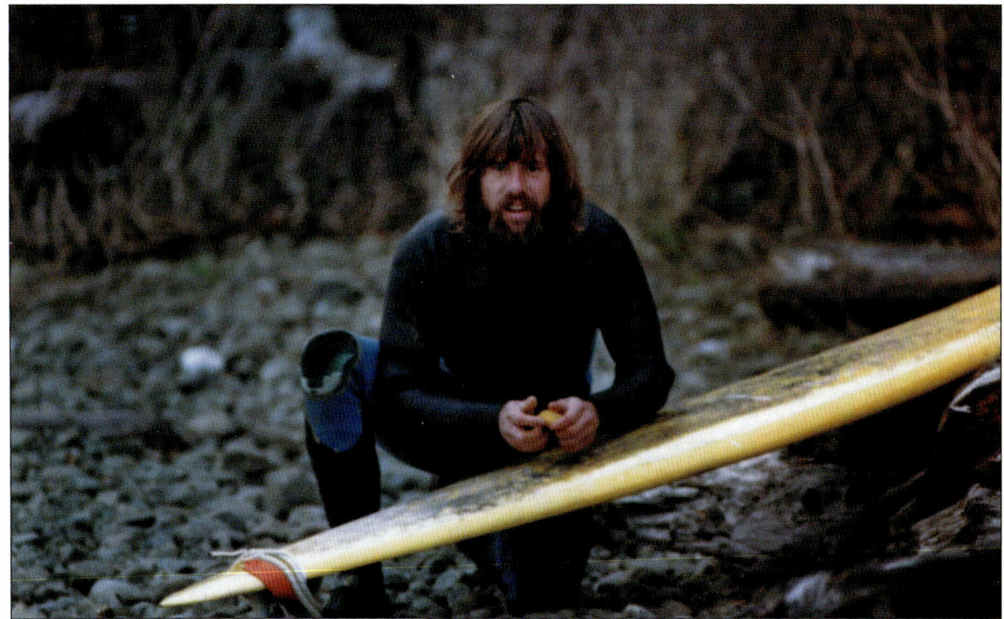

Kenny Doudt poses here at the Point in the early 1980s. On November 27, 1979, Doudt was savagely attacked while surfing at Haystack Rock, Cannon Beach. The white shark was estimated to be 17 feet long and 3,500 pounds. After returning to surfing, Doudt needed warmer water due to his injuries, and moved to Hawaii. He wrote a book, *Surfing with the Great White Shark*, about the experience. Doudt wrote, "It was just my lucky day to survive." (Courtesy of Bill Smith.)

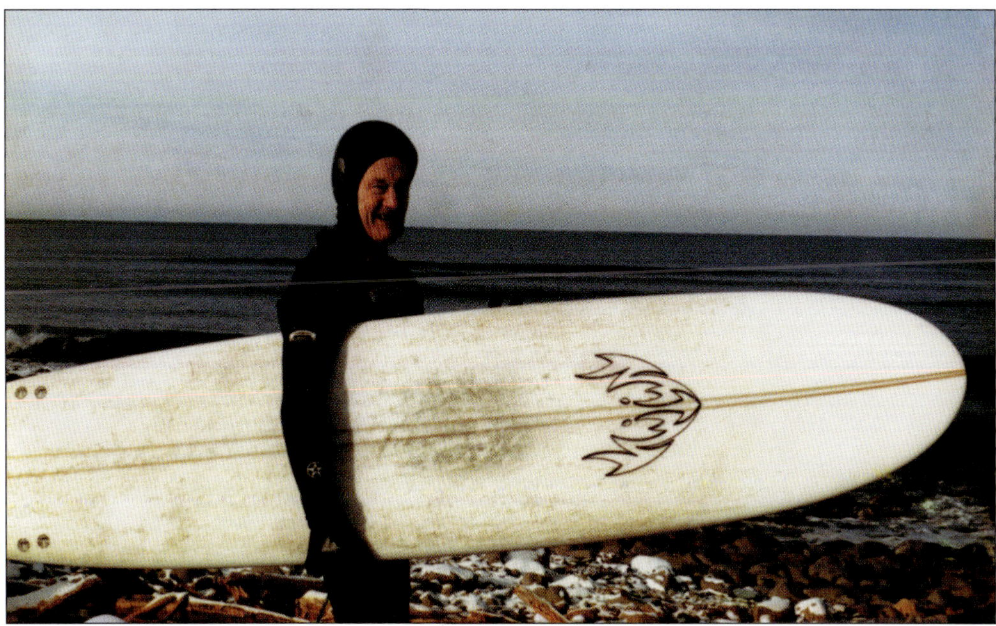

Pictured here in 1999 is 79-year-old Jack Brown, with a Tom Scott board, preparing to surf the Cove. Lexie Hallahan comments, "Jack Brown's presence every morning in the Seaside Cove at 8:00 a.m. for a 'surf check' was like clockwork and always a positive stoke. The waves might be small or slightly overhead, it didn't matter, Jack was paddling out for a session. He always had a great smile and shared his love of surfing with everyone!" (Photograph by Lexie Hallahan.)

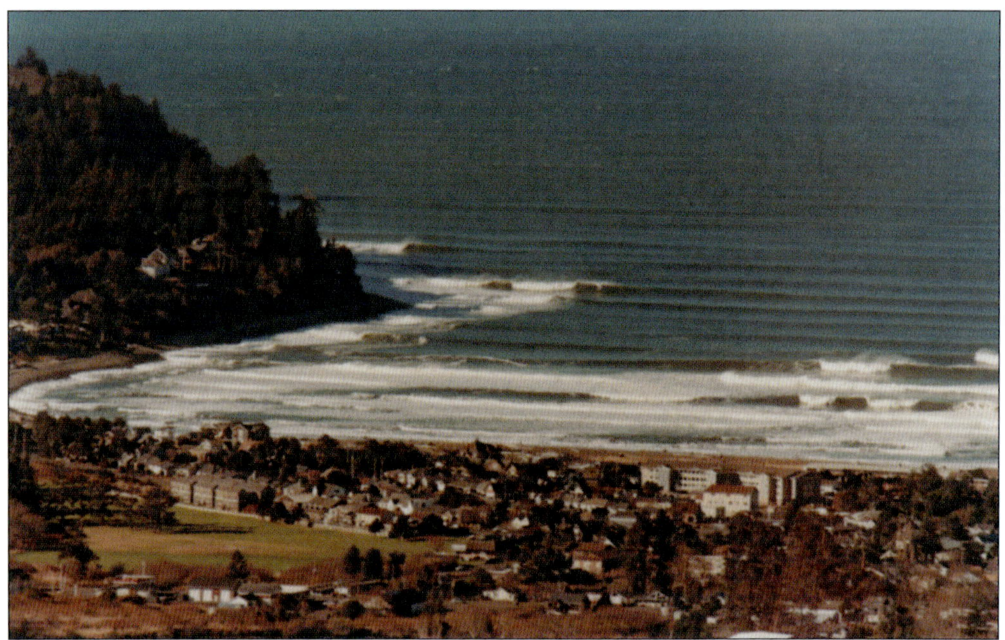

This view from the hills above Seaside captures the city, the Cove, Tillamook Head, and the Point. Scott Blackman comments, "The Point itself lies within the city limits of Seaside. The Point provides the possibility of very consistent waves when it's on. It allows all those who surf it regularly to improve their surfing skills on a very challenging wave. Surfers unable to surf the Point, surf the Cove." (Courtesy of Bruce Prator.)

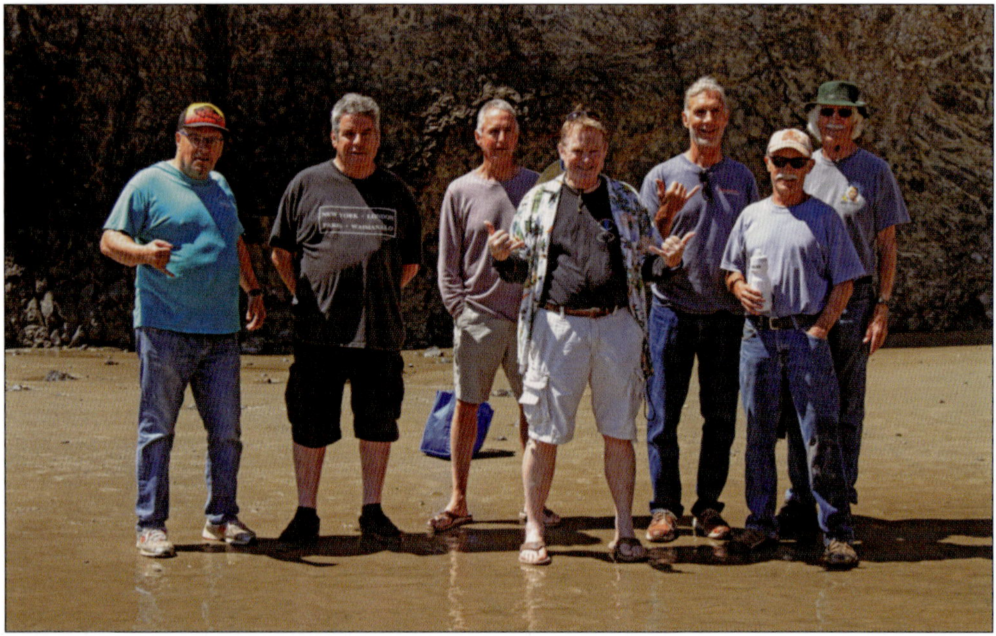

A group of pioneer Seaside surfers gather for a reunion at Agate Beach in July 2015. Many surfers from around Oregon attended the 50-year celebration of surfing at Agate Beach, north of Newport. From left to right are Steve "Red Trunks" Johnson, Scott Blyth, Peter de Turk, Greg Gosser, Randy Barna, Ron Hill, and Dick Wald. (Photograph by Scott Blackman.)

Two

Cannon Beach to Pacific City

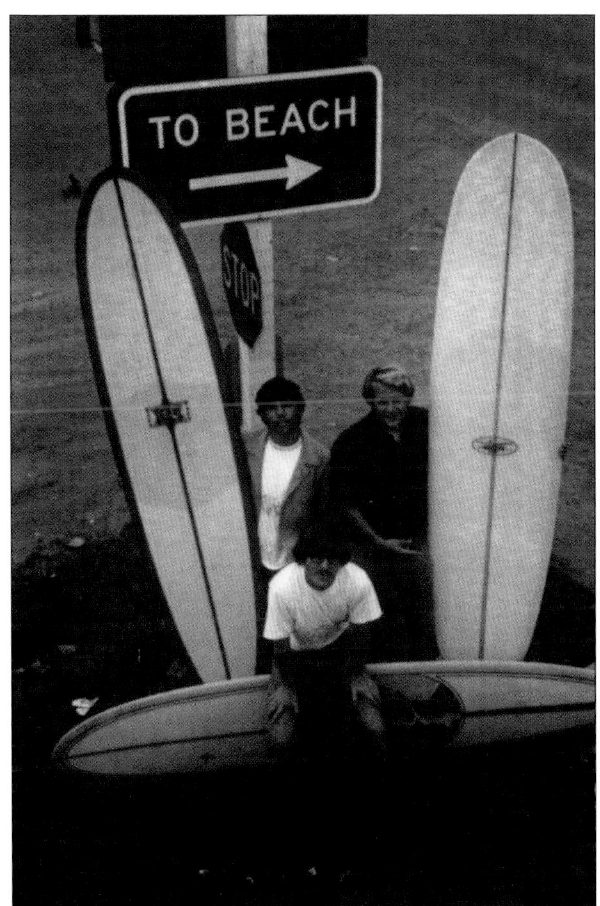

In the summer of 1965, Vince Morrison opened the first surf shop in Cannon Beach in a small area of the Coaster Theater. By the summer of 1967, Jim Sparks opened his surf shop down the street in the Morris Log Cabin on Second Avenue and Hemlock Street. Standing in front of Sparks's surf shop in November 1968 are surfers David Louis (back left) and Sandy Barrett. In front is Dick Borovicka, who remembers, "Sandy and I lived in the surf shop. I slept in the back and Sandy slept in the front next to all the surfboards." According to Knox Swanson, "In the early days of surfing, surf shops were fronts to get wetsuits and boards at cost. There were underground surf shops that came and went. You could get away with that back then. Beginning surf shops satisfied the demand of the time." (Courtesy of Max Justice.)

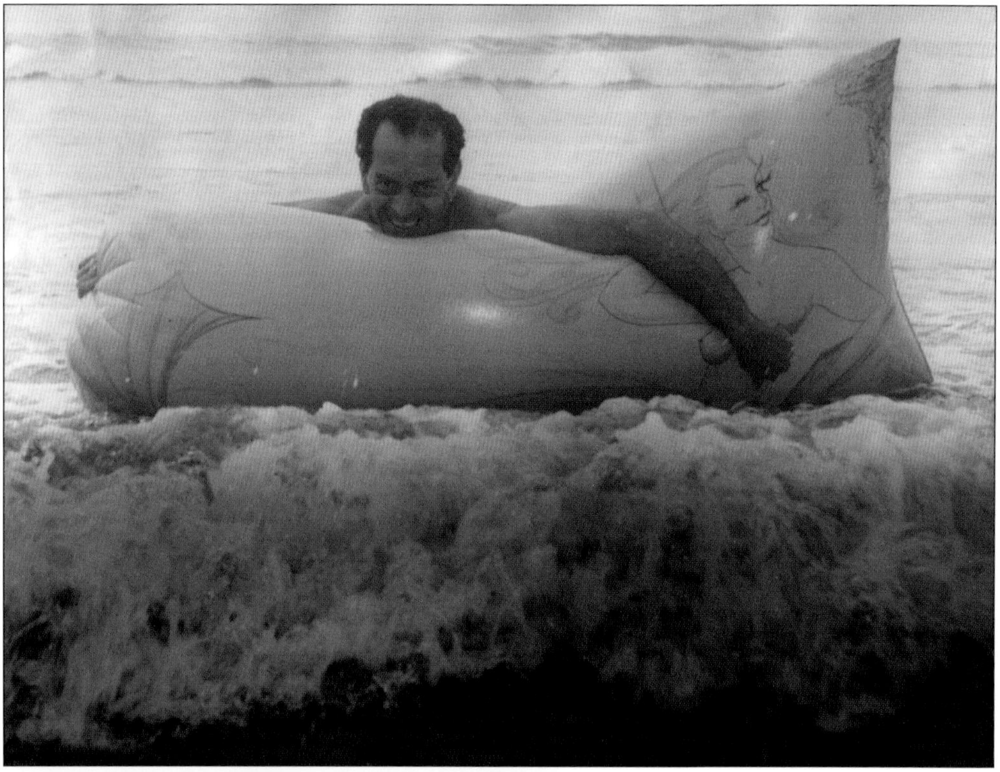

Max Allara is pictured here using a breaker bag at Cannon Beach around 1955. Mitch remembers, "My father, Max Allara, would hoist me to his back and shoulders as he body surfed his breaker bag on the whitewater waves at Chapman Point, the north end of Cannon Beach. The breaker bag was a bed sheet sewn together, making a large pillowcase." These were used as floatable devices to surf in Cannon Beach in the 1950s. (Courtesy of Mitch Allara.)

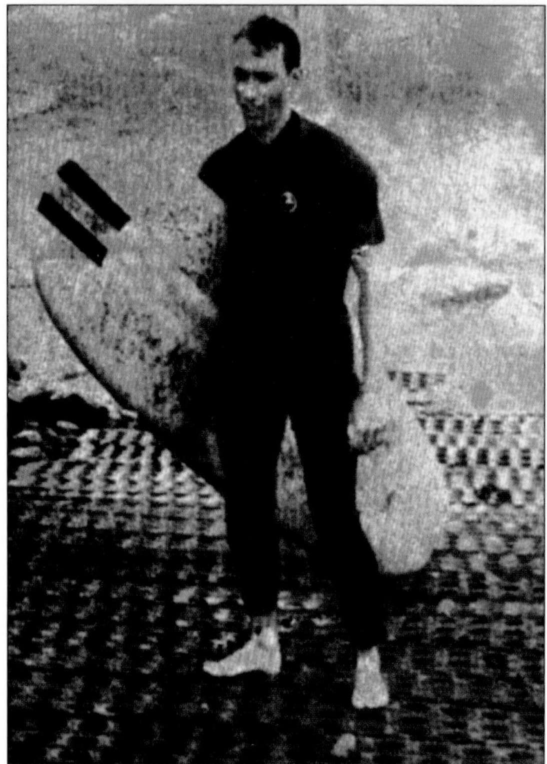

Mike Zalk was an entrepreneur and self-promoter. John Alto recalls, "Mike Zalk's family moved to Seaside in the early 1960s and he was a better surfer than all of us. Zalk had surfed in California and he showed up about the same time as Dana Williams. Zalk hired me to work concert gigs for Paul Revere and the Raiders, the Ventures, and Sonny and Cher at Oregon State University." (Courtesy of Jerry Alto.)

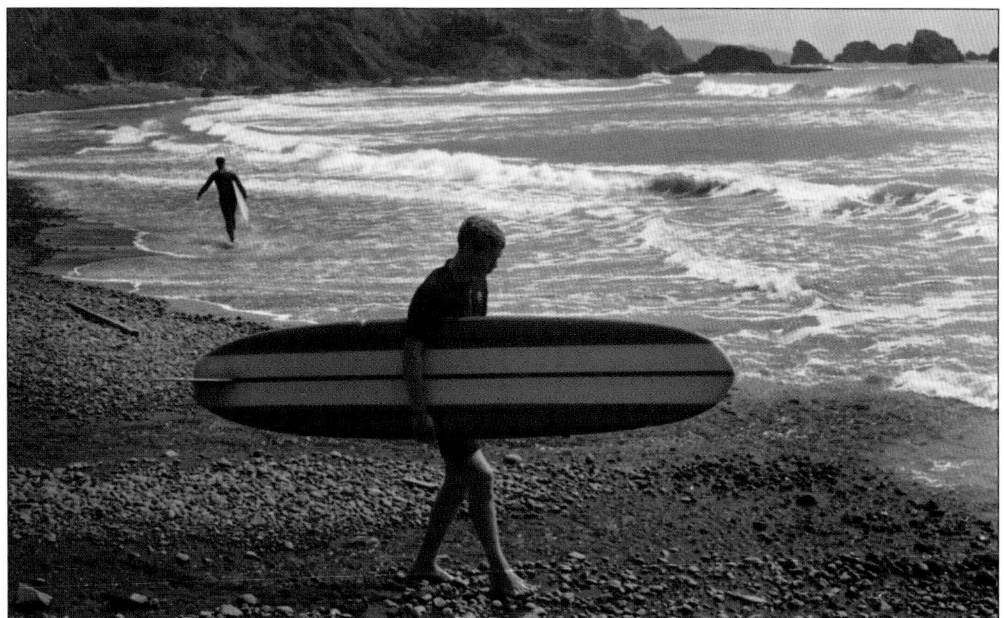

Seaside surfer Mark Hansen heads toward the water at Indian Beach in 1963. Mark comments, "Dana was the pivotal guy in Seaside starting in 1961. I played sports but I wasn't that good. Surfing was fun and better than football. Surfing was new and it made us different. My first board was a nine-foot-six Velzy. I've surfed every year for 50 years." Dana Williams taught Hansen to surf at Indian Beach. They surfed the Cove later. (Photograph by Jerry Alto.)

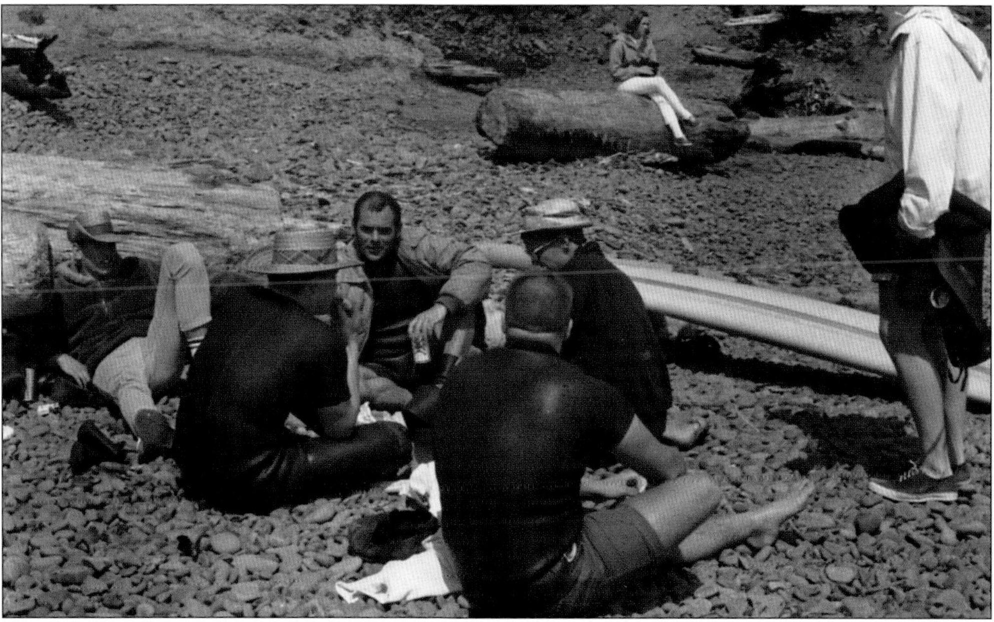

Surfers hanging out at Indian Beach around 1963 are, from left to right, Gary Hansen, Dallas Cook, unidentified, Pierre Marchand, Dick Wald, and Mark Hansen (partially obscured). Wald recalls, "I began surfing in July 1963. I surfed Indian Beach and met Dana Williams and the group. I came every weekend from Portland. That winter Dana called and we started surfing Avenue U and the Cove. That's when we first noticed the Point wave." (Photograph by Jerry Alto.)

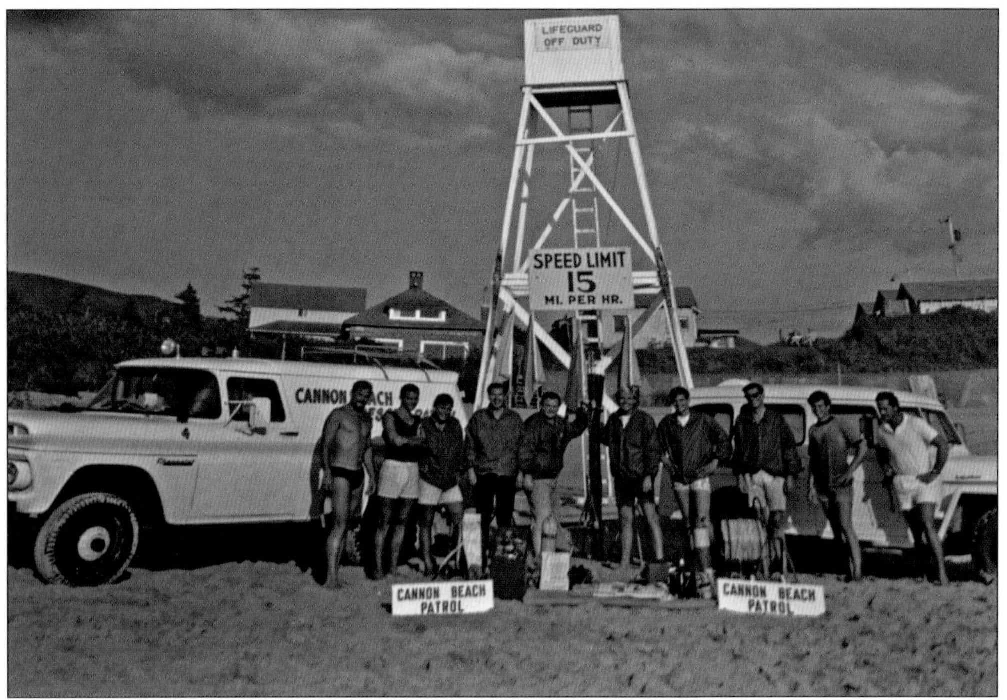

The 1964 Cannon Beach Patrol poses in front of a lifeguard stand. From left to right are Malcom Cant, Peter Lindsey, Tim Lindsey, Sam Foster, Bruce Doran, Tim Riddle, Pieter Van Dyke, Bruce Luzader, Paul Dueber, and Tony Knight. Many of the Cannon Beach Patrol, including Tim Riddle and Pieter Van Dyke, surfed with Seaside surfers. Bob Malo remembers, "Lifeguards wouldn't allow any floatable devices south of Haystack Rock until I got permission from the city council." (Courtesy of Tim Riddle.)

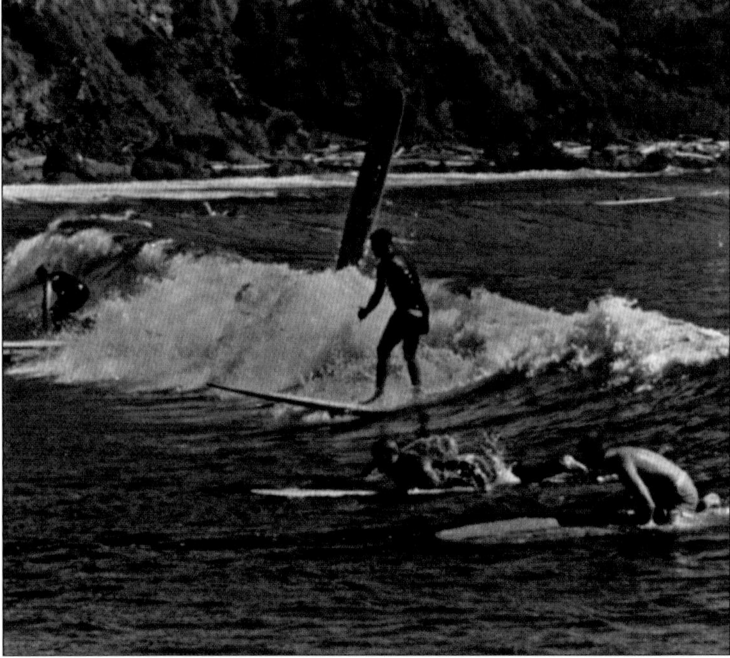

Jan Heron, standing in the center, and Dallas Cook, paddling to his right, are pictured here at Indian Beach in July 1965. Both Herron and Cook were local surfers who attended Seaside High School. Jan's brother Mike Herron recalls, "We built bonfires and surfed in our short wet suits or diving tops until our skin was purple. Then we would get out and warm up, only to go back for more waves." (Courtesy of George Daggatt.)

John Alto is pictured here at the Indian Beach parking lot in 1968, after returning from the Vietnam War. Alto comments, "It was great to watch other surfers from the elevated parking lot at Indian Beach. No restrictions on beach fires and there was an accumulation of wood on the beach because of storms. We weren't concerned about sharks back then. We thought the water too cold and they wouldn't come in there." (Courtesy of John Alto.)

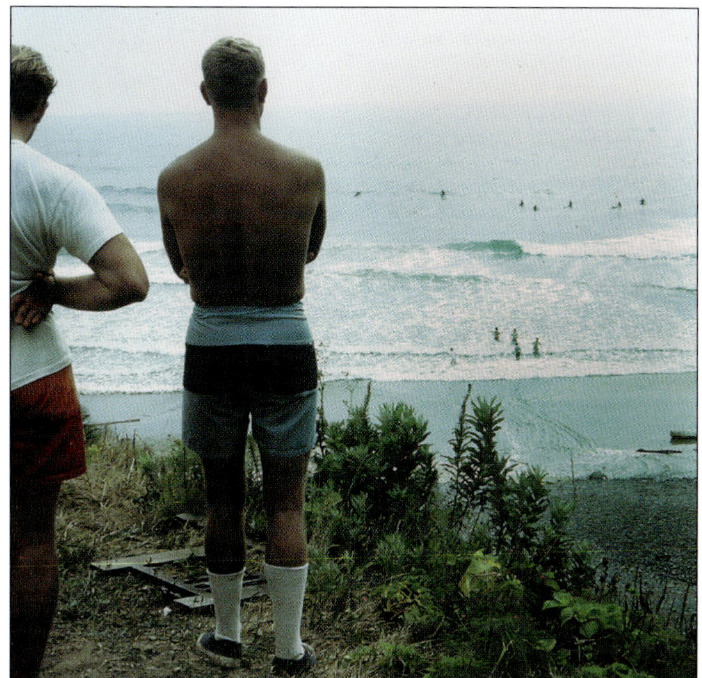

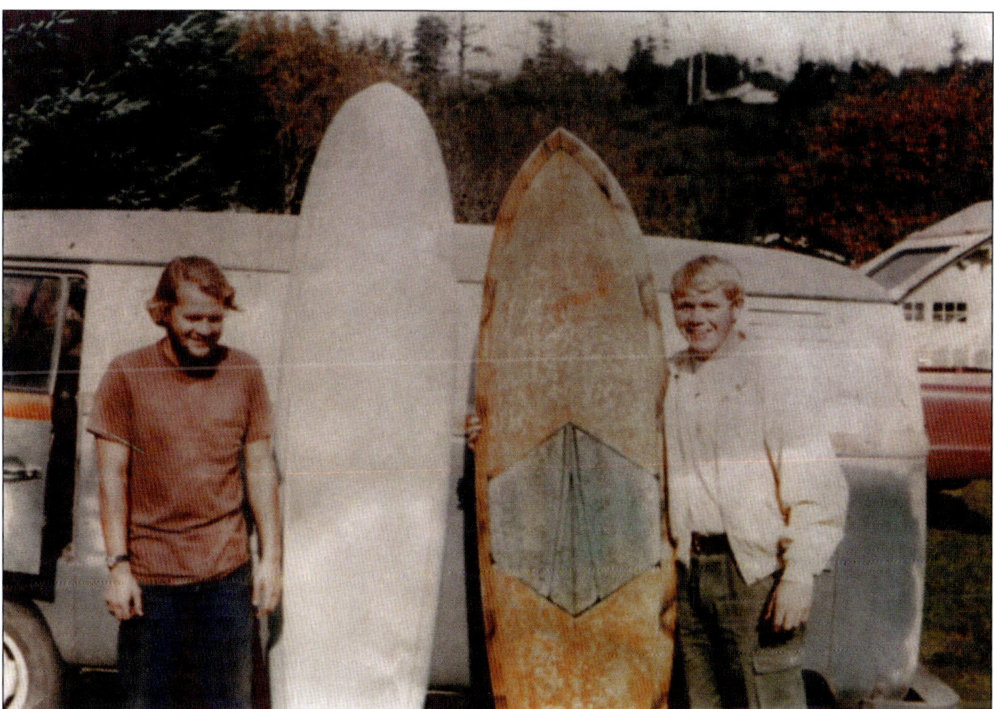

Pictured here with their boards and van are Bob Malo (left) and Sandy Barrett. Malo recalls, "My family owned the Malo's Burger Factory in Cannon Beach. My mom cooked a 'Surfer burger' and our place was a hangout for surfers. I met Sandy Barrett in the late 1960s, became friends, and he worked there. Mr. Gerald Gower of Gower Street helped me with our request to Cannon Beach City Council to allow surfing south of Haystack Rock." (Courtesy of Sandy Barrett.)

Bob Malo's North Shore Surf Club (NSSA) patch is displayed at Cannon Beach Surf Shop. NSSC members included brothers Bob and Jim Malo, Jim Martin, Tom Ladwig, Gordy Touer, and Jay Thurman. Bob Malo says, "The name was selected because of the beach north of Cannon Beach. Our hangout was Indian Beach and we surfed Short Sands some. Wally Parcels' surf shop in Seaside was our main surf shop." (Courtesy of Sandy Barrett.)

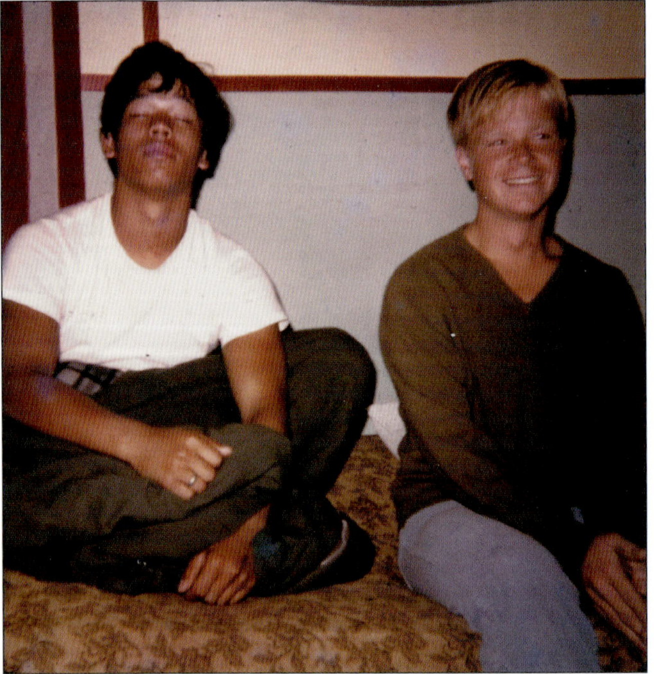

Relaxing at Captain Johnson's in Cannon Beach in 1968 are David Louis (left) and Bill Smith. Captain Johnson's inexpensive small cottages in Tolovana Park were a magnet for young surfers. Dick Borovicka remembers, "I came to the beach to hang out and found Peter Adamson, Bill Smith, Max Justice, and David Louis living at Captain Johnson's." David Louis recalls, "Bill Smith taught me how to surf in three days, then took me to the Cove." (Photograph by Barbara Garratt Castillo.)

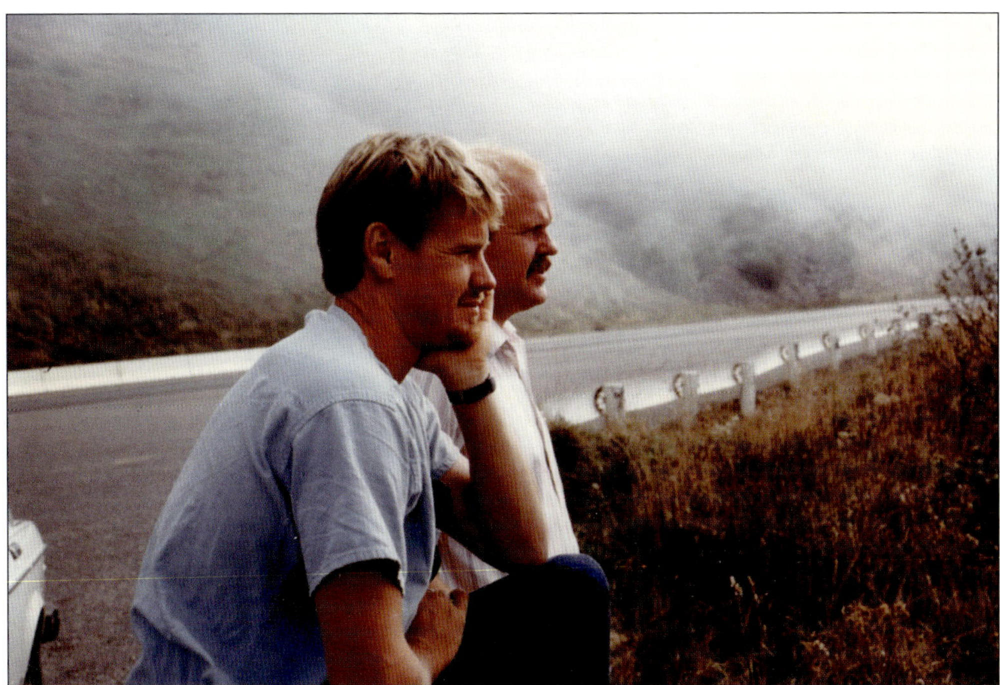

Mike Ehlen (foreground) and Bill "Seadog" Siewert are checking the lineup at Silver Point, south of Cannon Beach. Mike remembers, "Lots of spots were being discovered in those days and we even named a couple. The exploration aspect and the newness of the sport on the Oregon Coast made it exciting to be a surfer. We felt like pioneers, ocean adventurers. Seadog and I were tight surfing buds throughout the early seventies." (Courtesy of Mike Ehlen.)

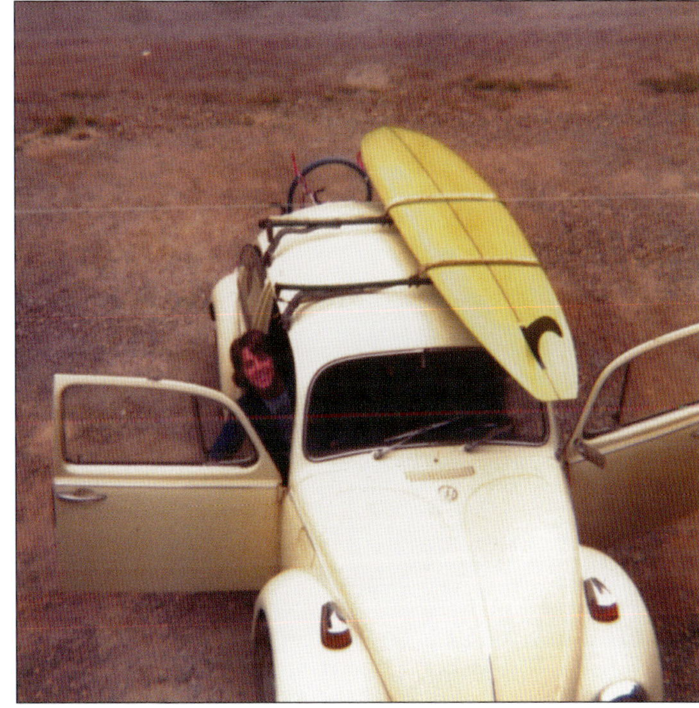

Peter Blyth peers out of his Volkswagen at Cannon Beach in the mid-1970s. Bob Malo remembers, "Driving on the beach was allowed past Silver Point to Hug Point, approximately four miles. Eventually beach driving was closed at all places." Mike Ehlen comments, "Peter truly holds a place in Oregon surfing history. Peter was always about style. He's always been completely into Dewey Weber, Harbour, Velzy, and so forth. He collects these boards and rides them." (Photograph by Dellanne McGregor.)

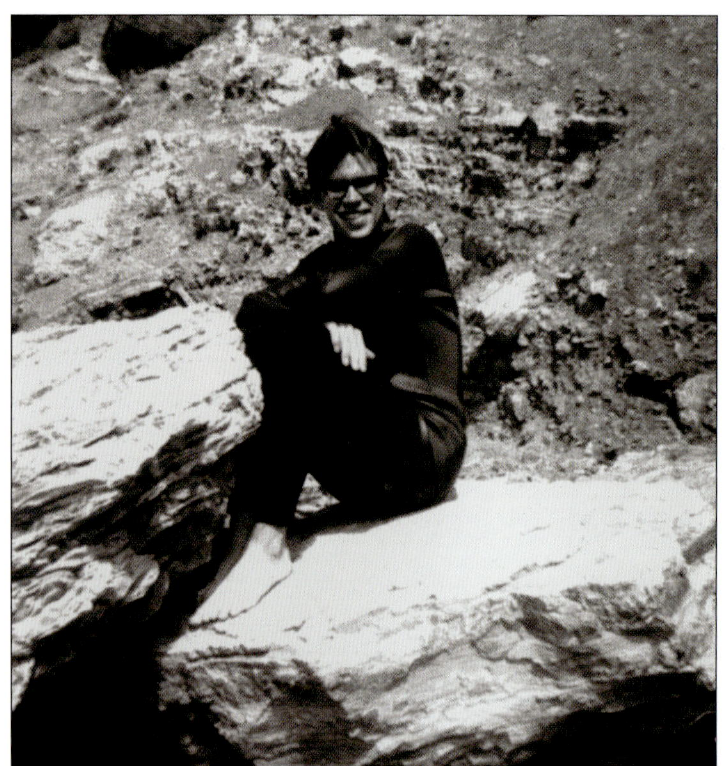

Peter Adamson relaxes on a rock at Short Sands in 1969. On July 23, 1964, the *Seaside Signal* featured Peter Adamson: "A member of the Seaside chapter of the North Shores Surf Club (NSSC), Adamson, an experienced surfer and author of several magazine articles on the fast growing sport along with manager, owner Phil Wilson of Portland's Foster Ski Chalet made a presentation to the Seaside Chamber of Commerce about the surfing organization." (Photograph by Barbara Garratt Castillo.)

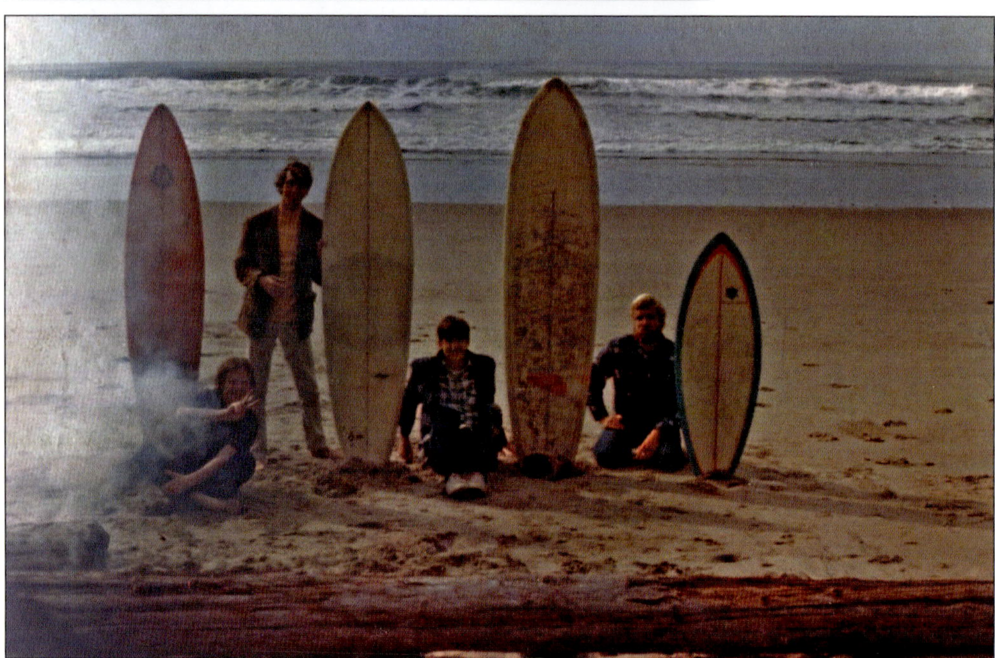

From left to right are surfers Greg Gosser, David McKinney, Steve Kraske, and Knox Swanson at Short Sands in the fall of 1969. Gosser recalls, "McKinney came from Florida and surfed here for 10 years. The board behind me was shaped by Jeff Hull and was one of my all-time favorites. A diamond tail with a slight dropped V!" (Photograph by Knox Swanson.)

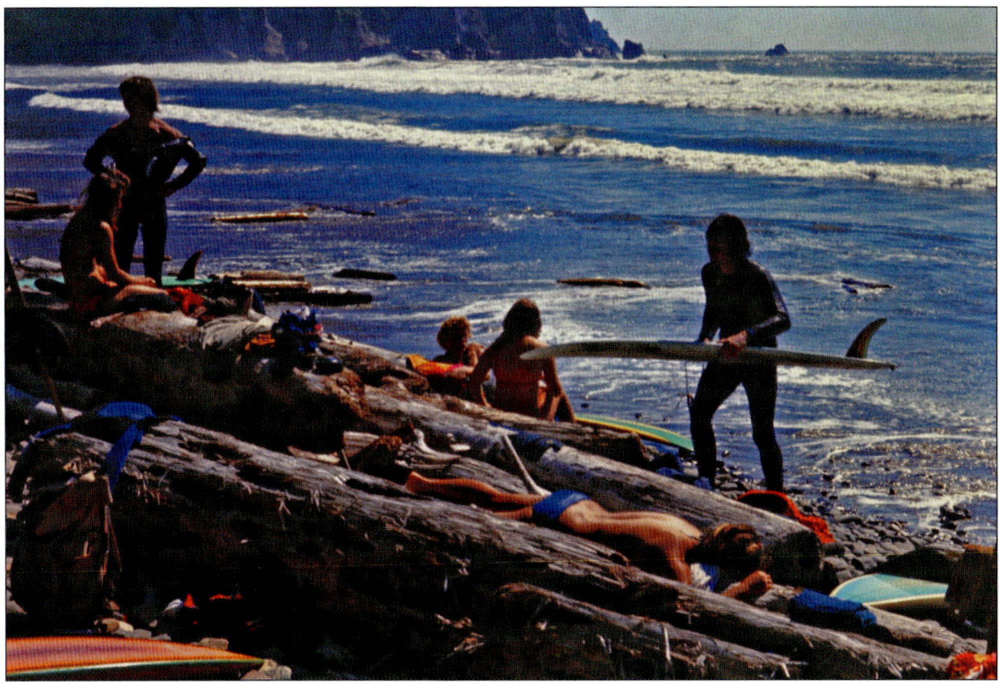

"This was a typical surfin' beach scene at Short Sands in the early seventies," according to Randy Barna. "Holding the board is Corky Carroll, upper left is Bill Barnfield and Wendy Van Sickle. In the middle is Cheer Chrichlow and Debbie Melville. Barely visible on the left is the tripod leg of Bud Brown's camera. Bud, the iconic surf filmmaker, had brought his crew north, and knowing Bill, hung out for a while." (Photograph by Randy Barna.)

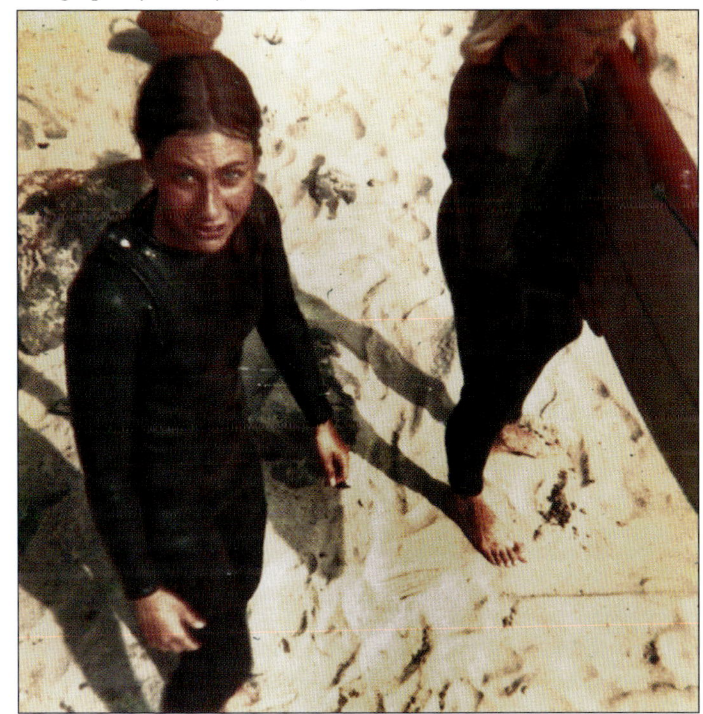

Wendy Van Sickle and Kent Wienker are pictured here at Short Sands in the late 1960s. David Louis recalls, "Kent Wienker swam like a shark, always moving, same style as Corky Carroll." Wienker came from Renton, Washington. Randy Barna comments, "Wendy's parents had a home at Arch Cape. We all shared the daily beach fire. Barnfield and Wendy were a solid couple, moved to Oahu North Shore together. They returned to get married and I was Bill's best man." (Photograph by Barbara Garratt Castillo.)

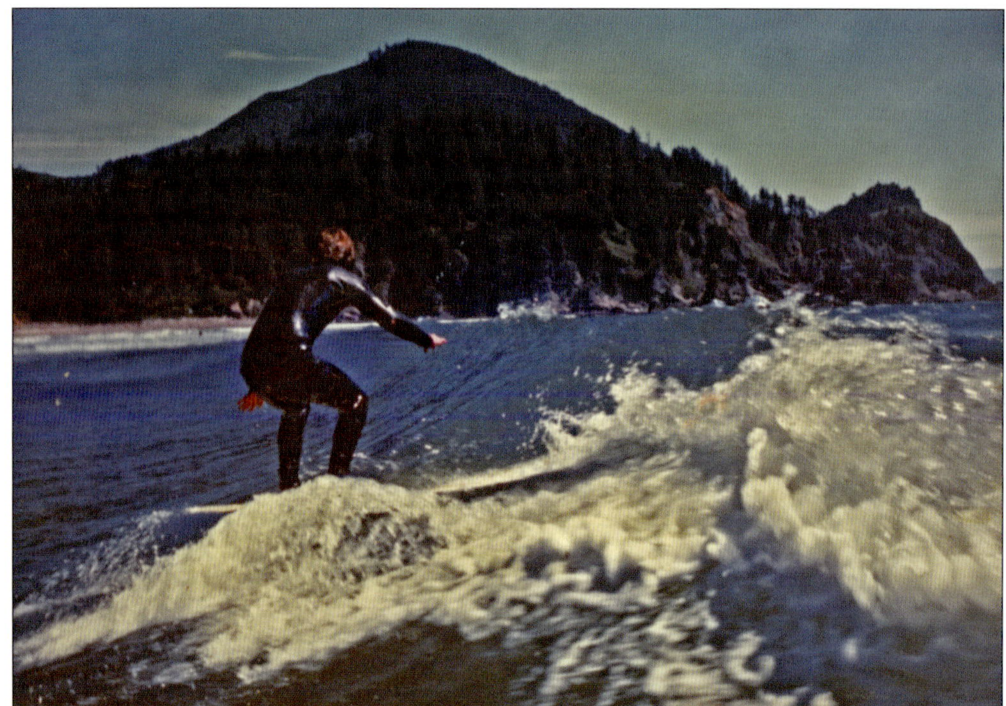

Tim Foley is pictured here surfing Short Sands in the early 1970s. Tim recalls, "I started surfing at Pacific City in 1964 as a junior in high school. I graduated from Grant High in 1965 and moved to Neahkanie Beach, living in a shed for the summer. I met Art Spence and his friend Bob Shaw at Short Sands." Foley eventually became part of the Tillamook Head crew. He recalls selling about 300 boards for Tillamook Head. (Photograph by Jack Molan.)

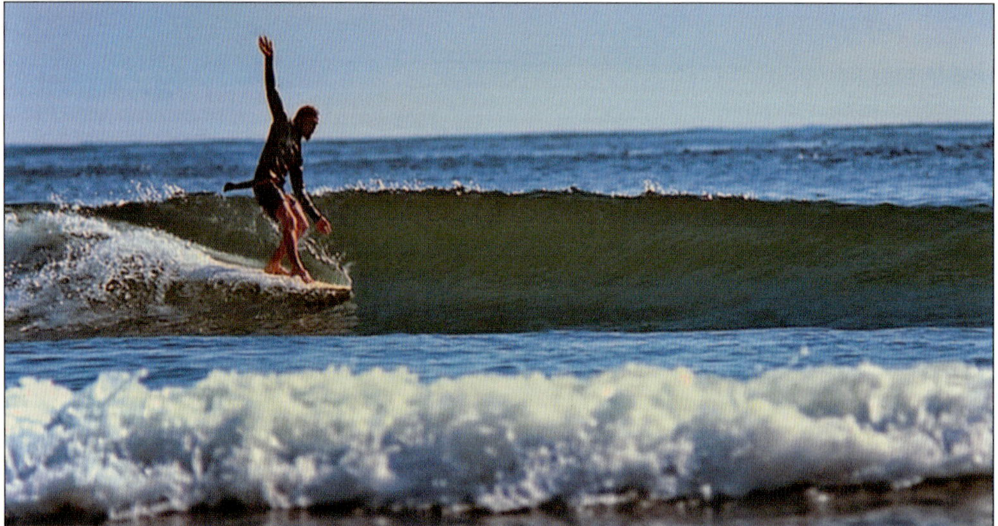

Art Spence is showing his style at Short Sands in the early 1970s. "I remember seeing Art Spence and California surfer Bob Shaw surfing Short Sands," Brand Dichter recalls. "Art was out in the water with sunglasses. He had that California look." Shaw remembers visiting Spence in Oregon. "Art Spence and I were best friends in California. I first surfed the Seaside area, summer of 1965. Art's parents had a summer house near the beach in Manzanita." (Photograph by Scott Blackman.)

Betty Abbott, or Mrs. A, as most surfers called her, was the owner of The Surfer. She took surfing lessons at Short Sands in 1970 with twins Rich and Randy Jenks, who recall her saying, "If I am going to sell surfboards I might as well get wet. Betty wasn't really mean but she did have an attitude. That's why we called her BA." Tim Foley remembers that Abbot was a no-nonsense businesswoman who studied the surfing magazines and sold hokey California boards. (Courtesy of Rich Jenks.)

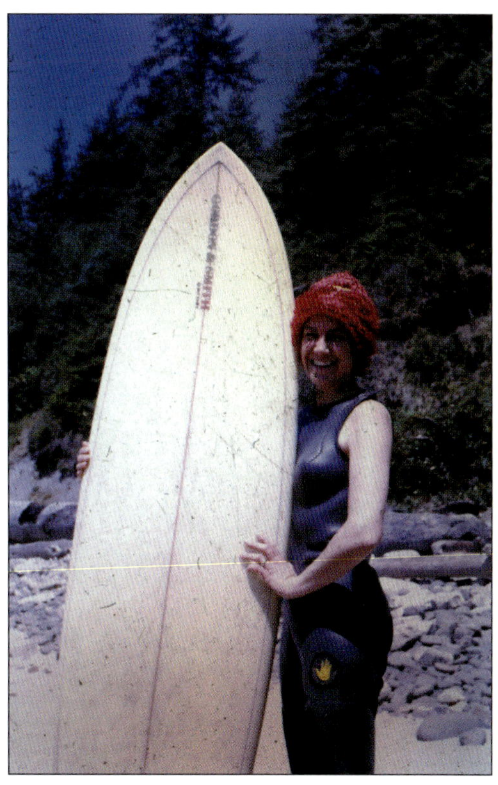

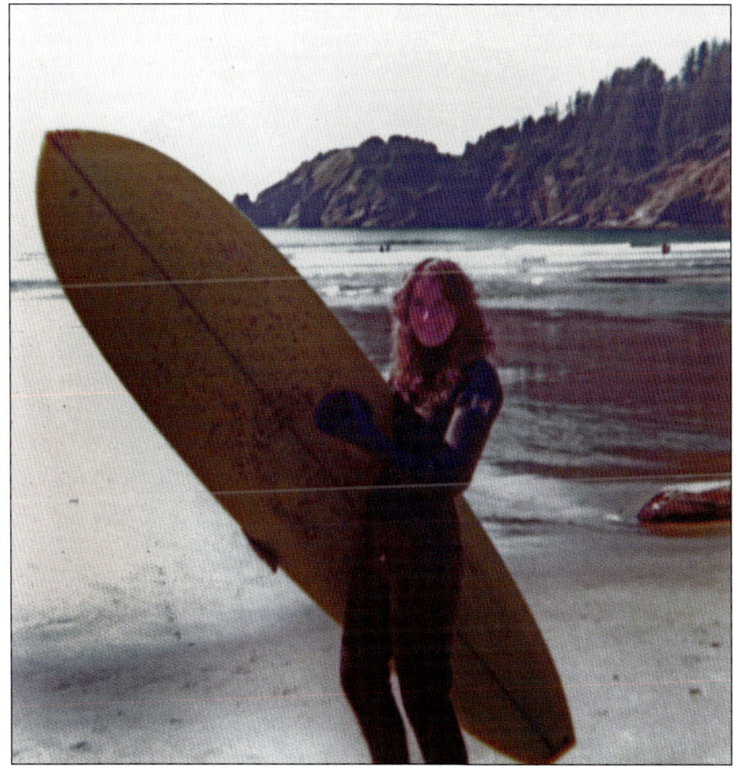

Dellanne McGregor appears ready to go surfing at Short Sands in 1978. Dellanne recalls, "My mom bought a funky cottage in Cannon Beach in 1965. During high school, my sister Louise and I came down alone all the time from Portland. Our mom trusted us. My first board was an O'Neil. I bought it off a surfer in the Short Sands parking lot for $100 in 1967." (Courtesy of Dellanne McGregor.)

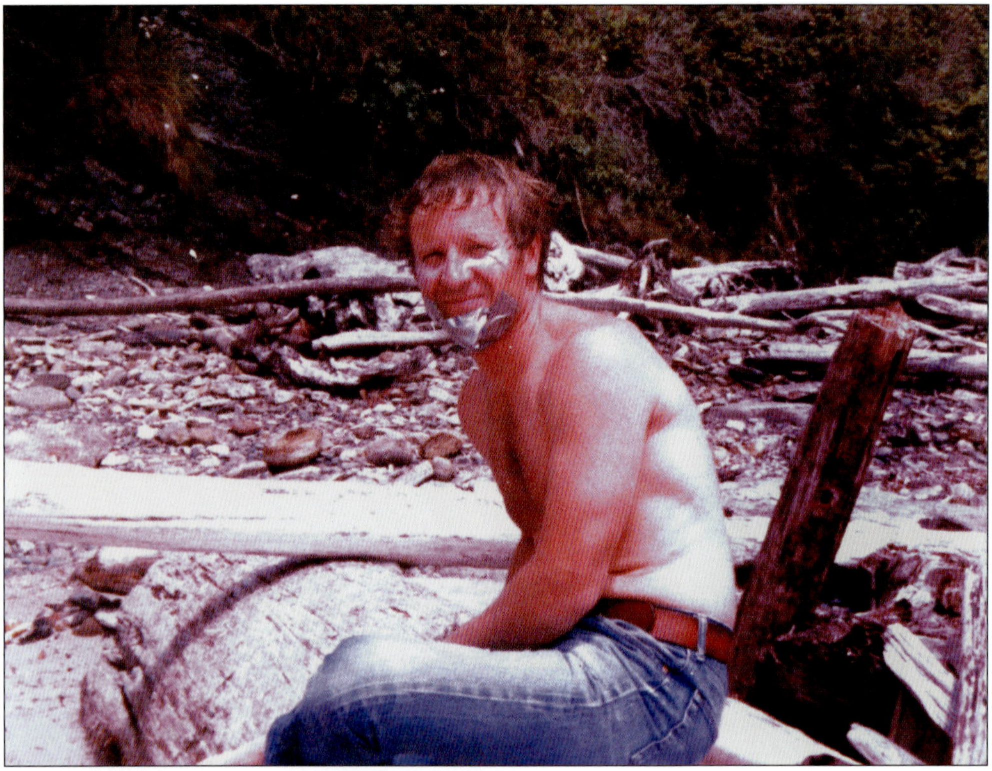

Kevin Kelty sustained a nasty cut at Short Sands in 1986. "I got a deep cut below my lip from my board when I pulled out of a large wave. Peter Blyth wrapped my jaw in duct tape and I got stitches later," Kelty explains. "Starting in 1963 I began surfing at Doheny Beach, California, when visiting my grandfather. In subsequent summers there I remember seeing Corky Carroll, Mickey Munoz, and Margo Godfrey while I was surfing." (Photograph by Dellanne McGregor.)

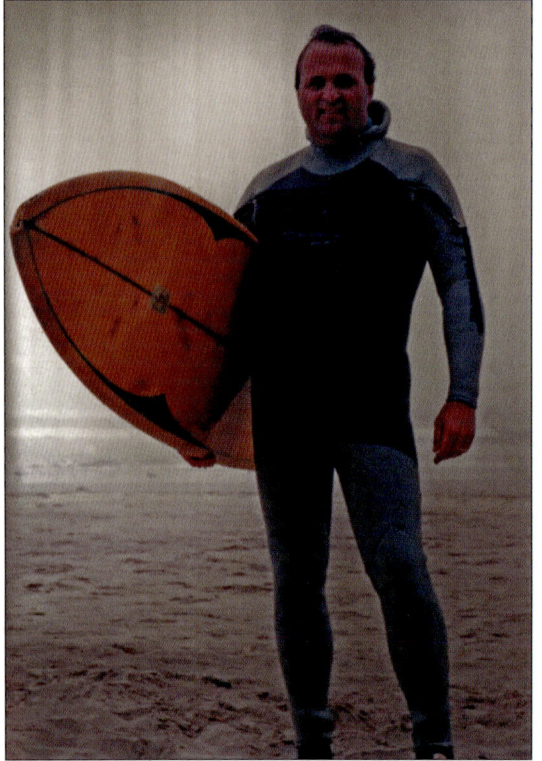

Mike Herron, pioneer surfer from the early 1960s, is pictured at Short Sands in 1994. Herron comments, "I was a 45-year-old pastor. I had an eight-foot-six Tillamook Head board made by Jerry Harrington in the late sixties and suit from the early seventies. In the fog paddling out, I looked like a ghost ship from the past to the young surfers on their four- and five-foot boards!" (Courtesy of Mike Herron.)

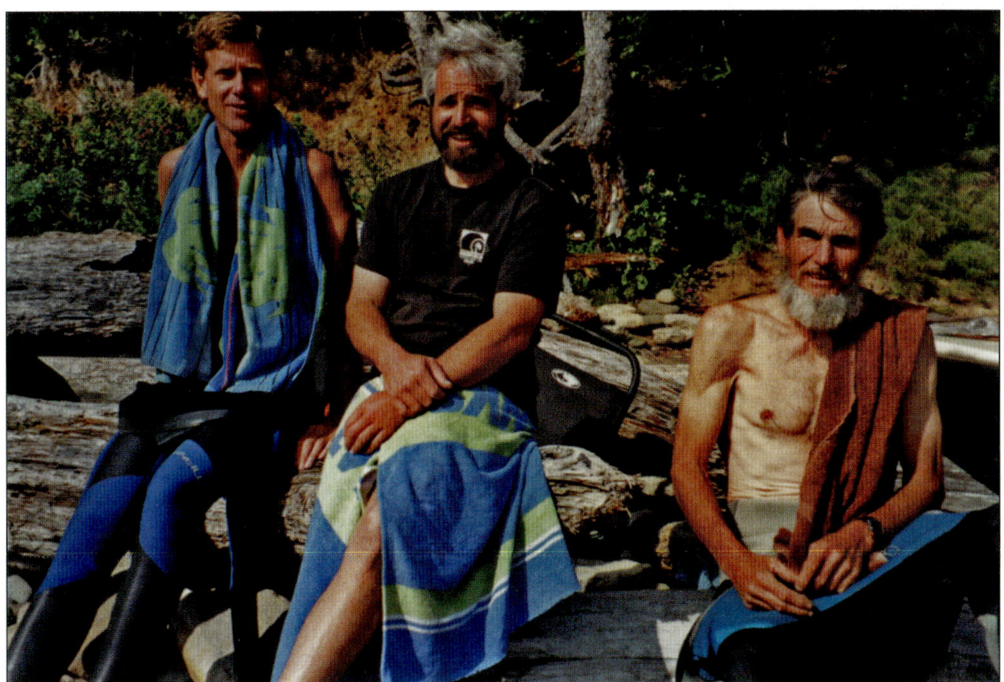

Sitting on a Short Sands log around 1990 are, from left to right, Randy Carman, Tom Burns, and Dana Williams. Burns remembers, "Many a summer day was spent with Jack Brown and Dana on the log at the middle creek at Short Sands talking life stories. I believe that log is still there and if it could talk, it'd spell forth volumes on the characters who sat there changing out of their wetsuits and talking surf." (Courtesy of Tom Burns.)

Knox Swanson (left) and Mike Burger are hanging out at Knox's home at Beerman Creek in 1986. Knox comments, "The car is Mike's, a '63 Oldsmobile that he inherited from his in-laws. We were heading to some surf spot in Cannon Beach. On top is a four-pack of Yater longboards—our preferred brand at the time." According to Knox, the Beerman Creek String Band, formed in 1974, played low-brow, old-time hillbilly music and got its name from this place. (Photograph by Knox Swanson.)

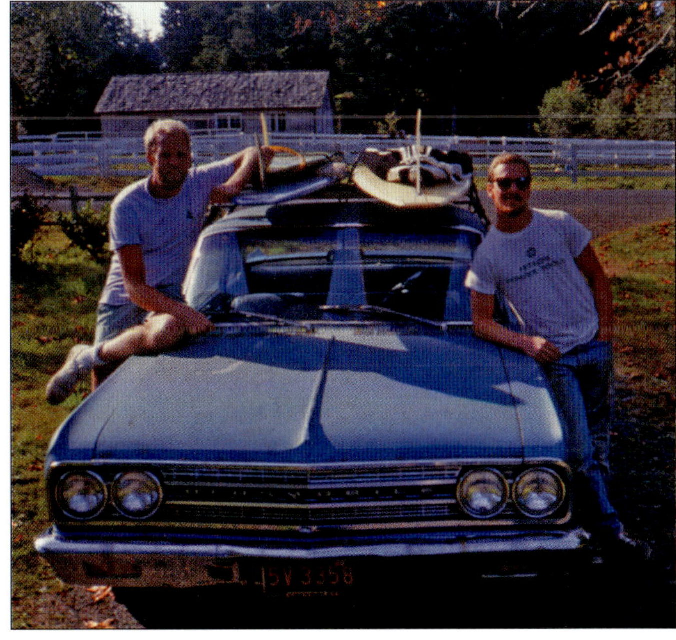

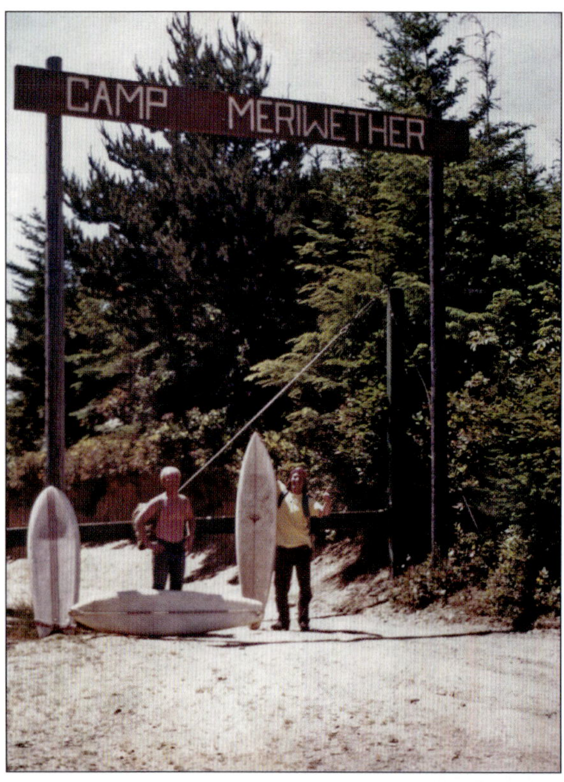

Bill Smith (left) and Mike Burger pose in front of the Meriwether Boy Scout Camp around 1975. According to Smith, "Boy Scout Camp, Camp Meriwether, Cape Look Out, and Seal Point are all the same place." Resourceful surfers were known to have bribed the camp caretaker, sneak onto the property, dismantle the locked gate, or descend a steep forest hill to reach the secret surf spot below the camp. (Photograph by Knox Swanson.)

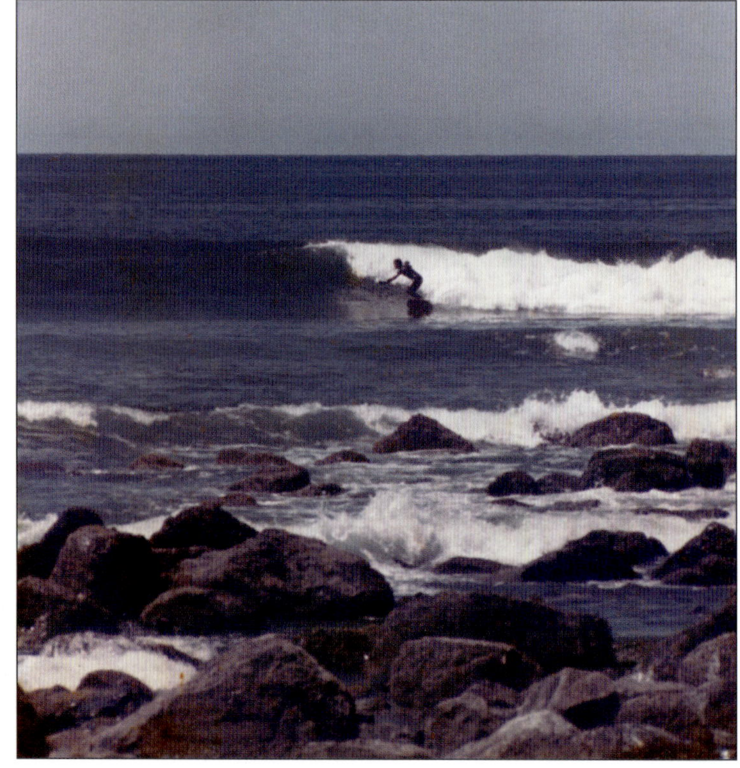

Pacific City surfer Jay Nicholls is pictured here at Cape Look Out in 1970. Nicholls migrated from Salem and joined the PCDC surfing crew. Jay recalls, "In early 1972 I did a header on the rocks at Cape Look Out, cracking two vertebrae. I couldn't surf for a year." Dave Guerena recalls, "Bird (Jay Nicholls) underreported surfing conditions to *Surfer* magazine's Surf Report. He got lots of beach cred for misleading them for years." (Courtesy of Jay Nicholls.)

These surfers are sitting at the base of the steep cliff below the Boy Scout Camp in fall 1981. From left to right are John Benson, Stan Hart, and Charles Carse. "The 'Benson Philosophy' was give a wave, get a wave, show respect Brah," Mitch Allara explains. "Benson was a regular at the camp long before the not-so-secret secret was out." John grew up in Neskowin and was a PCDC surfer. (Courtesy of Mitch Allara.)

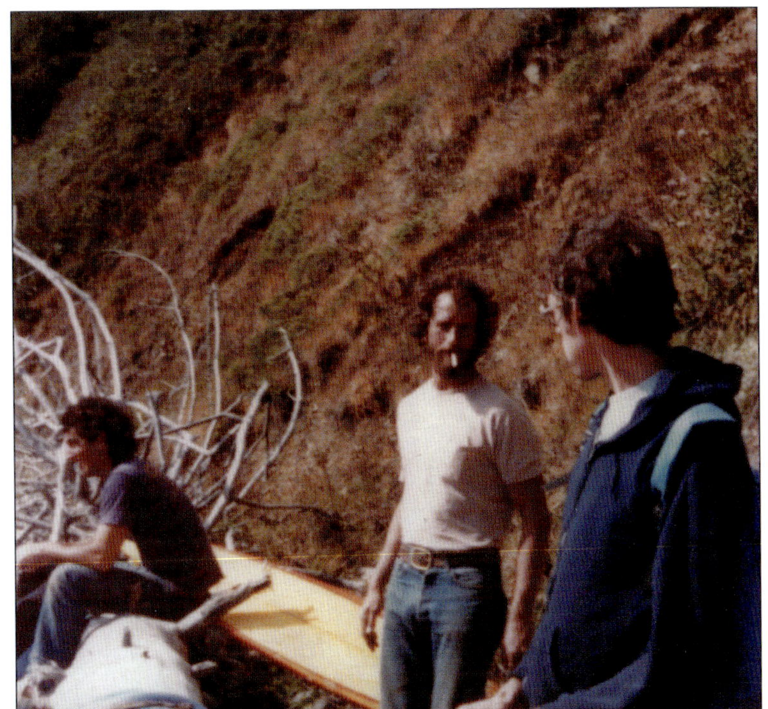

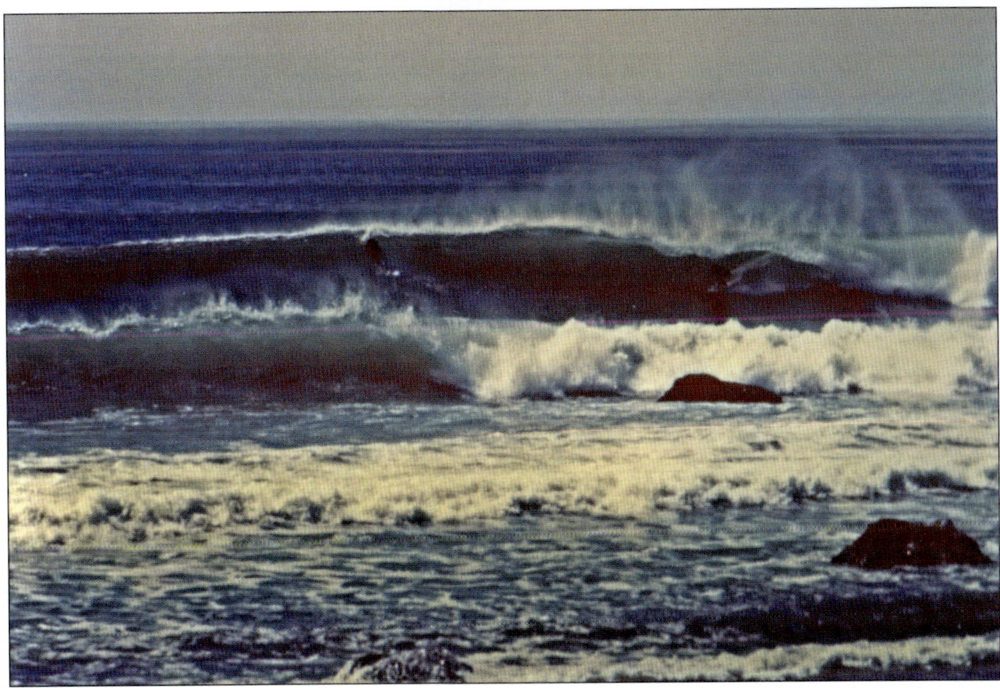

Mitch Allara (left) and Hawaiian surfer Charles Carse are pictured here in the tube at the camp in fall 1985. Allara comments, "Charles found his way to the camp and flashed a style suitable for the waves at the rocky point. The large wave felt the carve of his powerful turns and his speed down the line approach. The camp tube was the realm of Charles Carse and his constant infectious laughter." (Courtesy of Mitch Allara.)

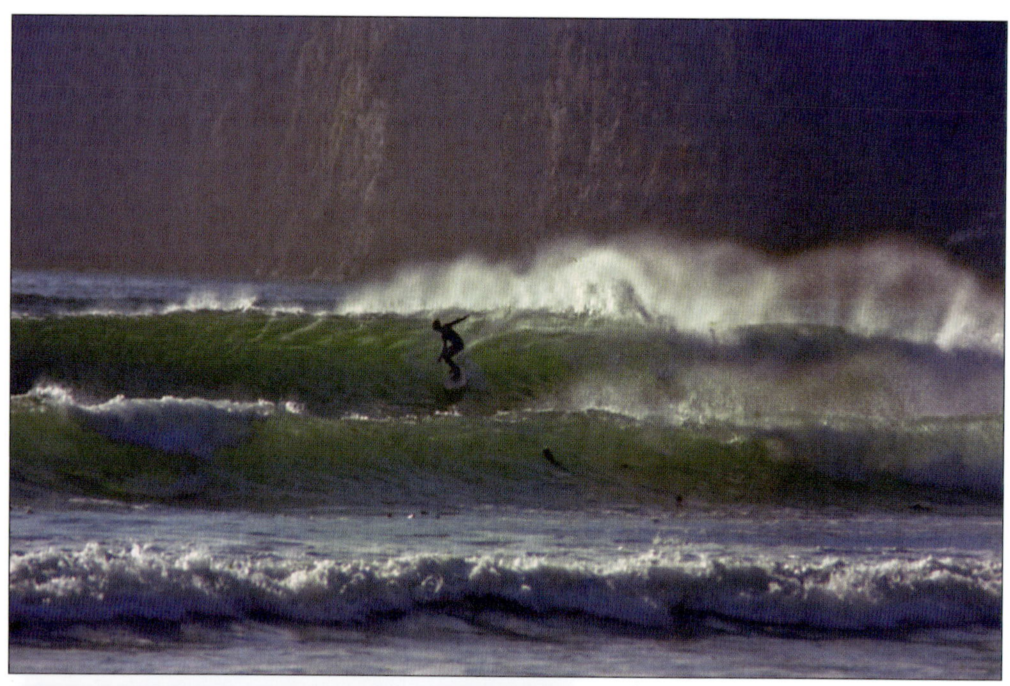

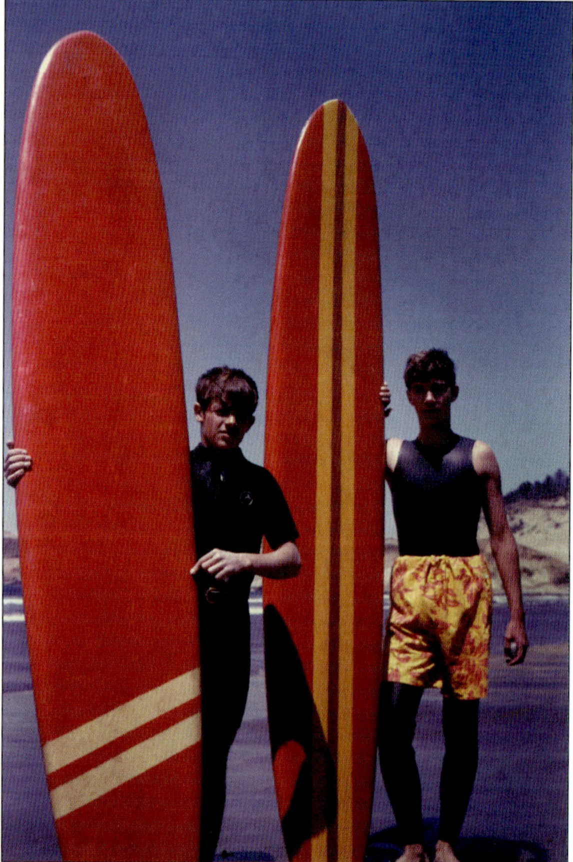

Rik Cederstrom is surfing Cape Lookout in the late 1980s. Rik recalls, "I set my camera and tripod on the beach and went surfing. Phil Mancill shot the rest of the roll while I was riding. I learned to surf in Santa Cruz, so for a while, I was called 'Santa Cruz Rik.' I made surfboards and Bill Fackerell sold them at his Raven surf shop. My logo was 'Cede,' which became my nickname." (Courtesy of Rik Cederstrom.)

Childhood friends Ron Hill (left) and Randy Barna made these boards in 1963 before they learned to surf. "We were only 13 and talked our parents into taking us to Pacific City," says Barna. "We made several boards from pre-shaped blanks. I liked boards, the shapes, and craft of making them almost as much as surfin' back then. Surfing was too cold until warm, flexible wetsuits came along and everything changed." (Courtesy of Randy Barna.)

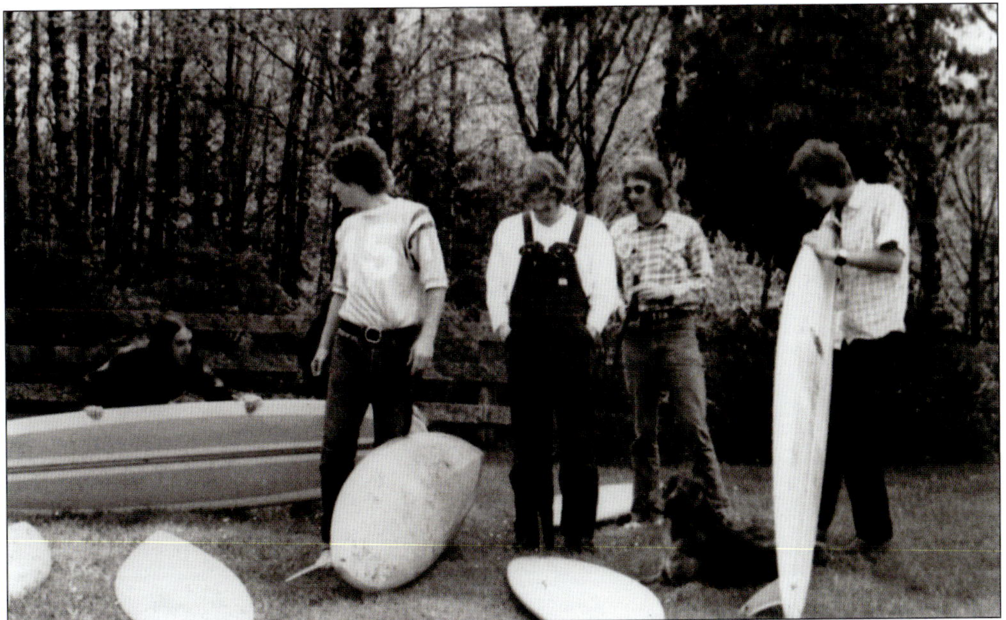

Glenn Kellow, raised in Pacific City, was an early 1960s surfer. Glenn remembers, "My father called us the PCDC, an acronym for Pacific City Dirt Crowd." Checking their boards at Glenn's place located on Miles Lake just off of Sandlake Road between Woods and Tierra Del Mar in 1974 are some of the PCDC. From left to right are Gerry Day, Peter Greene, Glenn Kellow, Jerry Sandal, and Bob Adams. (Photograph by Gerry Day.)

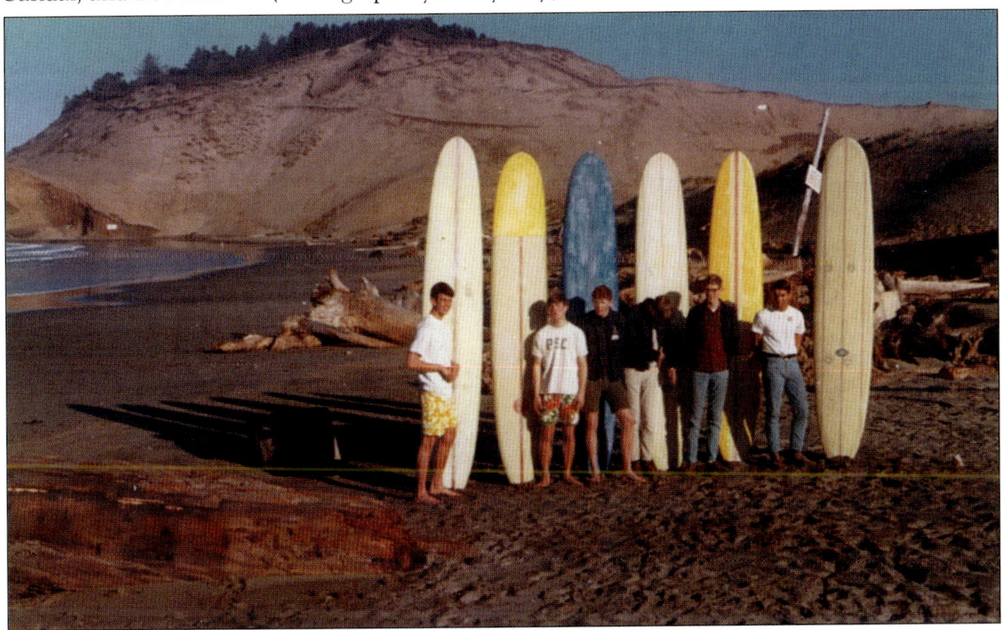

Members of the Sunset Surf Syndicate are pictured here on the beach at Pacific City in March 1967. From left to right are Stan Hart, Joe Mineau, Jay Howe, Paul Keller, Bob Archibald, and Tim Mack. Paul Keller writes, "While all of the late 1960s surf club members attended Sunset High School in Beaverton, Pacific City became our 'home' beach. In fact, our club jacket emblems read: Sunset Surf Syndicate—Pacific City and Portland Oregon." (Courtesy of Paul Keller.)

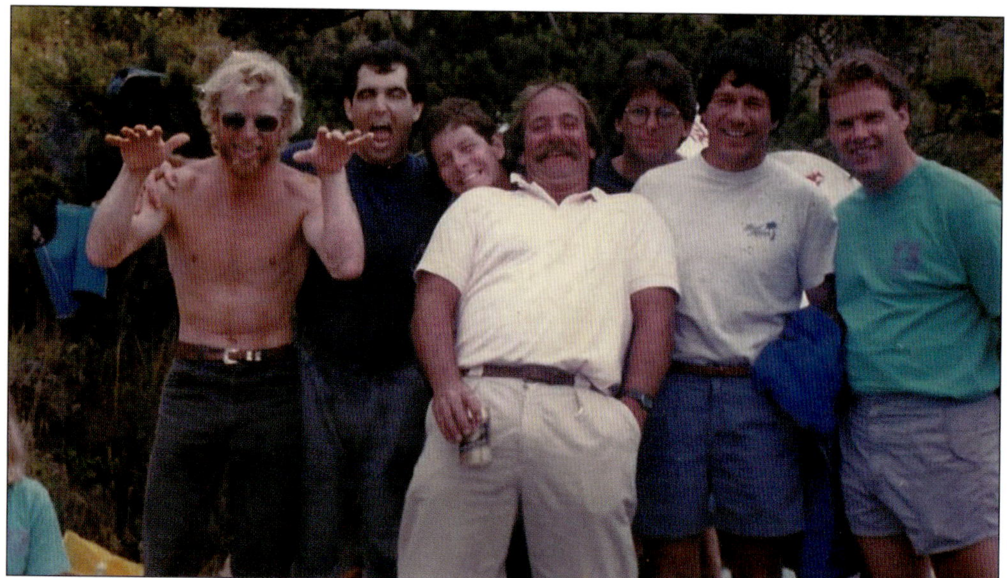

Pictured here are Pacific City surfers and friends attending the 1988 Cowabunga Surf Contest. From left to right are Chuck Swanson, John Benson, Tony Franciscone, Eddie Beers, David Guerena, Kani Rowland, and Glenn Kellow. Glenn Kellow, raised in PC and an early 1960s surfer, comments, "To quote Rob Machatto, 'Once you feel the glide you're a part of the tribe.' I did organized sports but none of them compared to surfing. Surfing is a communal feeling." (Courtesy of Glenn Kellow.)

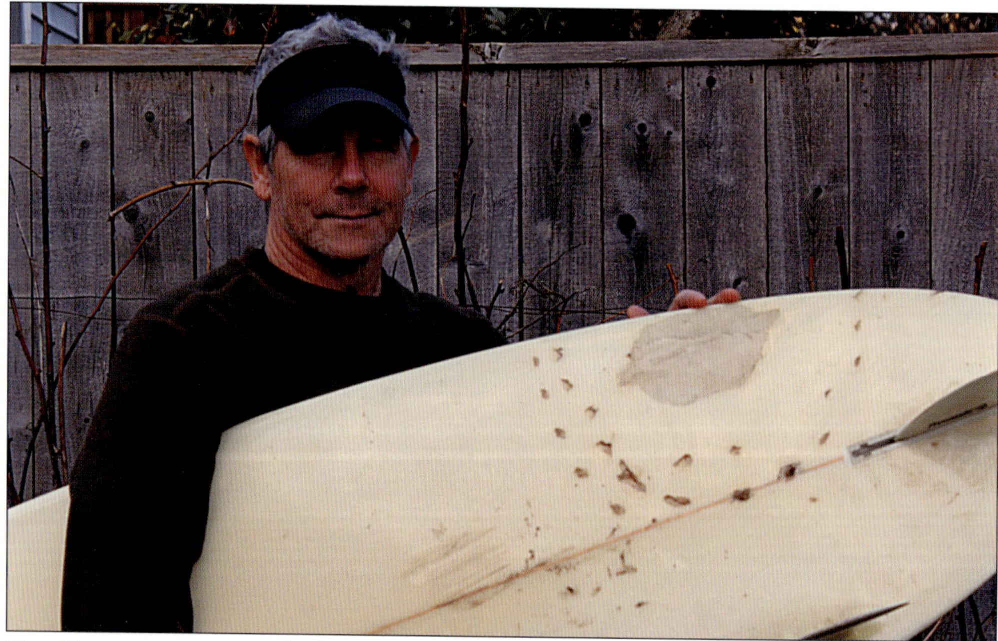

Tony Franciscone poses with the board from his shark attack at Neskowin on February 24, 1991. Surfing with John Benson, Tony recalls, "I was propelled helicoptering into the air. I turned, saw a huge set of gills. Time slowed. I was being pulled under by my leg, but eventually released. I thought 'No way am I going to die being a fish's lunch.' After being released, I made it to shore without injuries." (Courtesy of Tony Franciscone.)

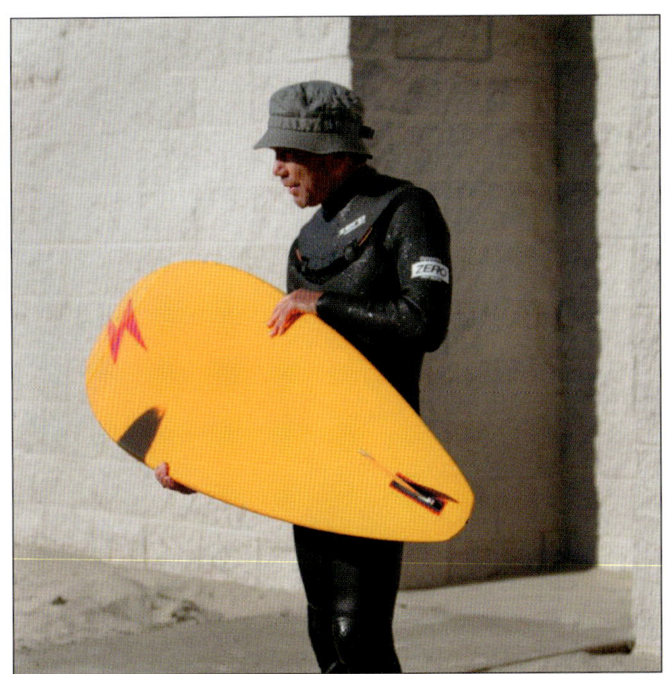

Gerry Lopez admires Glenn Kellow's Lightning Bolt at Pacific City in February 2011. Kellow bought the board from the Cal Hobie shop in 1975. Kellow states, "It's never been used. It's a collector's item. Looking at it, Lopez commented 'You could sell this board and put your child through college.'" Gerry Lopez, one of Hawaii's more famous surfers, resides in Central Oregon and occasionally does stand-up surfing at Pacific City. (Photograph by Garry Link.)

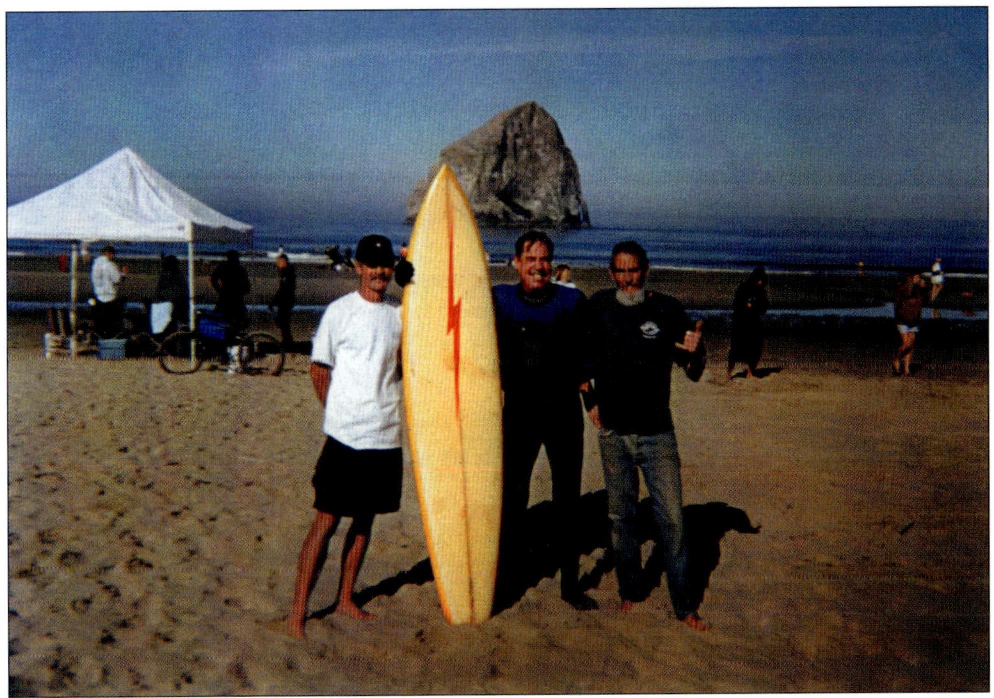

At Pacific City's 2005 surf contest are, from left to right, Bob Ledbetter, contest organizer; Rory Russell, Pipeline Masters winner in 1976 and 1977; and Dana Williams, the contest's head beach master. Bob and Michelle Ledbetter, while owning their South County Surf Shop, organized eight surfing contests from 1998 to 2005. No contest was held in 2006. Bryan Bates sponsored contests in 2007 and 2008. Jeff Mollencop of Moment Surf Company sponsored contests from 2011 to 2015. (Courtesy of Dana Williams.)

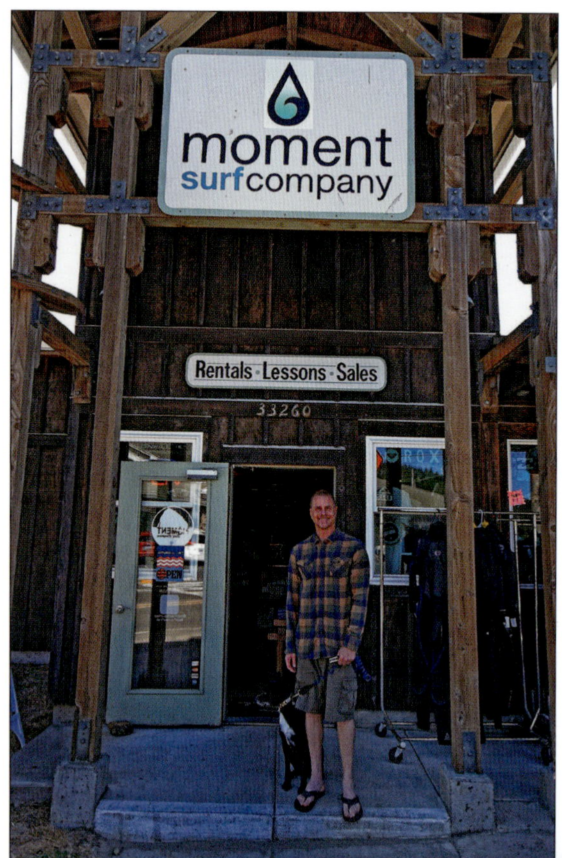

Jeff Mollencop has been co-owner of Moment Surf Company and Ben & Jeff's Restaurant next door since March 2010. Jeff explains, "I work the surf shop and Ben Johnson, my business partner, works the restaurant, which brings new customers into the surf shop. Surfing makes me happy. I've learned to enjoy the simple things in life and that's why it's called Moment Surf Company." (Photograph by Scott Blackman.)

Many of Oregon's pioneer surfers attended the 50-year celebration of surfing at Agate Beach in June 2014. Representing some of the pioneer surfers from Pacific City are, from left to right, (first row) Mitch Allara (back to camera), Tony Franciscone (kneeling), John Benson, Steve "Red Trunks" Johnson, and Dick Wald; (second row) Dennis Pearson and Glenn Kellow; (third row) James Burton, Stan Hart, Mike Mullin, and John Muller. (Photograph by Scott Blackman.)

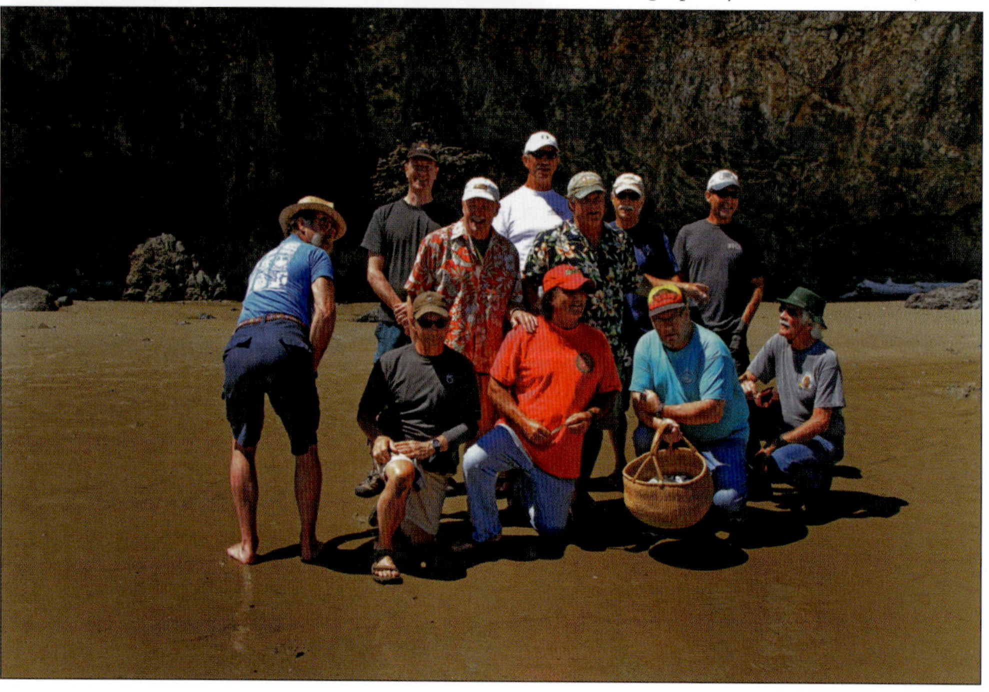

Three

Surfing Culture

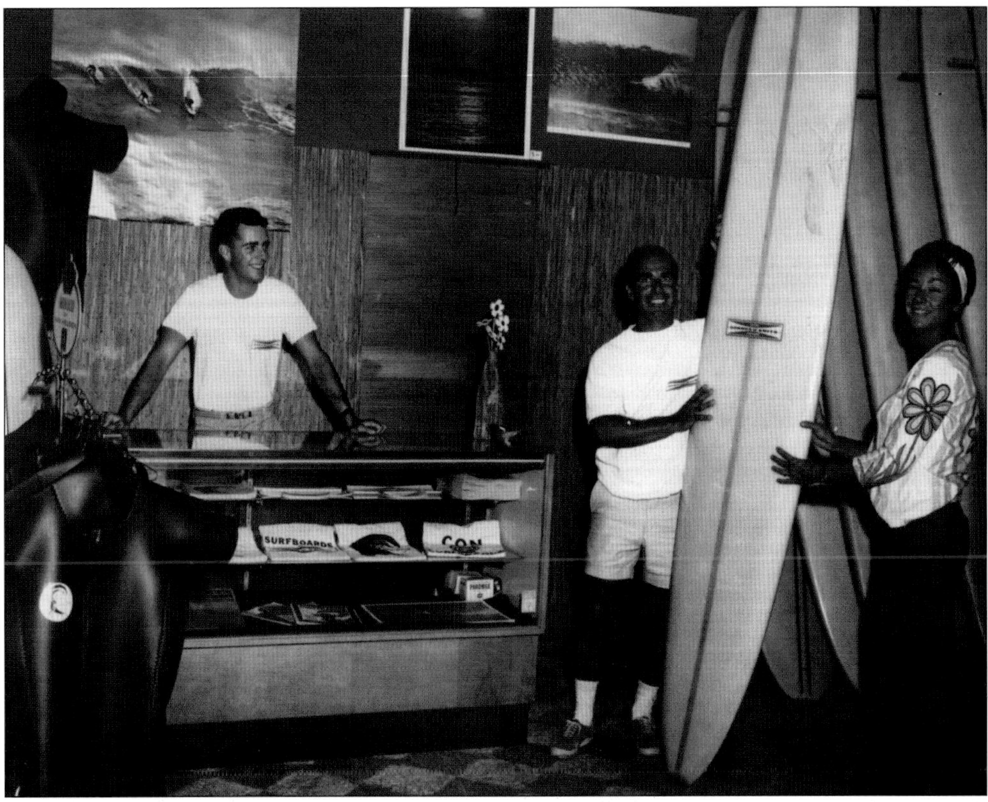

Owners of the first surf shop in Seaside were Bill Theiring (left) and his older brother Jim with his wife, Linda Theiring. George Daggatt comments, "The first surf shop, where the Seasider was, now the Shilo, sold Gordon and Smith boards. Bill had a pilot license, was older than us, and we'd check surf going flying." The Theiring brothers were entrepreneurs and had four surf shops in Coos Bay, Portland, and Seaside and one in California during the 1960s. Bill recalls, "I sold my 1957 Corvette and bought surfboards for the Seaside Surf Shop. Jim had the shop at Pleasure Point, Santa Cruz, California, and sent boards up from there." Jim Theiring says, "We financed Bruce Brown's trip to Oregon to show his movie *Endless Summer* at Benson High School in Portland and Coos Bay in 1965." (Courtesy of Bill Theiring.)

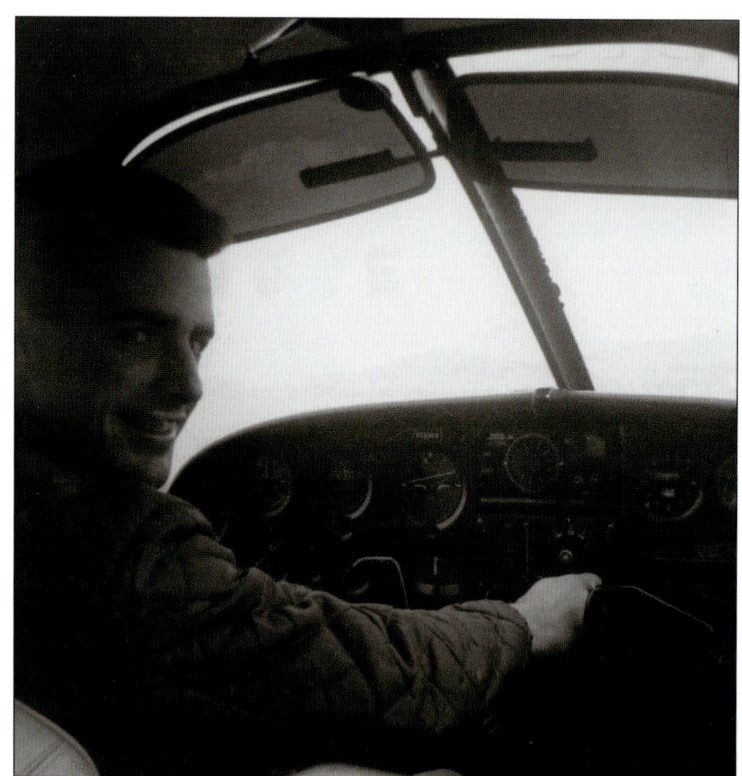

Bill Theiring checks the surf from the air. Calling in reports to Portland's KISN radio station was a great way to advertise the shop. Bill recalls, "We flew from Astoria to Agate Beach. Surfin' and flying, we had such good times. Looking at my pilot log I see early surfers who came with me: Sandy Barrett, Brad Corrtright, Bill Gleeson, Mike Weybright, Tom Bailey, George Daggatt, Zac Ramey, Pam Webber, and Myra and Jim Furnish." (Courtesy of Bill Theiring.)

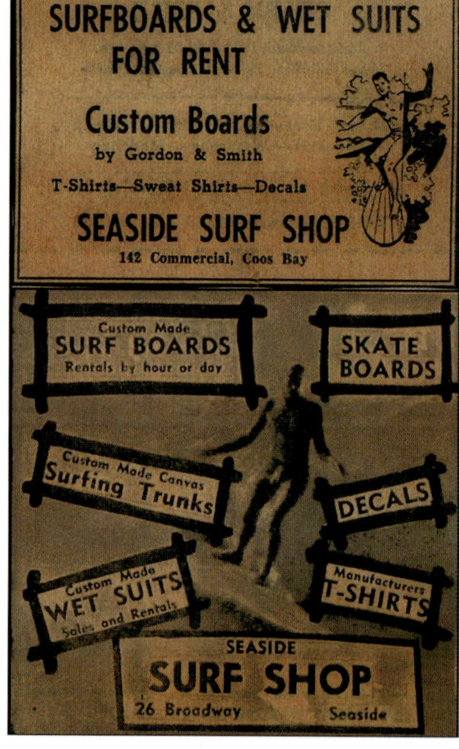

Here are two advertisements for the Theiring brothers' surf shops in Seaside and Coos Bay. Bill Theiring recalls, "I'd open the surf shop in Seaside on Broadway, Memorial Day through Labor Day weekend. I slept in the back of the shop. I'd move the Seaside Surf Shop to Coos Bay and run Seaside Surf Shop there the rest of the year. Our surf shop was open in Seaside for three summers from 1964 to 1966." (Courtesy of Bill Theiring.)

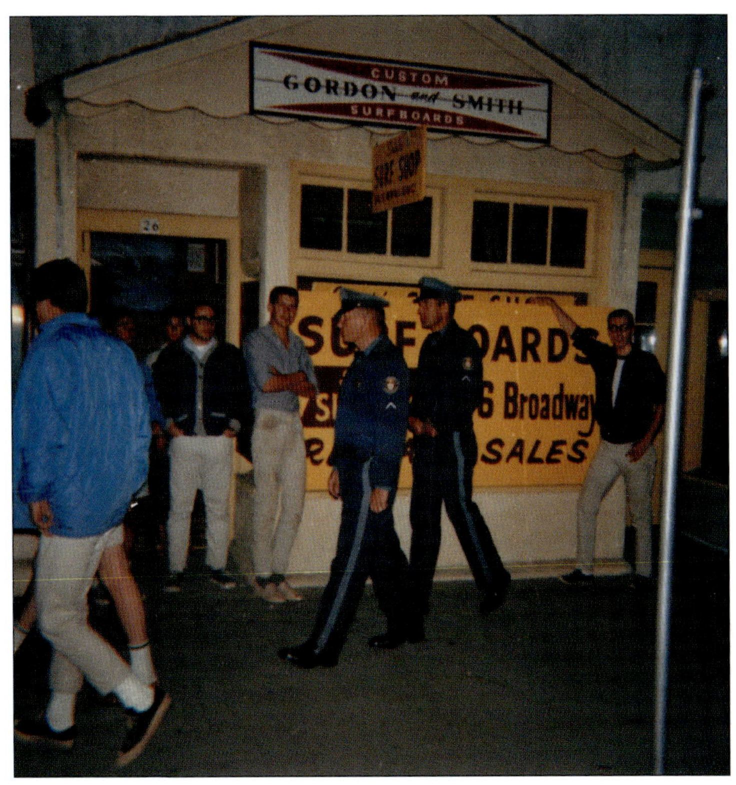

Seaside Surf Shop is pictured here on Labor Day weekend 1965. "The Seaside Riots broke out for three years in Seaside on that weekend," Bill Theiring recalls. "State police walked in pairs. We would step outside every time the television cameras came by. Similar images appeared on Walter Cronkite and Huntley Brinkley's national news." From left to right in the doorway are Jim and Linda Theiring and Joe Shank; to the right of the sign is Bill Gleeson. (Photograph by Bill Theiring.)

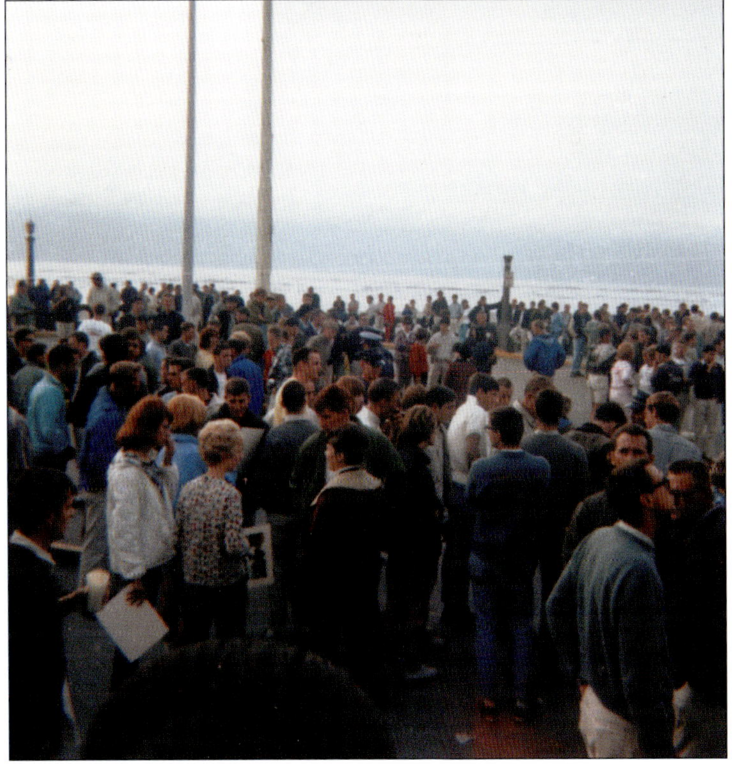

Pictured here is a gathering at Seaside's turnaround on Labor Day weekend 1965. Bill Theiring remembers, "The riot squad had driven the mob from the turnaround onto the beach. National Guard was on rooftops, martial law declared, and loudspeakers announcing 'you are all under arrest.' " SSA president George Daggatt states, "The Seaside Riots got us organized as a club and putting on surfing contests during Labor Day weekends, gave kids something to do." (Photograph by Bill Theiring.)

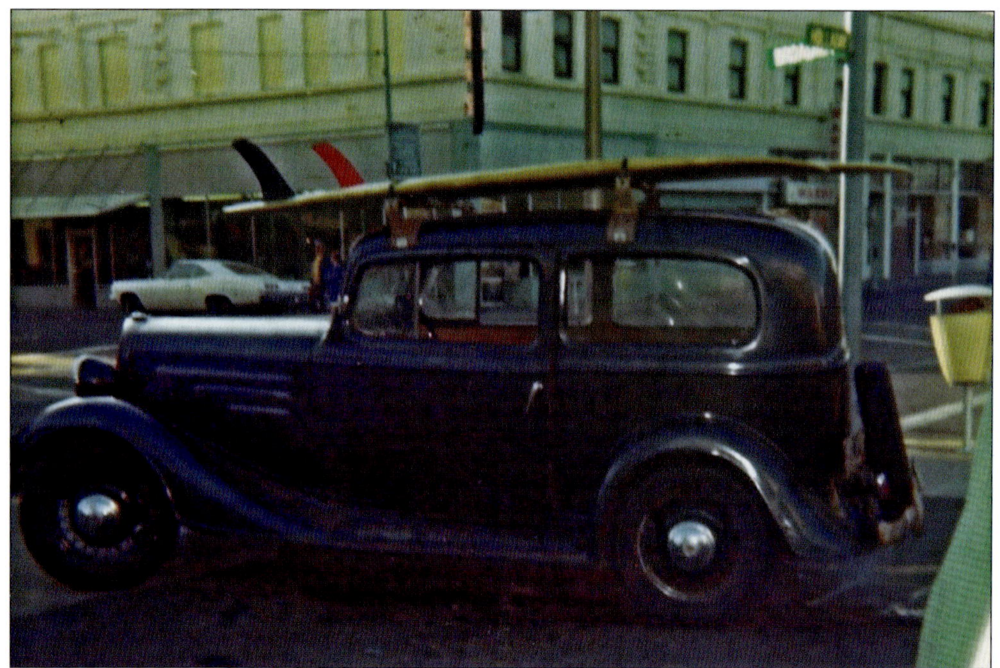

Brothers Mike and Jan Herron's 1935 Chevy is parked in the Piggly Wiggly parking lot on the corner of Holladay Drive and Broadway Street in 1965. Mike recalls, "Our car was a familiar sight around Seaside. We kept boards on the car continuously, ready to surf at the Cove, Point, Indian, and Short Sands. We and our buddies would 'drag the gut' endlessly talking to friends and girls; sometimes they would stand on the running boards as we drove around." (Photograph by Mike Herron.)

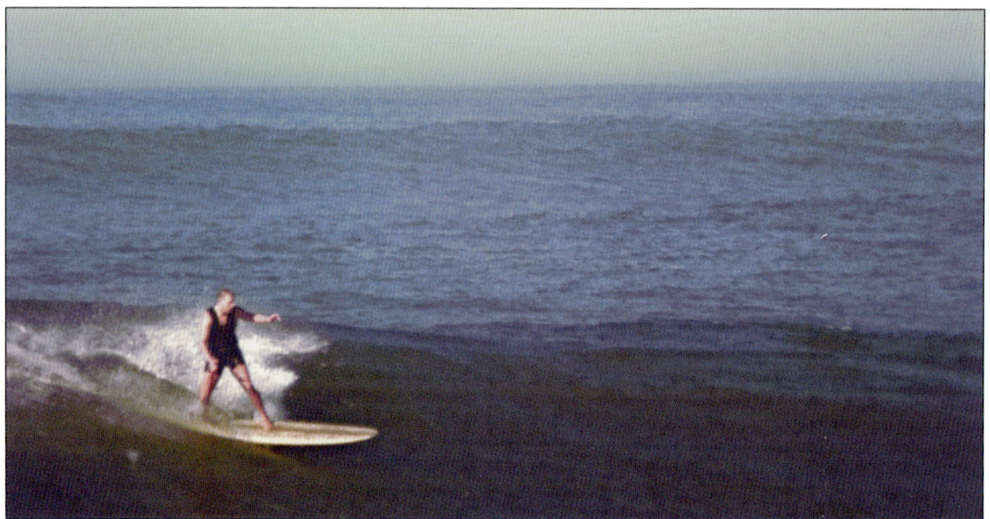

The first Seaside surfing contest, on February 20, 1966, "was sponsored by the OSD Sea Lions, a local skin diving club whose members helped start surfing in Oregon, the summer of 1963" writes Dick Wald. "Eighteen surfers participated, from Marty Skriver, 14, to Cal Hal, age 45." The winners were Sam Beck, first; Larry Tucker (pictured), Agate Beach Surf Club (ABSC), second; Dick Wald, third; Mark Hansen (SSA), fourth; Rick Baley (ABSC), fifth; and Marty Skriver (ABSC), sixth. (Photograph by Scott Blackman.)

Pictured here are a few 1960s surfing logos. The Hillsboro Surfing Association patch was donated by Richard Petrich. Members of the club included Richard, his brother James Petrich, Ron Reedy, Charlie Cook, and Warren Flink. They surfed Short Sands, Indian, Seaside, and Pacific City. Theiring's surf shops in Oregon featured Gordon and Smith boards; the decal was donated by Bill Theiring. The Jensen decal was donated by Brand Dichter. Jensen, a California board maker, lived around Seaside during the 1960s. (Authors' collection.)

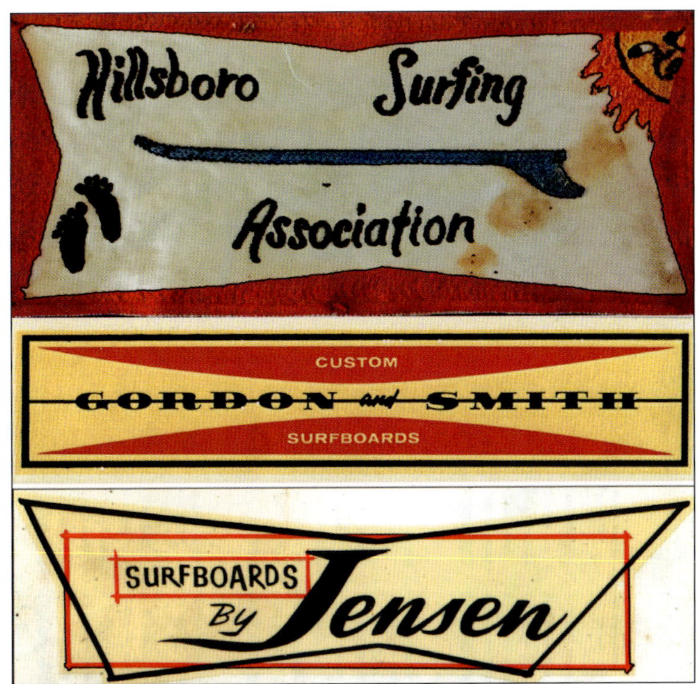

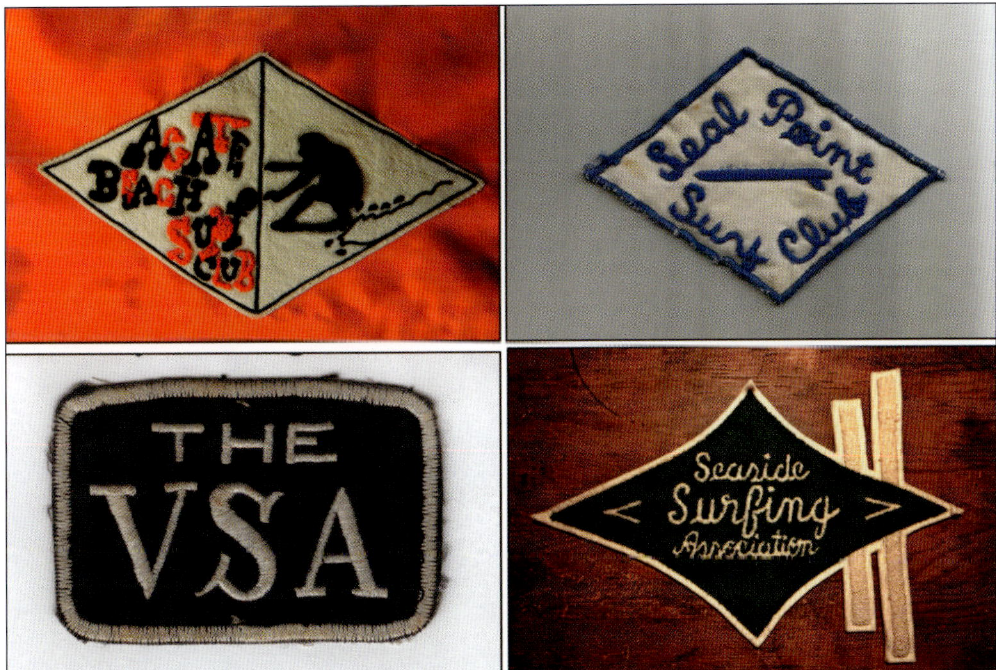

Clubs represented here that surfed North Coast are Agate Beach Surf Club (ABSC), logo designed and donated by Scott Blackman; Seal Point, donated by Glenn Kellow, Pacific City; VSA (Valley Surfing Association), donated by Ron Sandstrom, a member from Salem; and Seaside Surfing Association (SSA), donated by Gary Hansen. George Daggatt recalls, "Members other than charter members were Wally Parcels, Dallas Cook, Bill Fackerell, Pierre Marchand, Jerry Harrington, Robin Hinton, and Bob Jensen." (Authors' collection.)

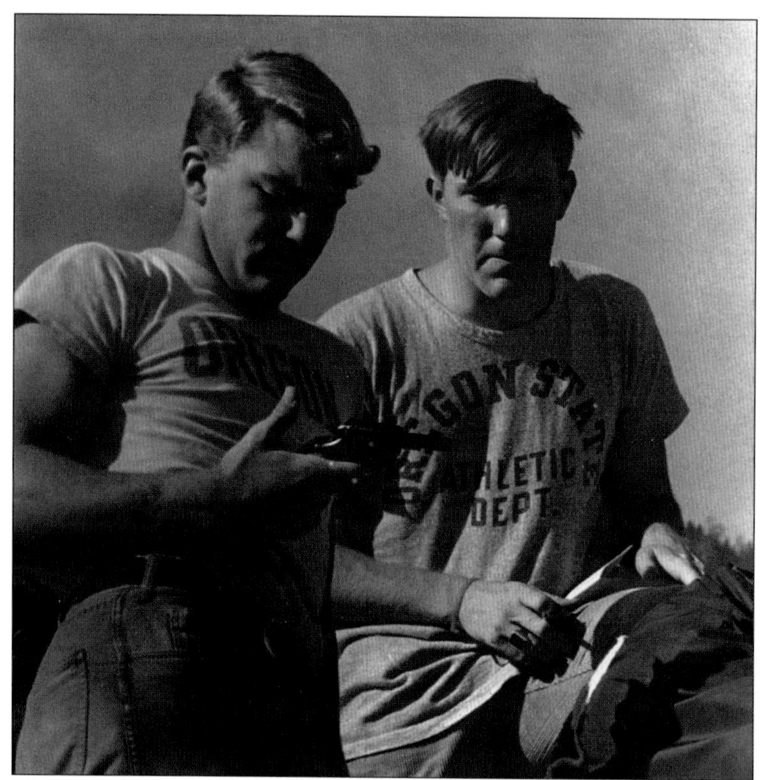

SSA members Dallas Cook (left) and George Daggatt are running heats during the 1966–1967 Surf Contest. Cook and Daggatt graduated from Seaside High School in 1964, returning home during the summers from college. Daggatt recalls, "The SSA had a spaghetti feed annually, and we went to the city council to get approval for the surfing contest. The chamber of commerce donated money in 1966 for the trophies." (Courtesy of George Daggatt.)

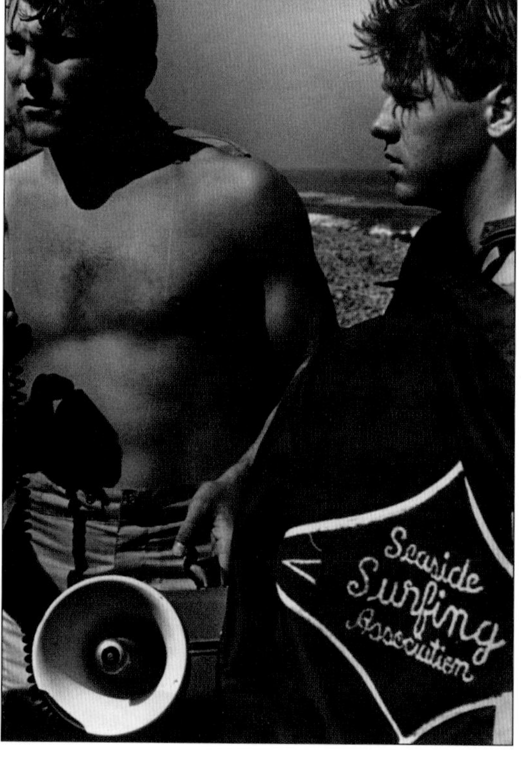

Dallas Cook (left) and Wally Parcels are pictured here at the 1966–1967 Seaside Surf Contest. "Wally and I ran it," recalls Dallas, who was getting a degree in recreation at the University of Oregon. "We took turns running the heats and then we'd also surf. Some Hawaiian kid won it. Wally owned the Surf N' Cycle Surf shop first and then the Surf Hut. Dick Borovicka bought Wally's inventory when it closed." (Courtesy of George Daggatt.)

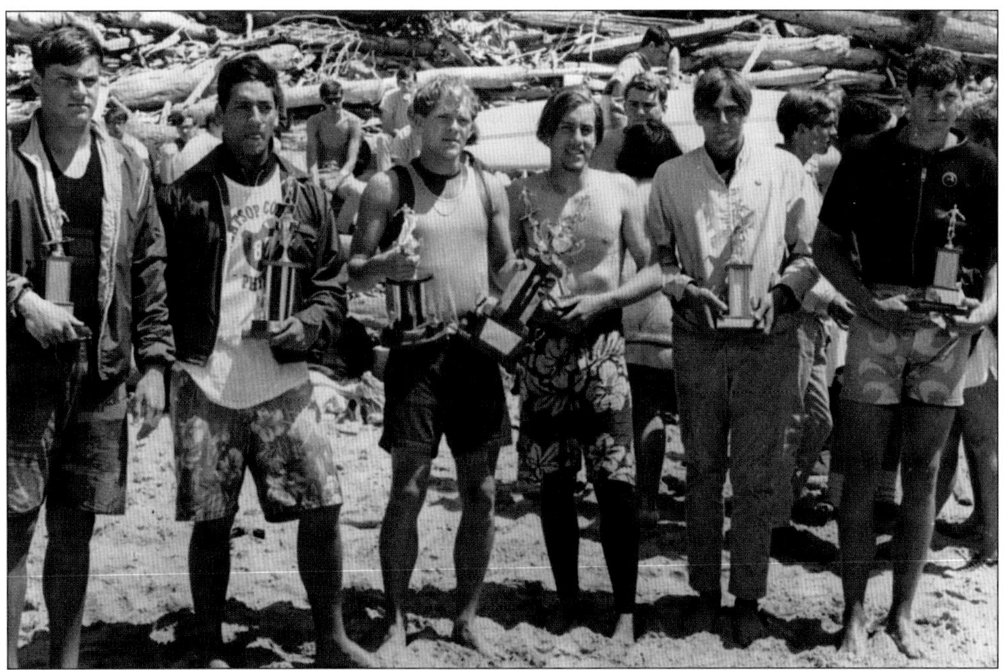

Pictured here are the 1966 Labor Day Seaside Surf Contest winners. "I had just graduated high school. I'd won at the Indian Beach contest and had to compete at the senior level," recalls Gary Hansen. From left to right are Paul Kafoury, ABSC, third-place junior finalist; unidentified junior finalist; Sandy Barrett, Seaside, second-place senior finalist; Larry Morris, first-place senior finalist; Bill Fackerell, Seaside, junior finalist; and Gary Hansen, SSA, Seaside, third-place senior finalist. (Courtesy of George Daggatt.)

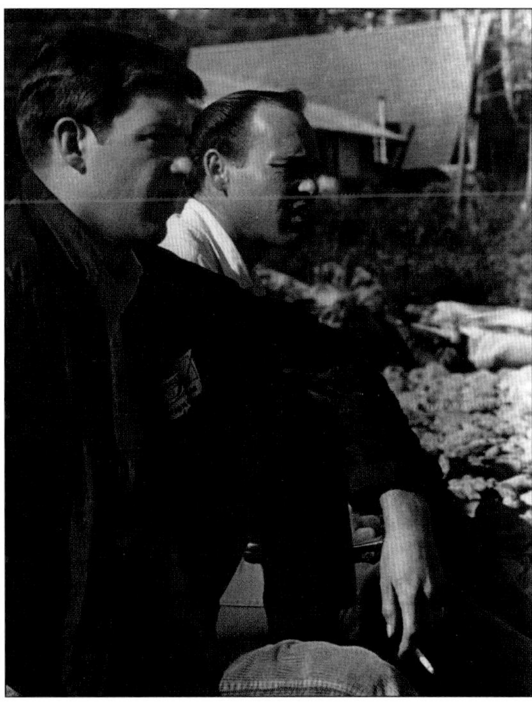

Bruce Combs (left) and Bob Jensen are pictured here at the 1966–1967 Seaside Surf Contest. According to George Daggatt, Combs served as SSA president after him. Dallas Cook recalls, "Combs and Jensen didn't surf much. Jensen shaped boards for Morey-Pope, Gordon and Smith in Southern California before moving here." Larry Tucker recounts, "Jensen was older than us, lived up some nameless logging road with his family where he made boards. He was a craftsman and made beautiful boards." (Courtesy of George Daggatt.)

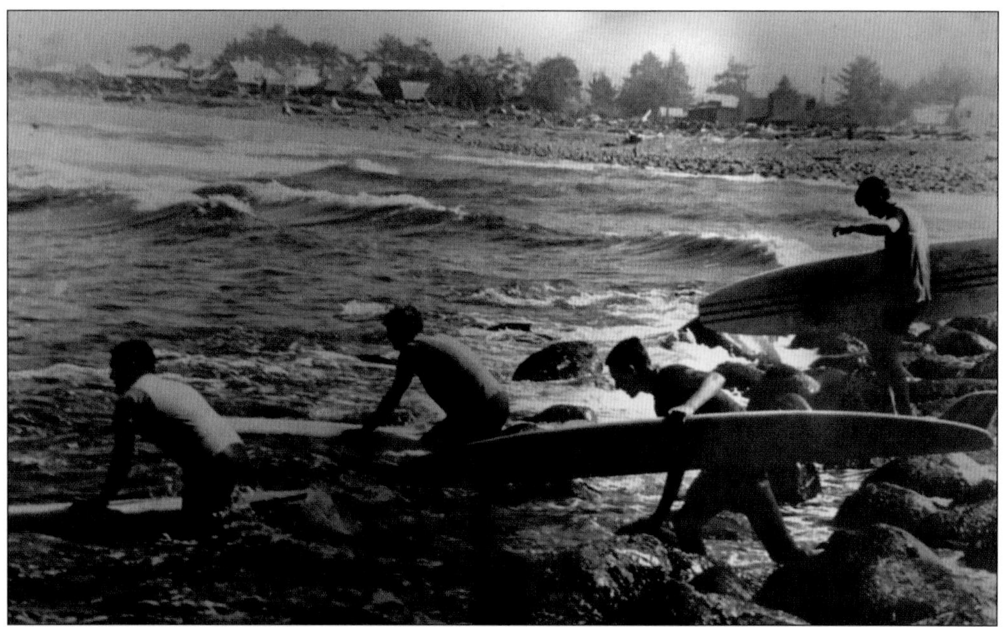

Pictured here are 1967 Seaside Surf contestants entering the water. George Daggatt explains, "The Seaside Surf Association held the contest Labor Day weekend. It was the Northwest's largest contest with 87 entered. We surfed the Cove during the morning but around noon each day it was blown out so we moved heats to Indian Beach. The Seaside Boosters donated the trophies. The paddleboard race was held in the Necanicum River." (Courtesy of George Daggatt.)

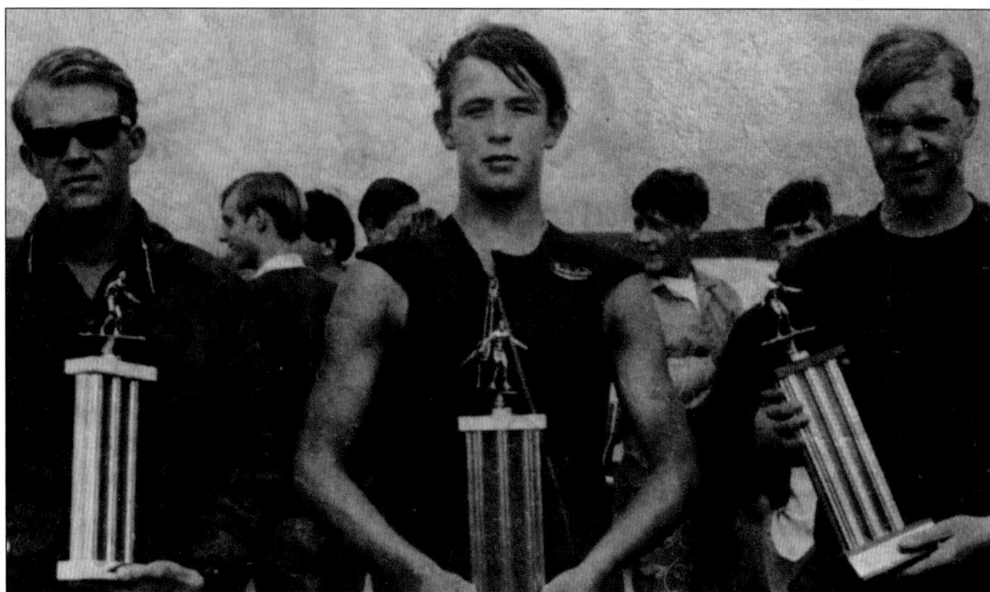

First-place winners of the Seaside Surf Contest are, from left to right, Sandy Barrett (senior division), Marty Skriver (ABSC, junior division), and Dave Holbrook (ABSC, novice division). This contest was most likely held in August 1967. "Barrett won it last year also. SSA and Seaside Boosters sponsored the contest, which was moved to Short Sands because of poor weather conditions," reports the newspaper article. The paddleboard winners were ABSC members Marion Bowers (first), Jeff Hollen (second), and Marty Skriver (third). (Courtesy of Knox Swanson.)

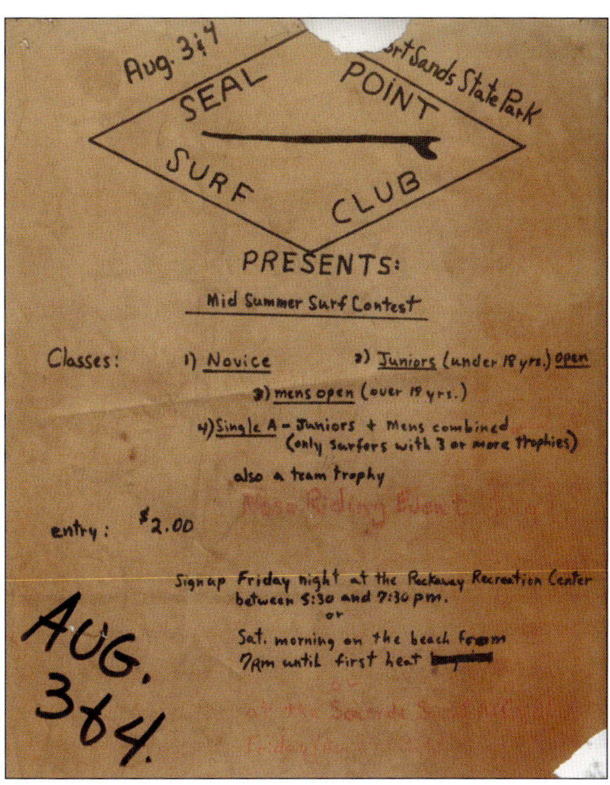

This is a 1968 Short Sands Surf Contest flyer. The newspaper listed the first, second, and third place winners of the various events. Novice: Mike Brisco (first), Bob Malo (second), and Marcus Lehrman (third). Junior: Dave Holbrook, Kurt Capri, and Scott Carlich. Men's: Mike Brisco, Rod Hamman, and George South. "A" event: Sandy Barrett, Marty Skriver, and Charlie Yates. The Seal Point Surf club, Tillamook, with the cooperation of KSWB radio and the Surf N' Cycle surf shop, sponsored and ran the contest. (Courtesy of Knox Swanson.)

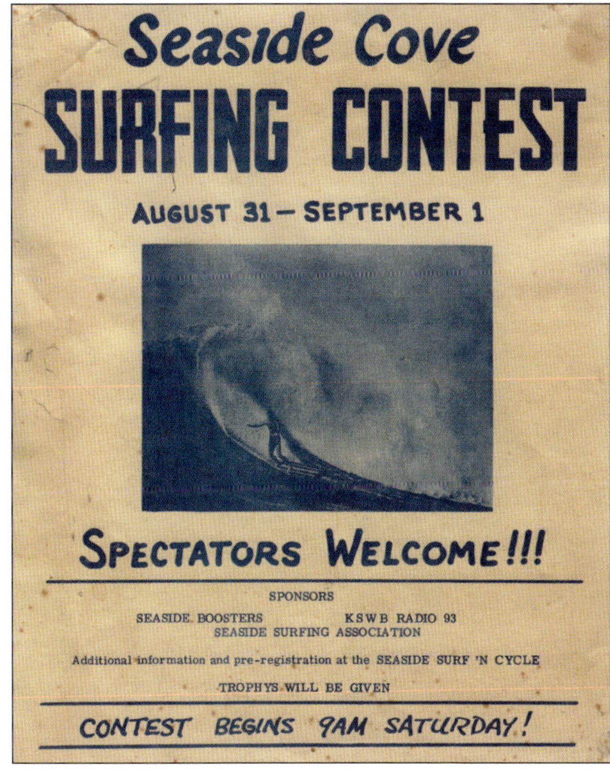

Here is a 1968 Seaside Labor Day Surf Contest flyer. The newspaper listed the winners: senior men's, Wally Parcels (first), Greg Van Sickle (second), and Wayne Schrunk (third); junior men's, Kurt Capri (first), Perry Shoemake (second), and Tim Harrington (third); advance men's division, Sandy Barrett (first) and Charlie Yates (second); novice division, John Kelsey (first), Jack Harroun (second), and Ellis Lark (third). The flyer and newspaper article listed KSWB radio and Seaside Boosters' involvement with the surf contest. (Courtesy of Knox Swanson.)

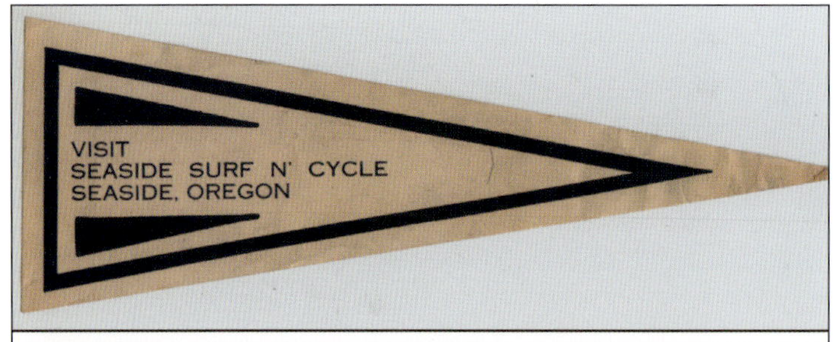

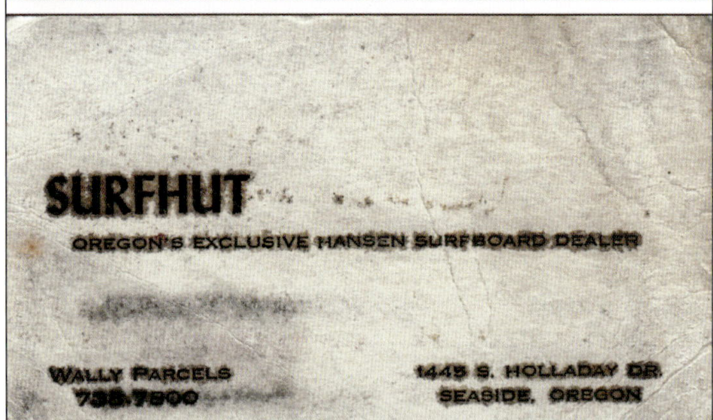

Pictured here are Wally Parcels' two surf shop logos. Wally comments, "I relocated from Seattle to Oregon in 1964 and worked with Tony Price at Troy's Surf Shop in Portland. I opened up the Seaside Surf N' Cycle in late spring 1966. We worked with Hansen surfboards. After returning from a winter surfing the North Shore of Oahu, for the next two summers operated as the Surf Hut on the Highway 101 entrance of Seaside." (Courtesy of Knox Swanson and Wayne Schrunk.)

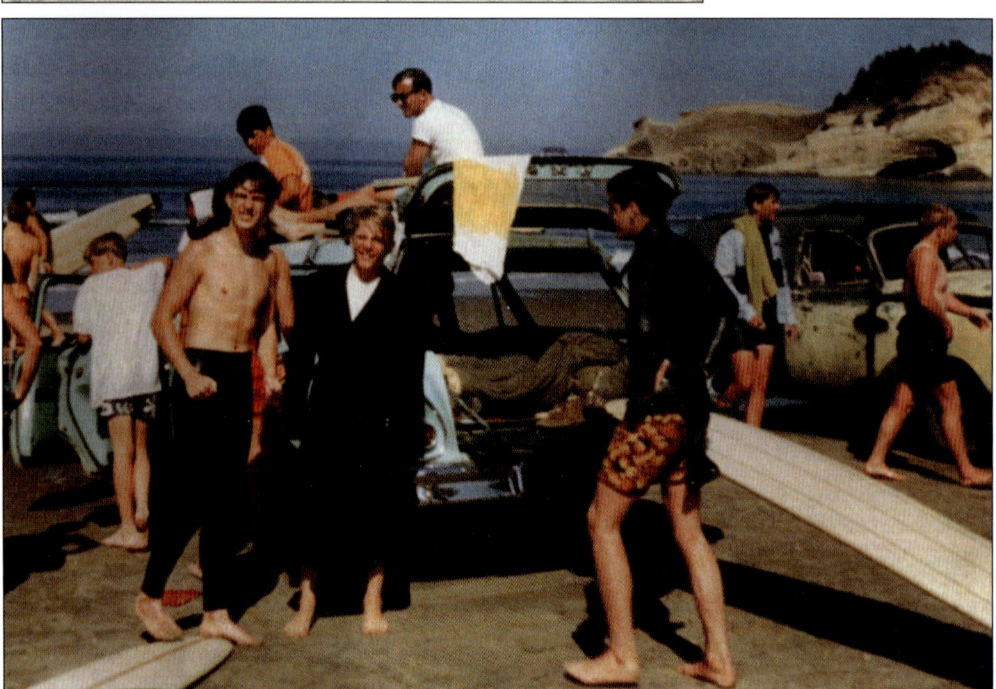

Observers and participants at the 1966 Pacific City Surf Contest are, from left to right, Salem surfer Mike Mullin (far left), and ABSC members Bruce McEntee and contest judge Scott Blackman on Mullin's 1958 Chevy Brookwood wagon. In back of the wagon are Portland surfers Steve "Red Trunks" Johnson (in wetsuit bottoms), Rich Gruetter, and Mitch Allara in bright jams. To the far right are Portland surfers Mark Miller (left) and Max Justice. (Courtesy of Steve Johnson.)

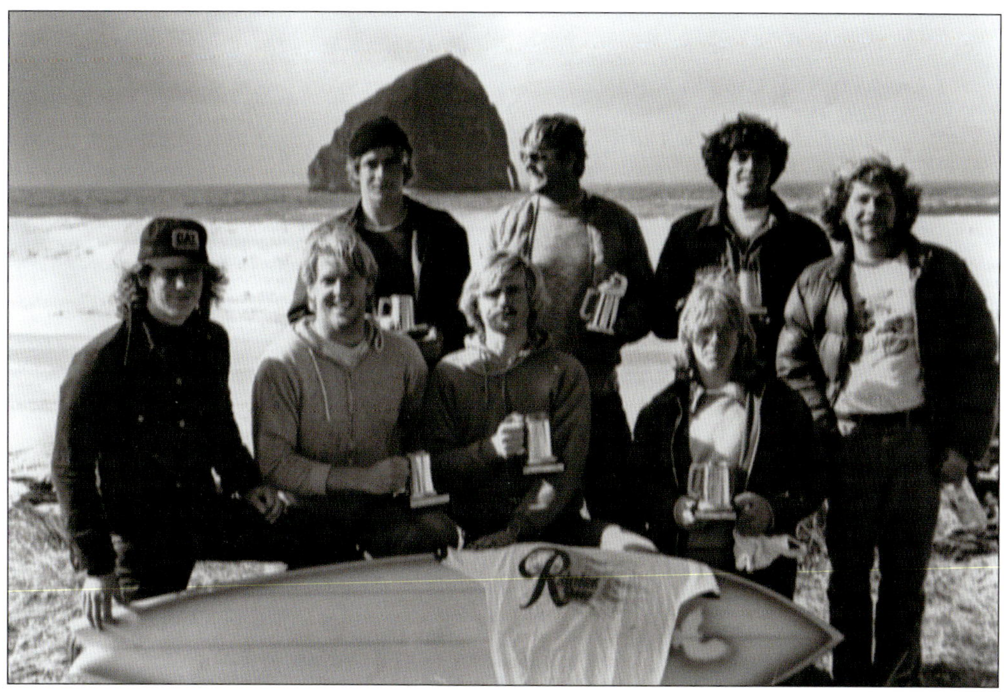

The 1973 Oregon State Rainier Beer Surfing Championship was held in Pacific City. Pictured here are, from left to right, (first row) Nick Stevens and Coos Bay surfers Wayne Schrunk, Ellis Lark, and Ed Ellingson; (second row) Agate surfer Jack Skriver, Coos Bay surfers Charlie Yates and Memo Jasso, and non-surfer Del Patrick. Schrunk recalls, "We were all finalists except raffle winner Stevens, and Patrick, who was intoxicated and wandered into the photo." (Courtesy of Wayne Schrunk.)

Dana Williams is pictured here in Pacific City in 2000. Dana recalls, "I judged in Oregon, Washington, California, Hawaii, and Long Island, where we got paid, wined, and dined in those days. Judged my first contest in the winter of 1962–1963 in Southern California. I was involved with Hoppy Schwartz in California, who was starting United States Surfing Association [USSA]. Also glassed surfboards six to seven nights a week. I believe the Seaside Surfing Association was the third club in the USSA." (Courtesy of Tom Burns.)

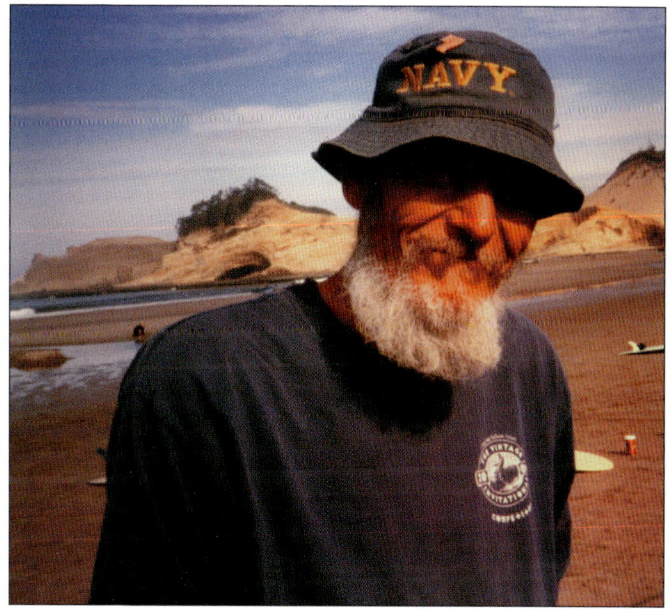

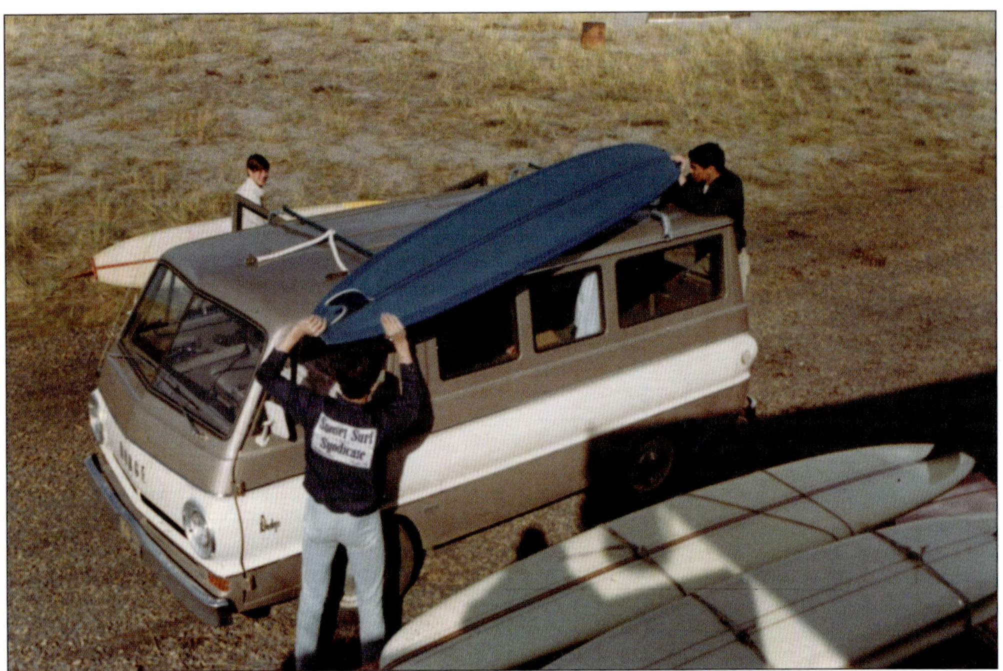

Members of the Sunset Surf Syndicate in Neskowin are pictured here during spring break 1967. Males from Portland's Sunset High School formed a surf club and surfed along the North Coast often. "The dodge van was Jay Howe's" recalls Tim Mack. "Stan Hart and I are loading or unloading Jay's Harbour surfboard. That is Joe Mineau, another Sunny High surfer, in the background. The Sunset Surf Syndicate logo is visible on Stan Hart's jacket." (Photograph by Forbes Mack.)

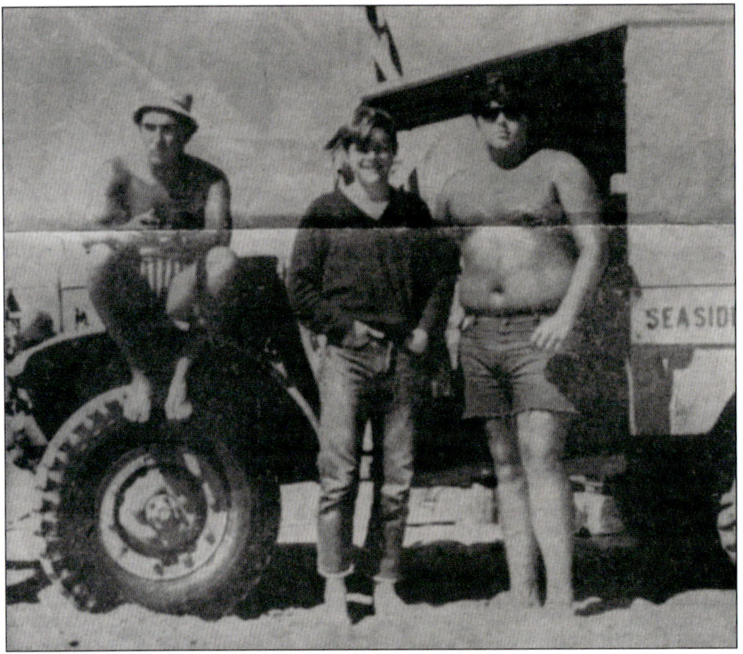

On July 18, 1968, Greg Gosser (center) reported seeing a shark in the Cove to lifeguards Jay Oakman (left) and Dennis Moody (right). Gosser recalls, "A wave came up and there was a shark. I paddled in fast and ran up the beach yelling, shark, shark, shark! Wally Parcels who owned a local surf shop at the time, wasn't too happy with me. No one would rent any surfboards all weekend." (Courtesy of Greg Gosser.)

Jim Sagawa stands in front of Portland's Underwater Sports in the summer of 1965. Sagawa recalls, "This is when I first started shaping boards under the SAG logo and using a Surfboards Hawaii template from Dick Brewer. Dick Wald and I rode the Point together in the early 1960s, without leashes. We had good times drinking Wald's homemade wine from Cragmont soda bottles before surfing the Point. Now I teach young dentists in the Philippines." (Courtesy of Mike Jipp.)

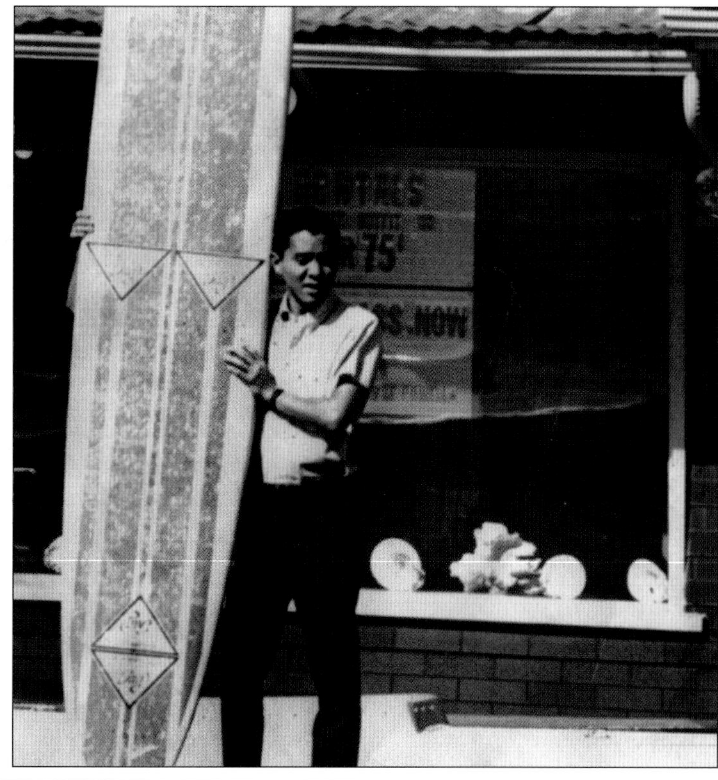

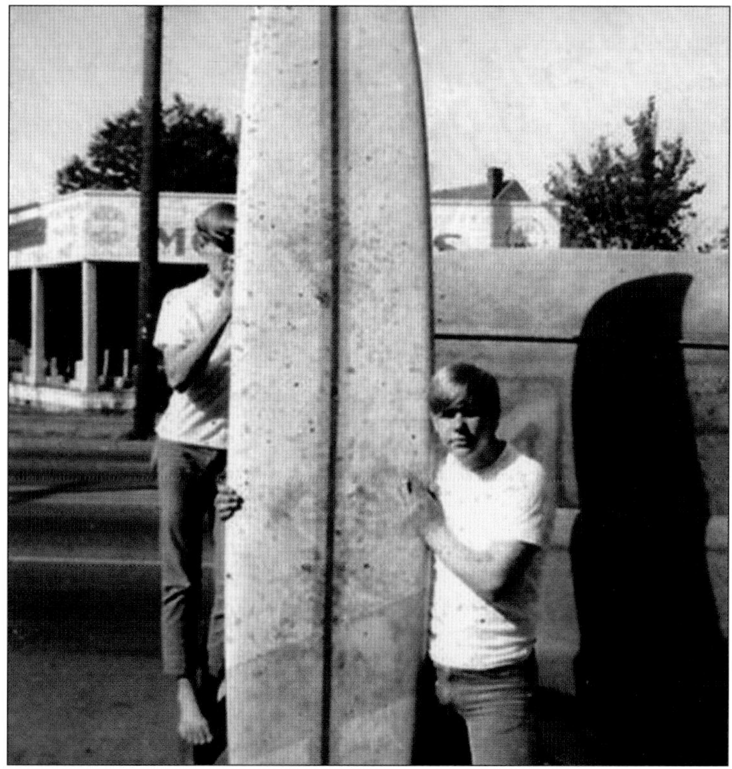

Pictured here in front of the original Troy's Surf Shop are Max Justice (right) with his 1951 panel truck and Dave Acker in 1966. Max recalls, "Troy's was about 68th and Foster S.E. in Portland for one summer in 1966. I forget why we named it Troy's. We then moved to 28th & Powell and Betty Abbot was our landlord there. She took over the shop a year later and ran it for about 15 years." (Courtesy of Max Justice.)

Custom Surfboards for the Oregon Coast

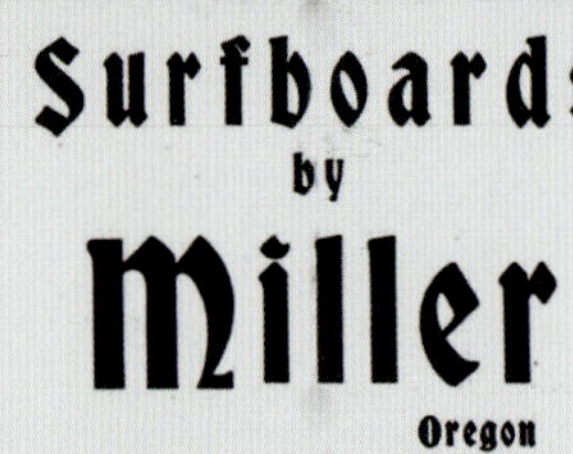

STOCK PRICE LIST

UNDER 9' 6"	$124.00
9' 6" to 9' 10"	129.00
9' 10" to 10' 2"	134.00
10' 2" to 10' 6"	139.00
OVER 10' 6"	Special Order

Price includes custom shaping, choice of 3/4" Redwood or 1/2" Balsa center strip, double glassing, clear finish, Clark foam blank, choice of glass or polypropolene fin.

Extras Available
(Price on request)

Any combination of Balsa - Redwood - Foam stringers available up to 7 strips.

Color - pinstripes - noseblocks - stripes

Surfboards by MILLER are Oregon made using the highest quality products available. Exclusively distributed in Oregon - Washington by
SEASIDE SURF N' CYCLE, Seaside, Oregon

This is a 1966–1968 Miller's flyer from Portland. Miller boards were made out of Troy's Surf Shop. "Tony Price was the only one old enough to rent these buildings and he ran the shop during the days. We called him our front man," Max Justice recalls. "Mark Miller, me, and Ray Jones built boards for three years. Mark and I were still in high school and we came in evenings and weekends to build boards." (Courtesy of Knox Swanson.)

This is The Surfer's business card. Mike Ehlen writes, "It was a pretty cool shop, across from Cleveland High School. It was our go-to place to buy wetsuits, boards, wax, etc. Mrs. A, as she was known, could be grumpy or your best friend. I knew her as both. Underneath her sometimes tough demeanor she had a big heart. I got to know her over the years and we became friends." (Courtesy of Knox Swanson.)

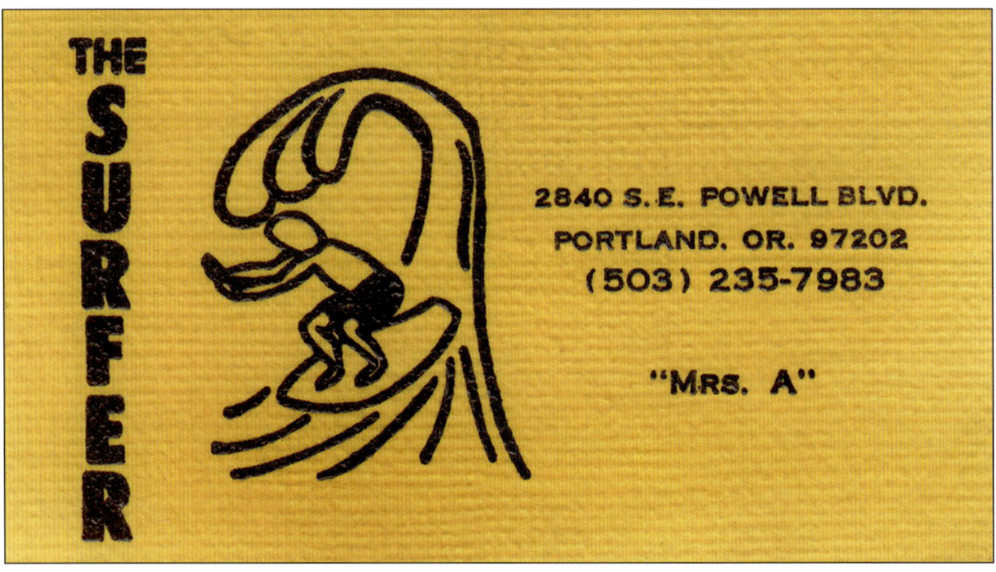

Jim Sparks is pictured here at Cannon Beach Surf Shop in 1968. Peter Lindsey writes, "Vince Morrison operated the first shop in Cannon Beach. Peter Adamson, Jim Sparks, and David Louis opened the next shop in the late sixties. The boys set up their shop inside the old Log Cabin Restaurant, carrying Haut surfboards." Knox Swanson states, "Jim Sparks ran the shop and it was a way to get O'Neil wetsuits at cost, and Haut surfboards too." (Photograph by Dick Borovicka.)

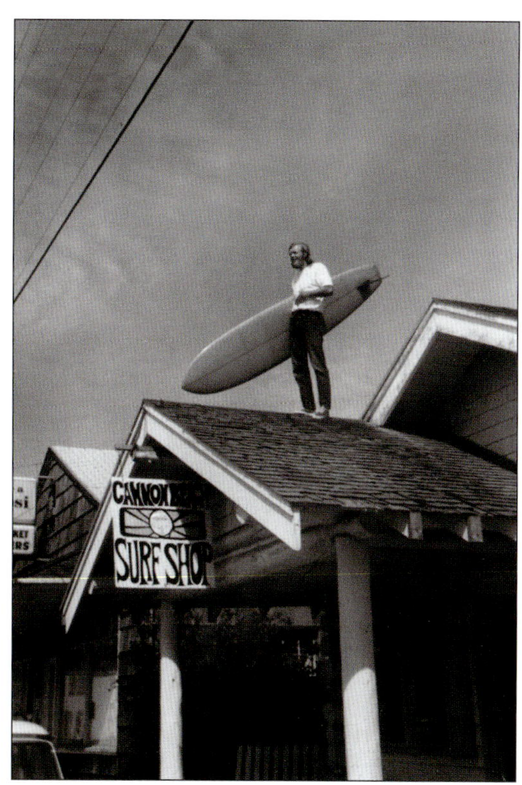

INDIAN SURF SHOP

CANNON BEACH, OREGON

NEW BOARDS BY:

Sundance Surfboard of California

Tillamook Head & Indian Surfboards

WETSUITS BY:

BODYGLOVE WHITE STAG

AVAILABLE NOW

DRI-DUCK DRY SUITS

Surf Warm and Dry All Year Round

Used Boards and Rentals

Blanks Cloth and Resin

Located 2nd Ave., Cannon Beach, Ore.

Pictured here is a flyer from the Indian Surf Shop in Cannon Beach from 1971–1973. Dave Kron recalls, "There were four partners in the beginning, Dave Hillis, Jim Porras, Mike "Bear" McClellan, and myself. I made Indian surfboards." Knox Swanson remembers, "It was located on Second Avenue between Hemlock and Spruce Streets. Kron worked in an old building next to the surf shop repairing and making boards. Jack Brown started a surf shop in the same location after Indian Surf Shop closed." (Courtesy of Greg Gosser.)

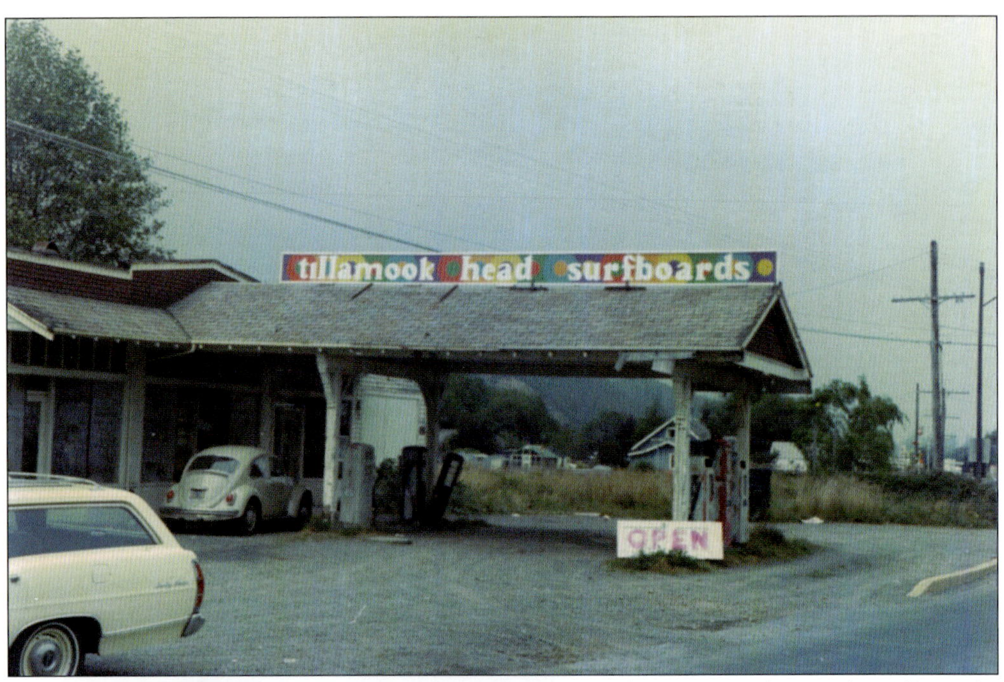

In the summer of 1968, the Tillamook Head crew lived three miles up the north bank, outside of Nehalem. Dan Matthews recalls, "Most of us left Seaside that winter and returned in the spring of 1969. We opened the Tillamook Head Surf Shop in an old gas station at the Cannon Beach Junction (pictured). Art Spence, Jerry Harrington, Tim Foley, and myself lived behind the shop in an old house." (Photograph by Dick Borovicka.)

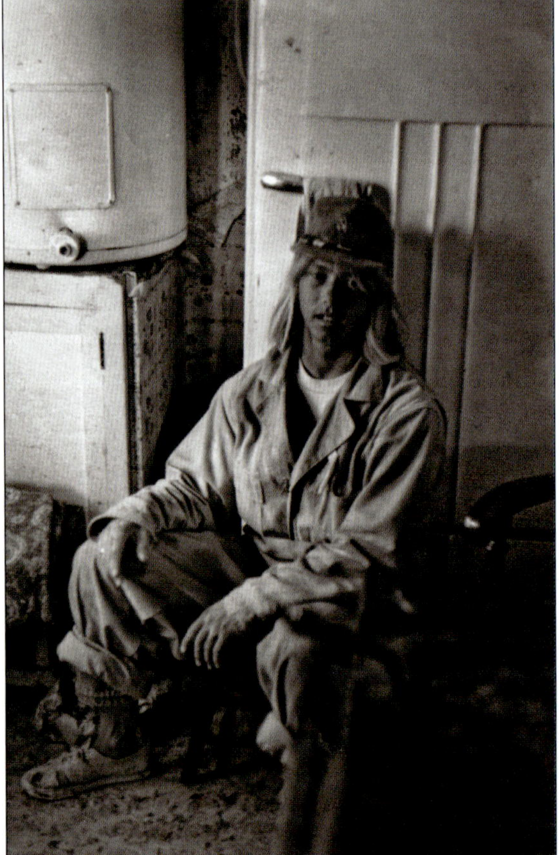

Bill Barnfield, sander, joined the Tillamook Head crew in spring 1969. Dan Matthews recalls, "Billy went over to Hawaii during the winter of 1971–1972 and started sanding for Gerry Lopez. Bill became a good glasser and good shaper. I went to Hawaii in 1989–1990 and spent the winter working for Billy. By that time Bill was the man on the North Shore. He had gotten in with the best and had learned about board making." (Photograph by Dan Matthews.)

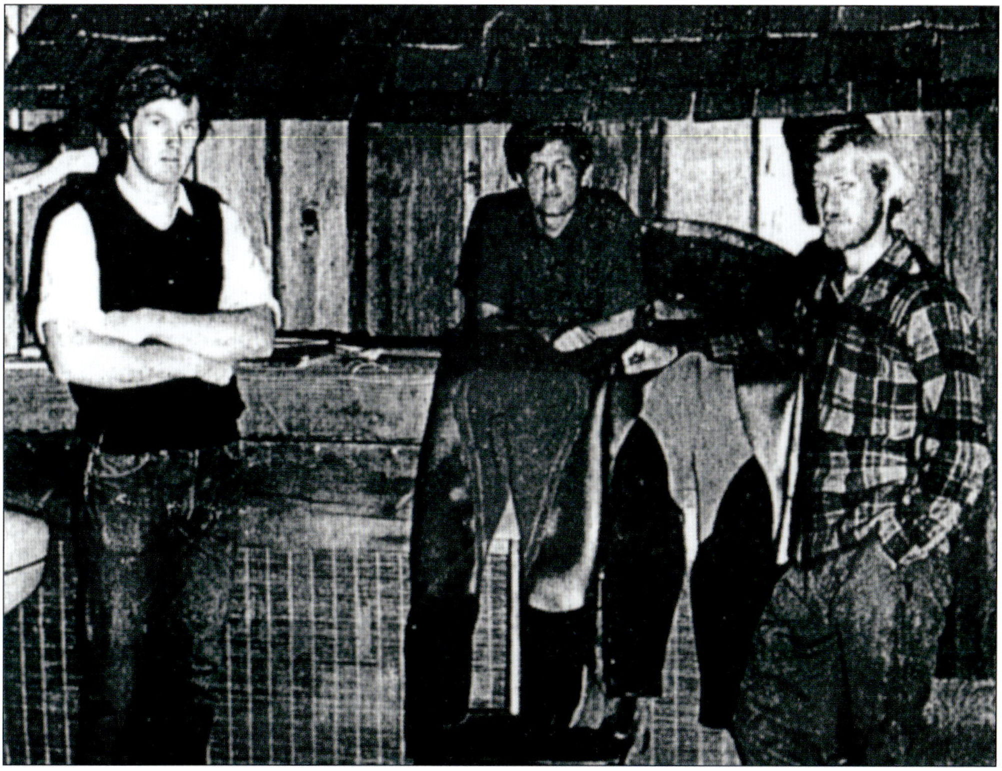

On September, 3, 1970, the *Seaside Signal* published an article on Tillamook Head Surf Shop. Co-owners Jerry Harrington (left) and Dan Matthews (center) were shapers, and Art Spence (right) was their glasser. Tim Foley sold boards, and Bill Barnfield was their sander. Scott Blackman recalls, "Tillamook Head was unique. While the group lasted, the shop and their boards were highly sought out by North Coast surfers. They were considered a creative group of board makers and surfers." (Courtesy of Mike Jipp.)

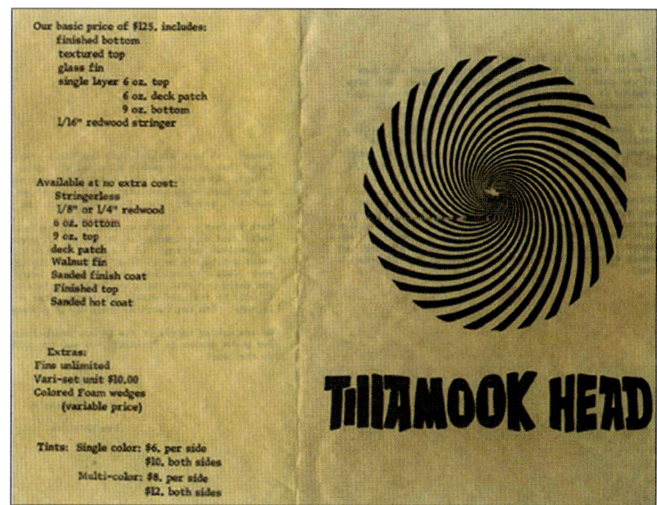

Our basic price of $125. includes:
finished bottom
textured top
glass fin
single layer 6 oz. top
6 oz. deck patch
9 oz. bottom
1/16" redwood stringer

Available at no extra cost:
Stringerless
1/8" or 1/4" redwood
6 oz. bottom
9 oz. top
deck patch
Walnut fin
Sanded finish coat
Finished top
Sanded hot coat

Extras:
Fins unlimited
Vari-set unit $10.00
Colored Foam wedges
(variable price)

Tints: Single color: $6. per side
$10. both sides
Multi-color: $8. per side
$12. both sides

TILLAMOOK HEAD

Pictured here is a Tillamook Head brochure, complete with prices and logo. Dan Matthews comments, "I still have one of the brochures that I wrote when we opened the shop at the Cannon Beach junction in 1969. That was the second year of Tillamook Head. The spiral logo was taken from the Tamari soy sauce label. Keep in mind, the Ford Mustang had debuted a couple of years earlier with a sticker price of $1,648." (Courtesy of Dan Matthews.)

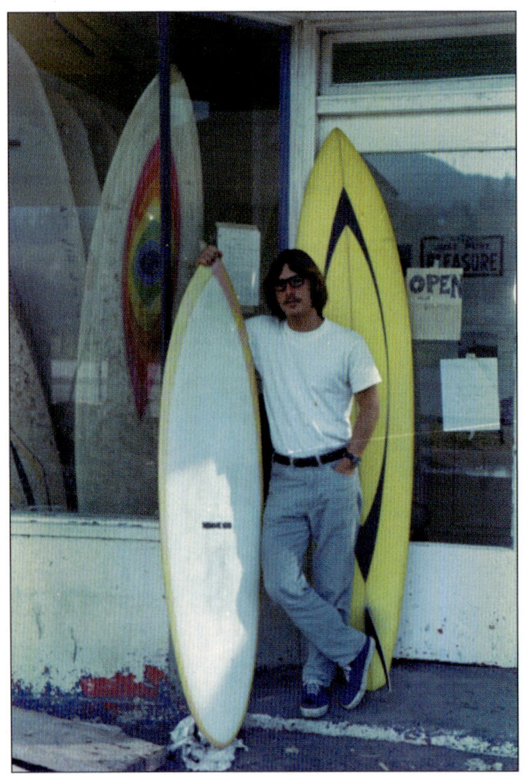

Dick Borovicka is pictured here in front of Tillamook Head Surf Shop, Cannon Beach Junction, in 1969. Remembering his first try at making a board, Dick comments, "I bought a blank from Mrs. A and made a mess at my parents' house. I didn't even shape the board, just glassed it. It was toxic, horrible. I had no mask. It stunk up the house and resin stuck to the basement floor." (Courtesy of Dick Borovicka.)

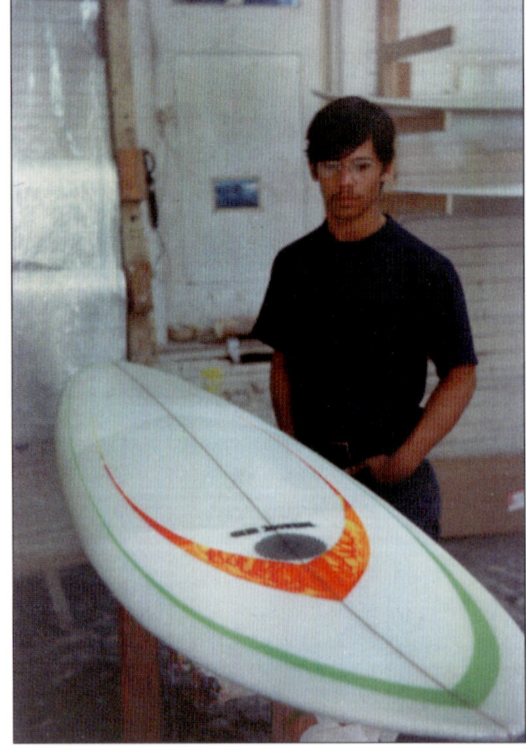

David Louis is pictured here with a Tillamook Head board in 1969. David recalls, "I met Bill Smith at Portland Community College and ran into him in Seaside in the spring of 1968. Bill taught me how to surf in less than a week at Indian Beach. I wore a short John, with no sleeves and short pants. Went to the Cove on the fifth day and surfed real waves. It was a kick in the butt." (Photograph by Dick Borovicka.)

Spence and Barnfield boards are strapped on top of Randy Barna's VW Beetle in 1970. Barna recalls, "The Swallowtail is a seven-foot Art Spence Sword for the Cove and Short Sands. The seven-foot-six pintail is a Bill Barnfield Point board with the Evergreen graphics. These were boards from the Tillamook Head shop with the shapers' branding and a new progression. VW Beetles were the ultimate popular surf vehicle—cheap to run and easy to fix, but slow." (Photograph by Randy Barna.)

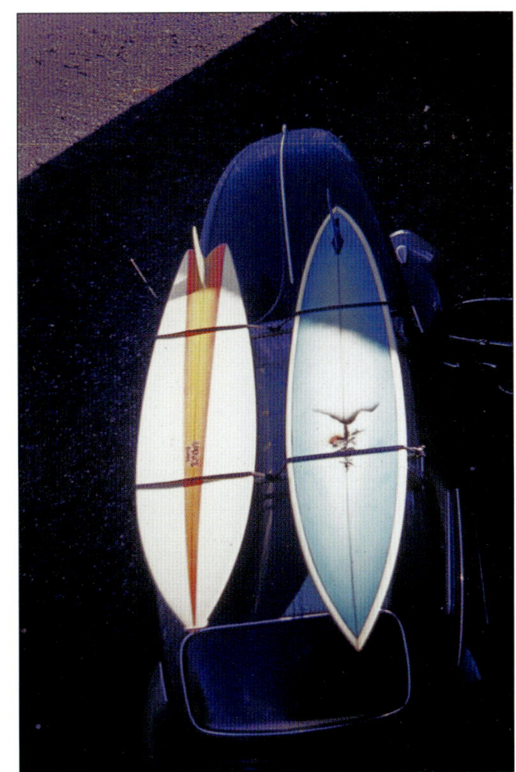

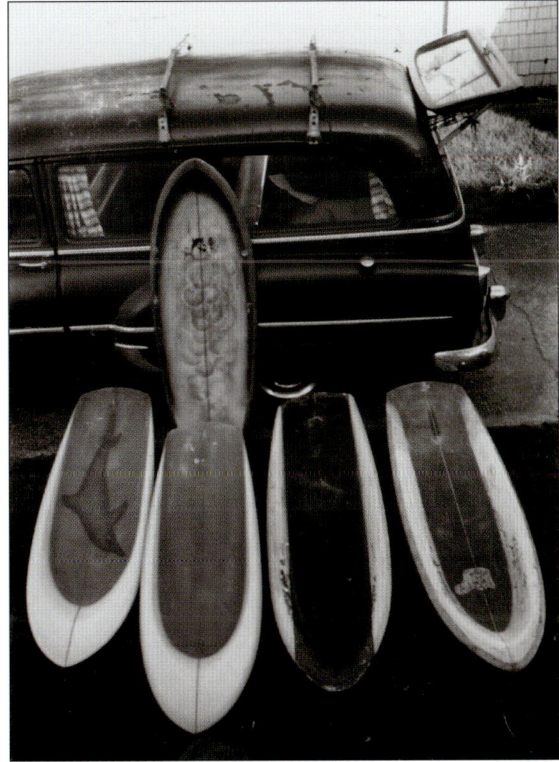

Knox Swanson's kneeboards and Chevy Wagon are pictured here in 1973. Swanson was known for using kneeboards at the Point along with Al Ritter and Mike Burger. Knox remembers, "Jeff Hull made them for me, and together we would figure out how to do them. As boards evolved, kneeboards were almost the same size as modern short boards. Surfing was always about whatever works." (Photograph by Dick Borovicka.)

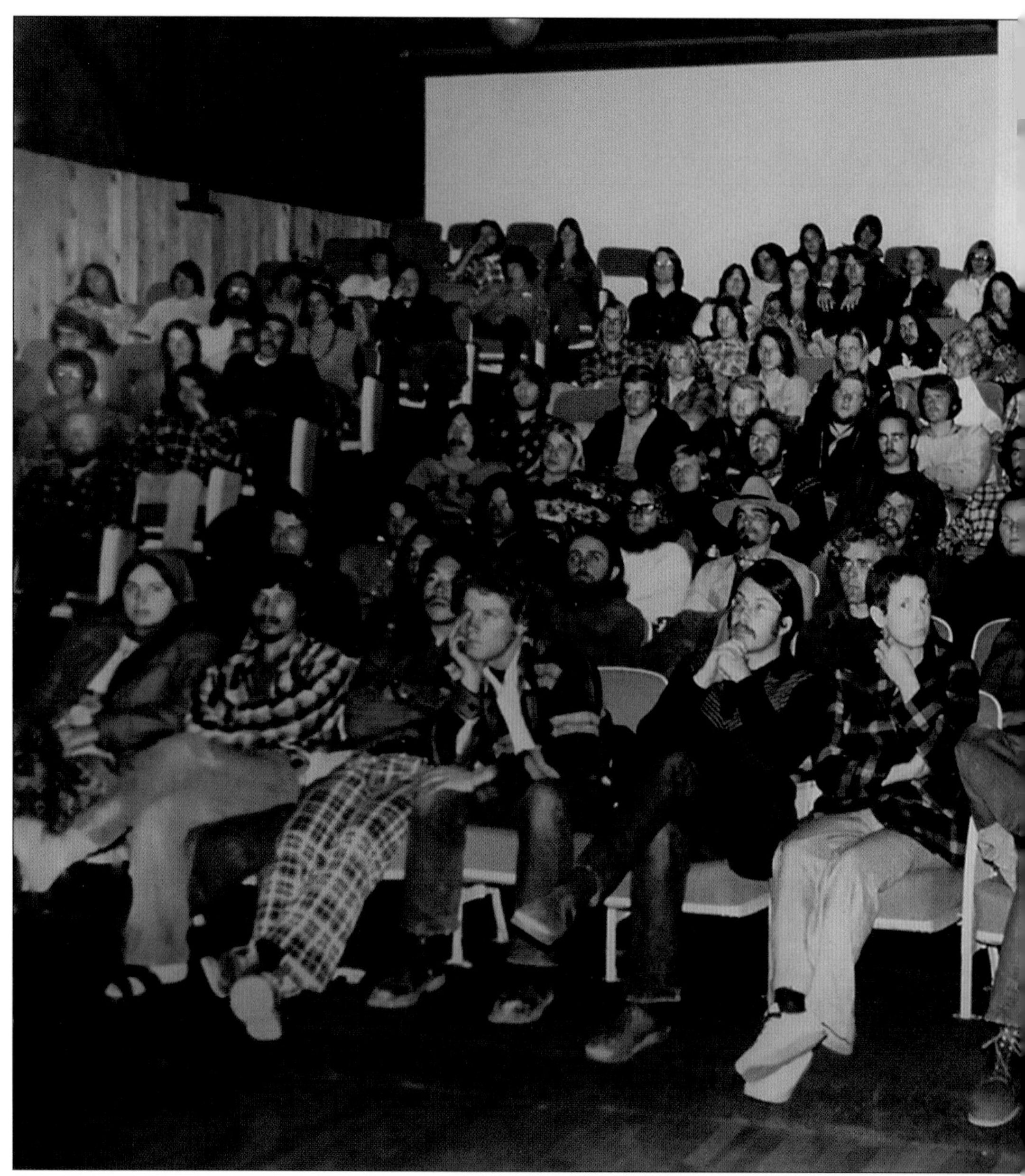

Sam Foster photographed these surfers watching *Salt Water Wine* in Cannon Beach's Coaster Theater in 1974. Jeff Hull comments, "A surf movie coming to the Oregon Coast in the 1970s was on a par with perfect conditions for epic surf. It happened once or twice a year. The difference was you could schedule it in advance and everyone would show up. David Kopra had worked with filmmaker Alan Rich on his movie *Salt Water Wine* and brought it to the North Coast, rented the Coaster Theater, and promoted it himself." Jeff Hull has identified some of the people, who represent most of the early pioneer surfers in Oregon: (first row) Cherly (Louis) Erikson, David Louis, Mike, Tim Foley, Peter de Turk, Dave Kron, and Mike Burger; (second row) Mike "Bear" McClellan, Jim Gray, Rod Bullier, and Rita; (third row) Jeff Hull, Dave Fee, Phil Mancill, Nancy Brown, Dave McKinney, and Steve "Red Trunks" Johnson; (fourth row) Rich Fencsak, Cliff Barber, Daryl Wood, Corky Wood, Sue De Bay, John De Bay, David Brice, Tim Mack, Art Spence,

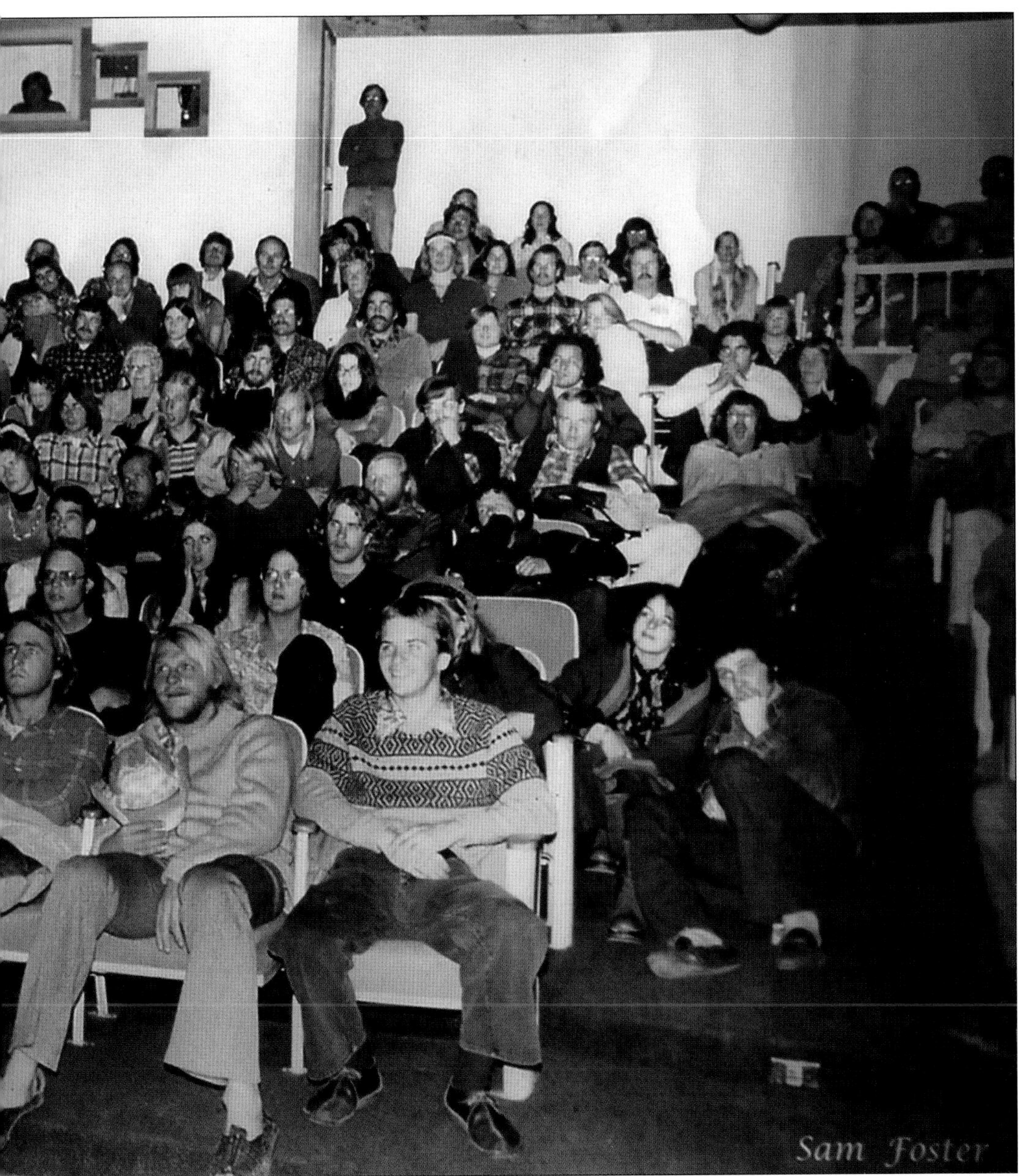

Steve Skriver, Jerry Holbrook, and Mark Hunter; (fifth row) Billy McKnight, Debbie Fackerell, Bill Fackerell, Pete Smith, Tim Holbrook, Perry Shoemake, Rich Gruetter, Dick Borovicka, Jim Smith, Al Ritter, and Jim Sparks; (sixth row) David Matthews, Serene Matthews, Darlene Mathews, Jeff Hite, Larry Ausman, Diana Schlavin, Lyla, Lyle, Lisa Schlavin, Grandma Kopra, Kevin Kopra, Olivia Kopra, and Jim; (seventh row) Johnnie Kopra; Mike Malis, Ron Chaloux, Connie Chaloux, Bruce Prator, Mark Tunno, Greg Gosser, and Steve Kraske; (eighth row) Geri (Natali) Gidian, Tom Palmrose, Jack Brown, Eveline Brown, Mike Ehlen, Paul Montgomery, and Bill "Seadog" Siewert; (ninth row) Cleve Rooper and Marilyn Rooper; (tenth row) Suzie Brown and Louie Wilson; (booth) Waco Kopra and David Kopra. (Courtesy of Seaside Museum and Historical Society.)

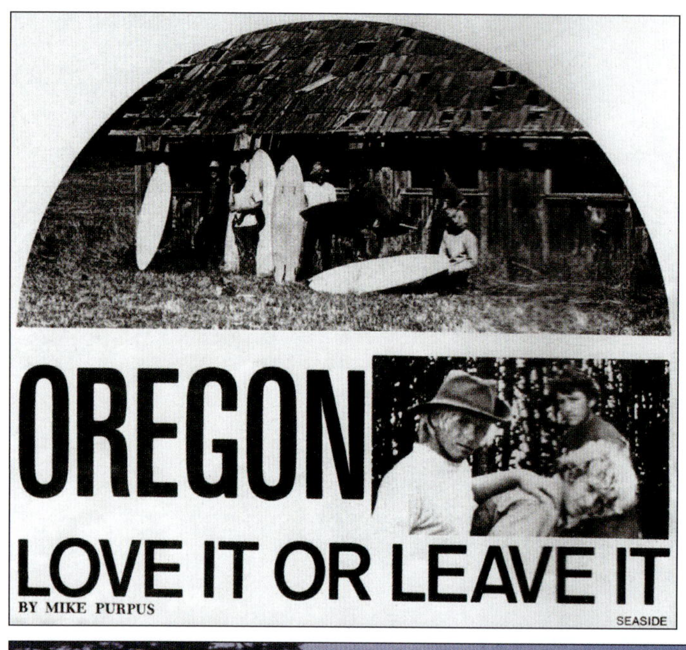

OREGON

LOVE IT OR LEAVE IT

BY MIKE PURPUS

SEASIDE

In 1972, Mike Purpus wrote an article titled "Oregon Love It or Leave It," for *International Surfing*'s February-March issue, accompanied by photographs by Dan Merkel. Before the Purpus visit, nonlocal surfers from California and around Oregon were welcome to surf the Point. Their advanced surfing skills were admired, and they brought innovation in equipment and boards. After the Purpus visit, outsiders were no longer encouraged to surf at the Point, only at the Cove. (Courtesy of Stan Hart.)

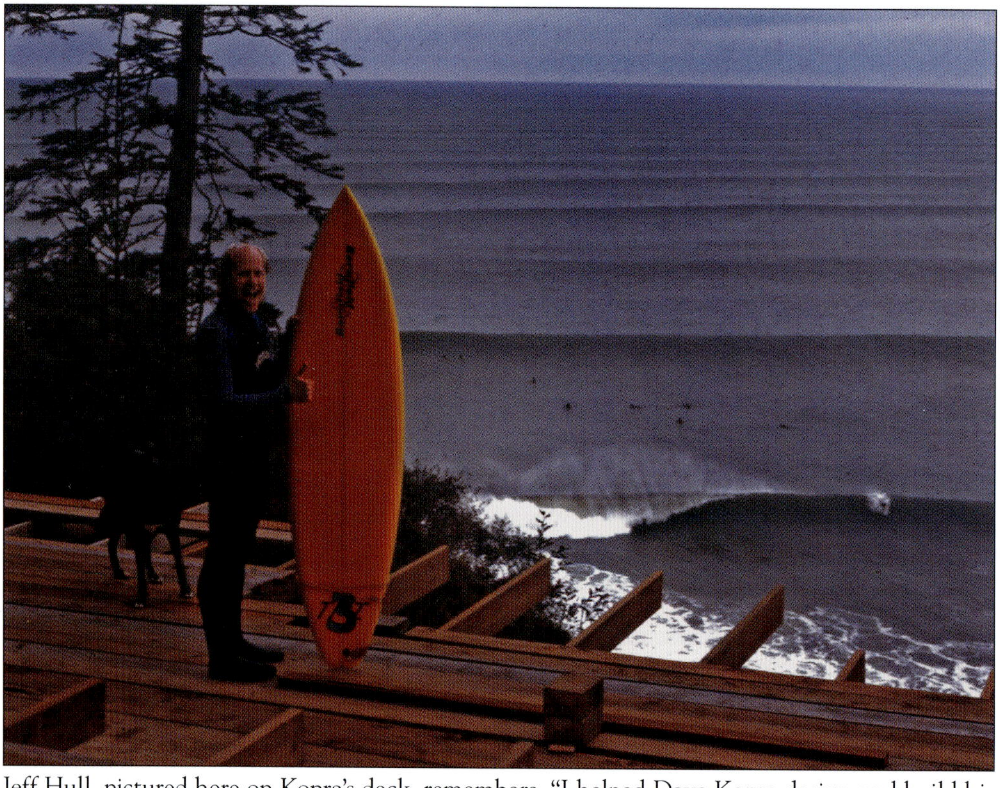

Jeff Hull, pictured here on Kopra's deck, remembers, "I helped Dave Kopra design and build his deck above the Point in the mid-1980s. Dave is one of the most generous guys I know and shared his good fortune with countless friends in the form of aloha spirit, Oregon style. He always welcomed me to his home above the Point, where a quick run down the trail put you in the lineup." (Photograph by Jack Molan.)

In the early 1970s Jeff Hull shaped and Max Justice glassed boards. "Their surf logo Hot Licks," Mike Burger explains, "was lifted from a band called Dan Hicks and the Hot Licks. I did a lot of drawings and doodling back then—some substance-inspired, some mental purging. I still have their Hot Licks board. It was backyard underground surfboard making at its best, or worst, depending on who you talk to." (Courtesy of Max Justice.)

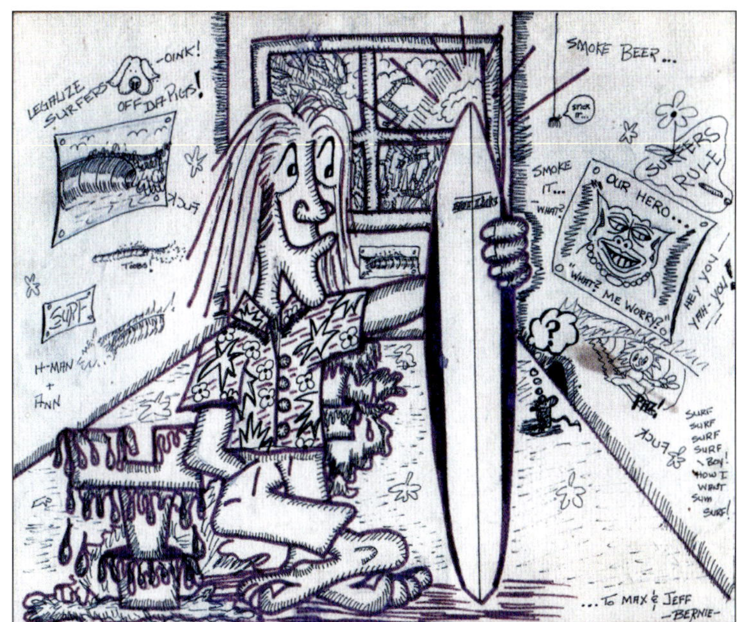

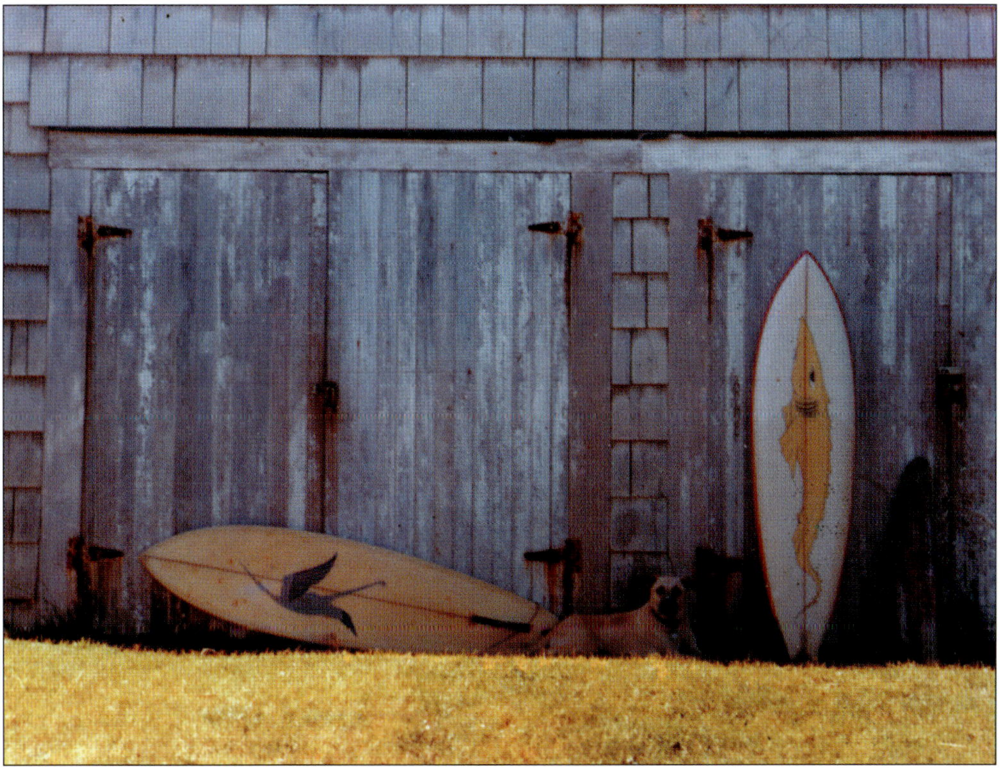

Pictured here is Scott Evansen's barn in Tolovana Park. Evansen recalls, "The barn was close to my grandfather's house, blocks from the beach. Jeff Hull shaped and I glassed and painted board designs in the barn. Our surfing friends would sleep upstairs. Cliff Barber, Larry Moore, Tim Sills, Rod Bullier, Richard Fencsak, Rob Laird, Jim Jarvis, and myself were the Tolovana surf gang during the 1970s. We mostly surfed Short Sands and Needles." (Photograph by Scott Evansen.)

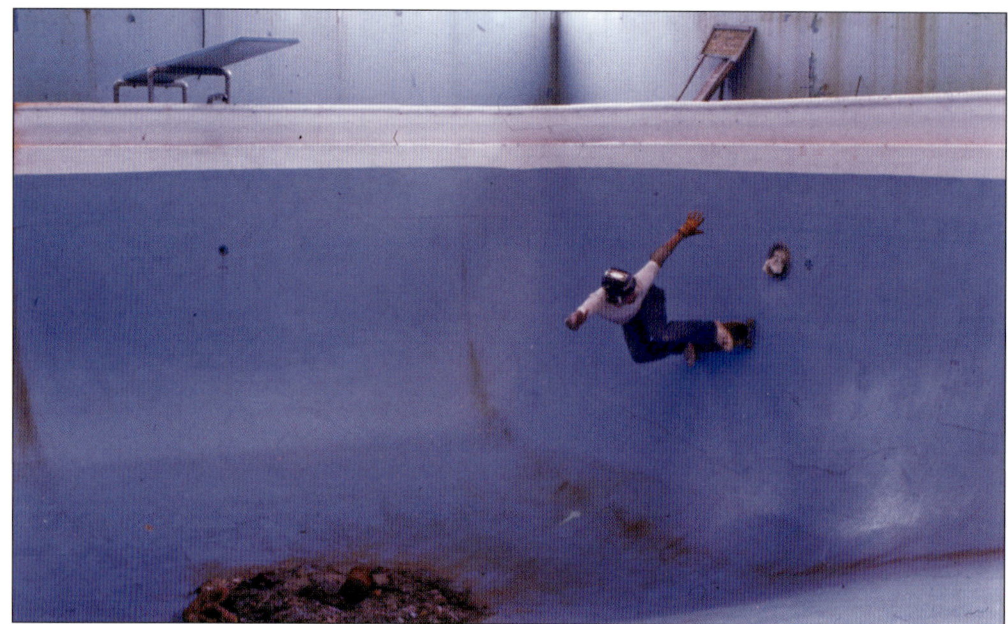

David Louis is pictured here skateboarding at Gearhart Swim Pool around 1972–1973, before it was covered with graffiti. This pool was a favorite place for many surfers. David Louis recalls, "I started skateboarding when I was eight years old. I got some metal skates, I flattened them out, nailed them on a two-by-four board I had found and started skating. I made skateboards in high school with clay wheels." (Photograph by Rik Cederstrom.)

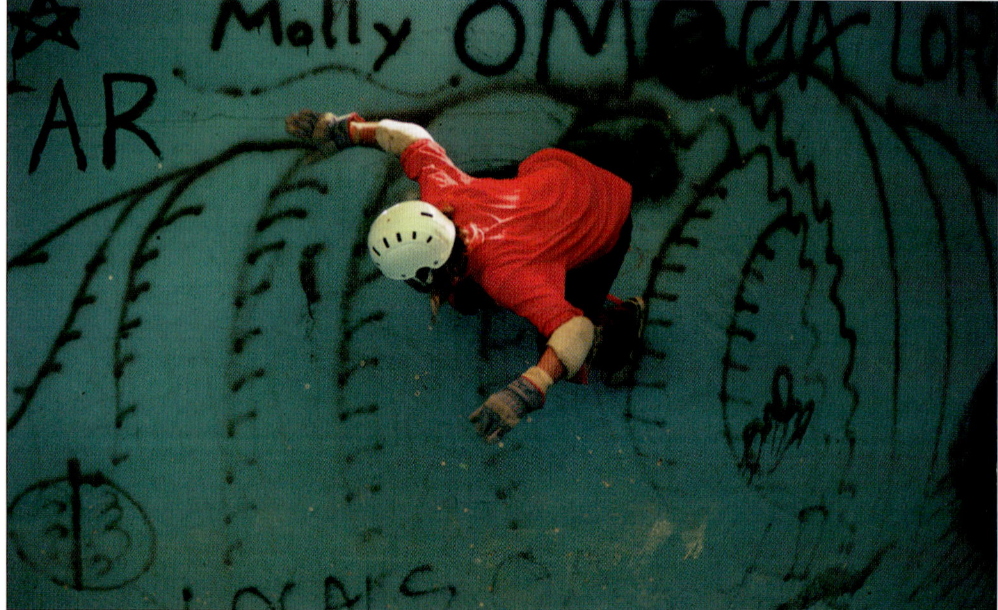

Art Spence is pictured here skateboarding at Gearhart Pool in 1977. The abandoned pool was a favorite spot for some surfers, and "We'd sneak in so people couldn't see us," Tim Foley recalls. "Spence got the speed wobbles on Saddle Mountain Road. He tried to bail, leapt for the shrubs, and shredded his knee. Went to Seaside Hospital, took over a year to heal. Got introduced to pain pills and was never really the same again." (Photograph by Tim Mack.)

Tim Foley is skateboarding in the mid-1970s at the abandoned and graffiti-covered Gearhart Pool. Tim remembers, "I started skating in Portland in 1961 with metal skates. Skating died until urethane wheels came along. I jumped on it along with Spence, Burger, and Gizdavich. We skated the Astoria hills, bank at Fort Stevens, trail out to Point at Ecola State Park, and the road to Saddle Mountain. Burger felt skateboarding and surfing mesh." (Photograph by Mike Burger.)

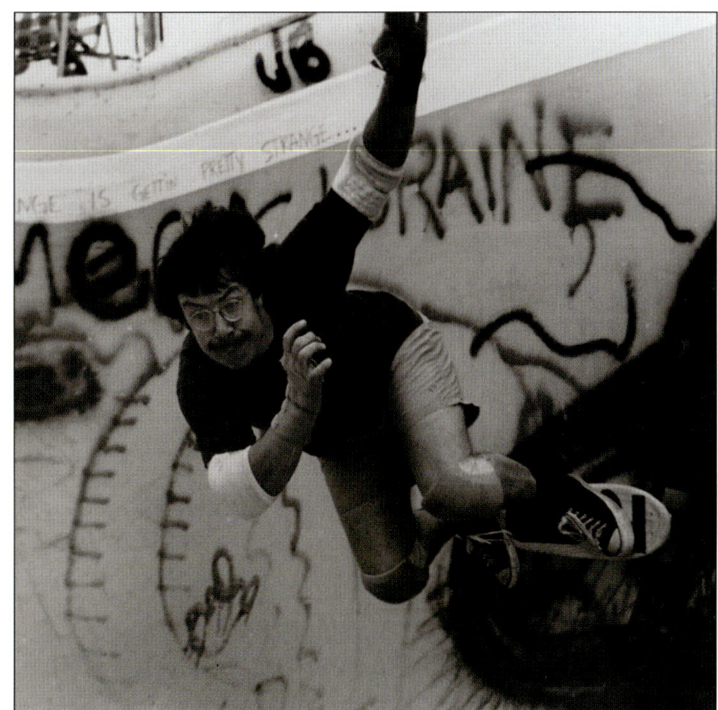

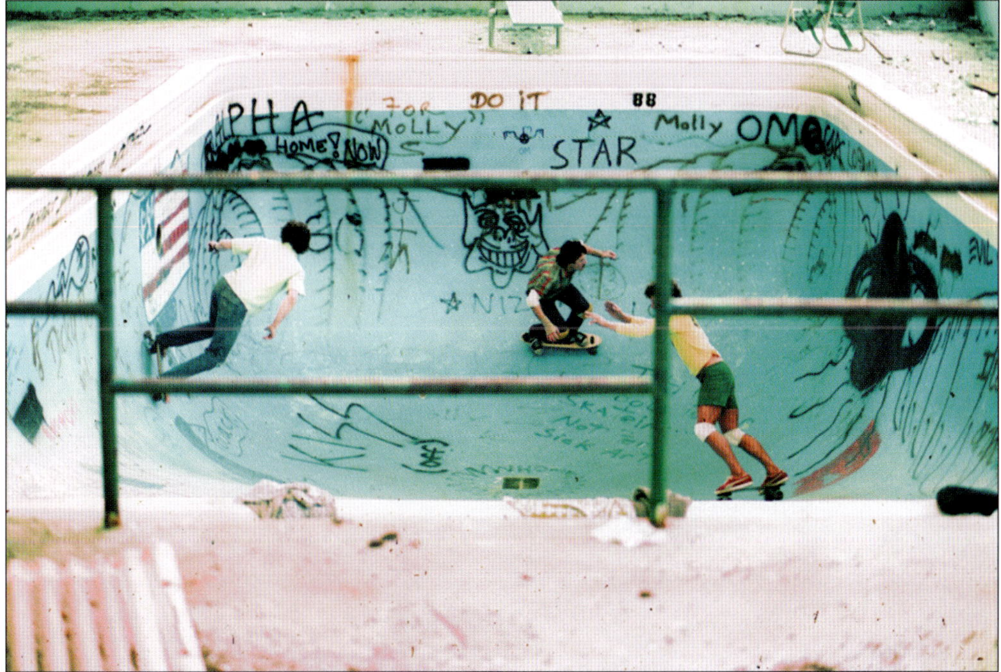

Skateboarding at Gearhart Pool are, from left to right, Jack Molan, Tim Foley, and Mark Hunter. "Molan and I bailed out the abandoned pool," recalls Josh Gizdavich. "It took us days to get all the water out. The roof was collapsing and it was condemned. We started skating in the pool around 1972–1973. The main rule—no noise. Condos around and we weren't supposed to be in there. If anyone made noise, they were kicked out." (Photograph by Tim Mack.)

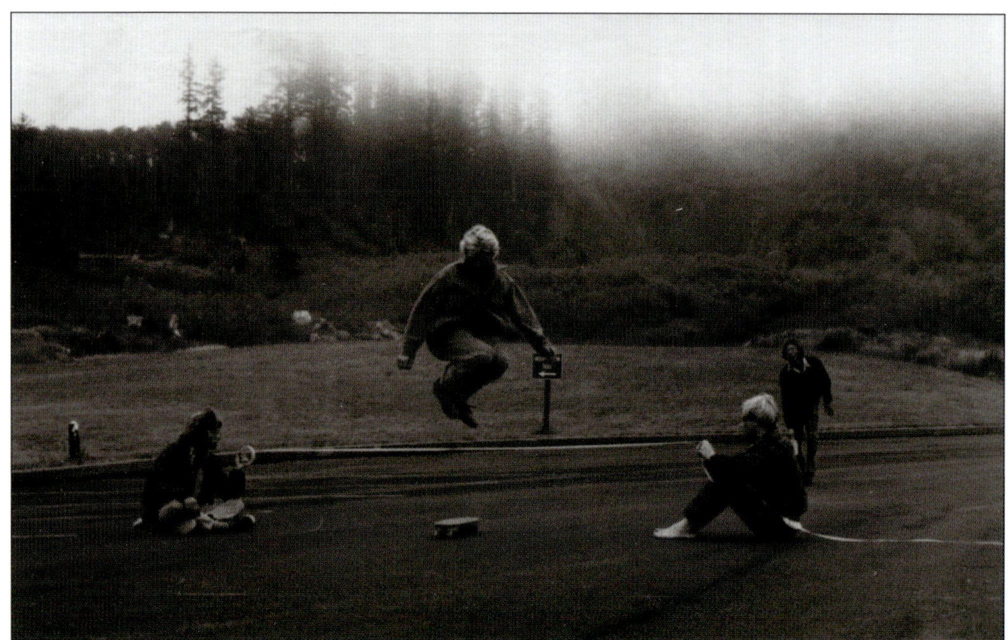

Kent Wienker is pictured here skateboarding in Ecola State Park. Wienker attended Washington's Renton High School with Mike Burger, who recalls, "Wienker looked like a surfer and disappeared to surf in Santa Barbara for a week, getting absences excused somehow. Very poised and good as a surfer." Wienker recalls, "Marty Skriver and I were in finals at Short Sands. He came out of the tube behind me on a center peak left! First place Marty!" (Photograph by Dick Borovicka.)

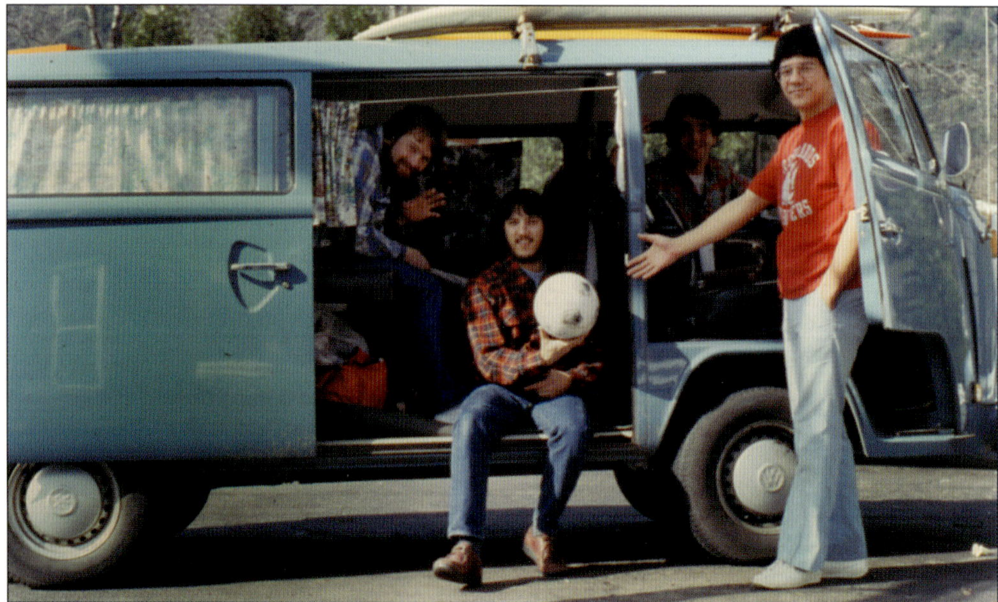

On a Pacific City Dirt Crowd (PCDC) Santa Barbara road trip in 1978 are, from left to right, Glenn Kellow, Gerry Day, John Benson, and Kani Rowland. "It was a spur-of-the-moment trip. Tim Mack and Perry Shoemake were going to surf the Ranch off Mack's boat and asked us to come," explains Day. "The only way to surf the place was to paddle in from a boat. We took off in Kani's VW. We were stoked." (Photograph by Gerry Day.)

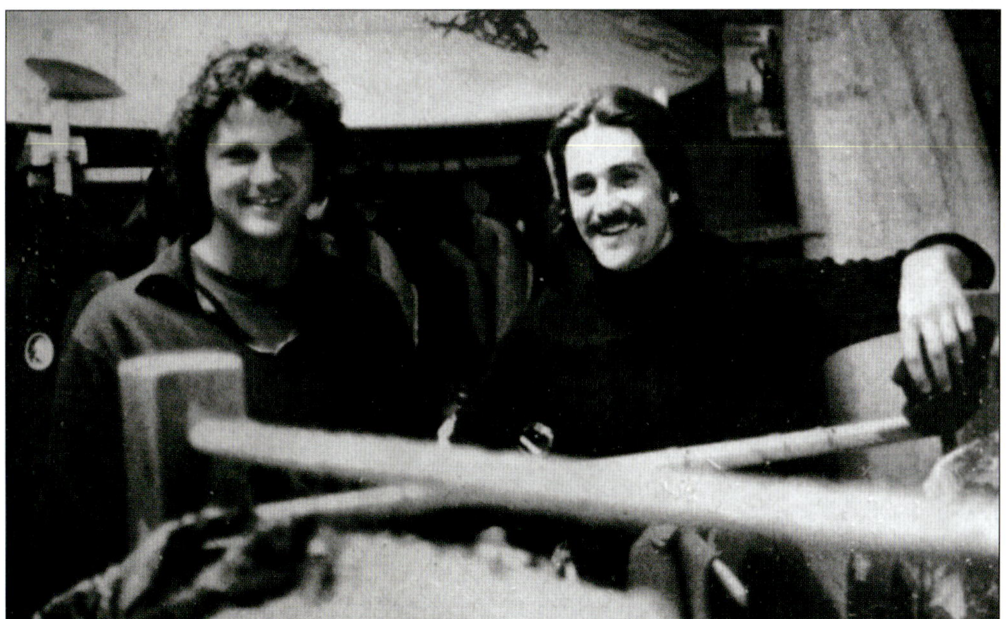

Seaside's Cleanline Surf Shop opened in August 1980 with co-owners Jack Molan (left) and Josh Gizdavich. Molan recalls, "We opened Cleanline, and both Josh and I were married that year. I kept fishing to pay the bills and Josh was a lead cook at the Crab Boiler to stay alive. We opened with three or four wetsuits, half a dozen surfboards." Molan and Gizdavich were in business together for two years. (Courtesy of Josh Gizdavich.)

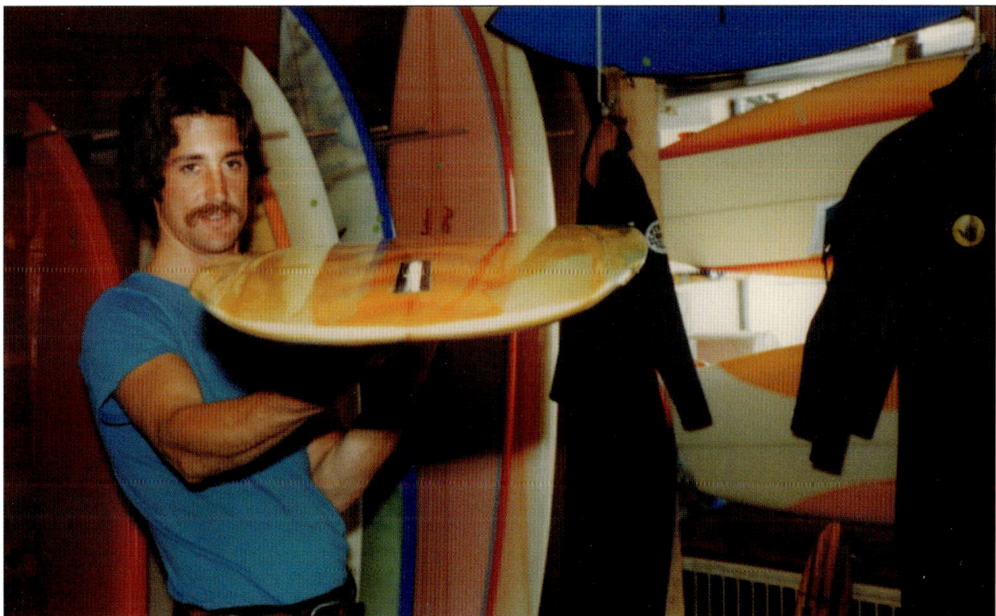

Josh Gizdavich is pictured here at Seaside's Cleanline Surf Shop in 1980. "The first shop was housed in my father's old medical office for 30 years. I moved the business into the old library building around 2012," he explains. "I made a list of possible names for the shop, and Josh picked Cleanline," Jack Molan recalls. "The name was a bit ironic, as the shop was next door to the local cleaners." (Photograph by Jack Molan.)

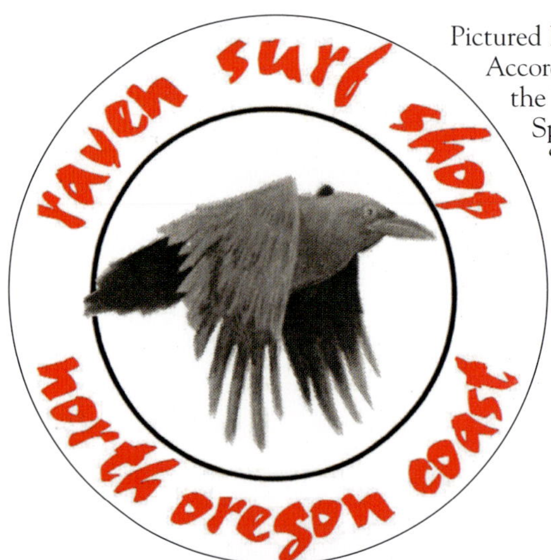

Pictured here is Bill Fackerell's Raven Surf Shop logo. According to Brand Dichter, "Reita Fackerell designed the Raven logo and Bill showed old movies of Art Spence on the wall." Rik Cederstrom explains, "Fackerell started the shop in the Old Fruit Stand south of town in the late 1980s. Raven was a local free spirit. Bill had a factory in Gearhart. He sold many of my boards and was open in 1994 when I left." (Courtesy of David Matthews.)

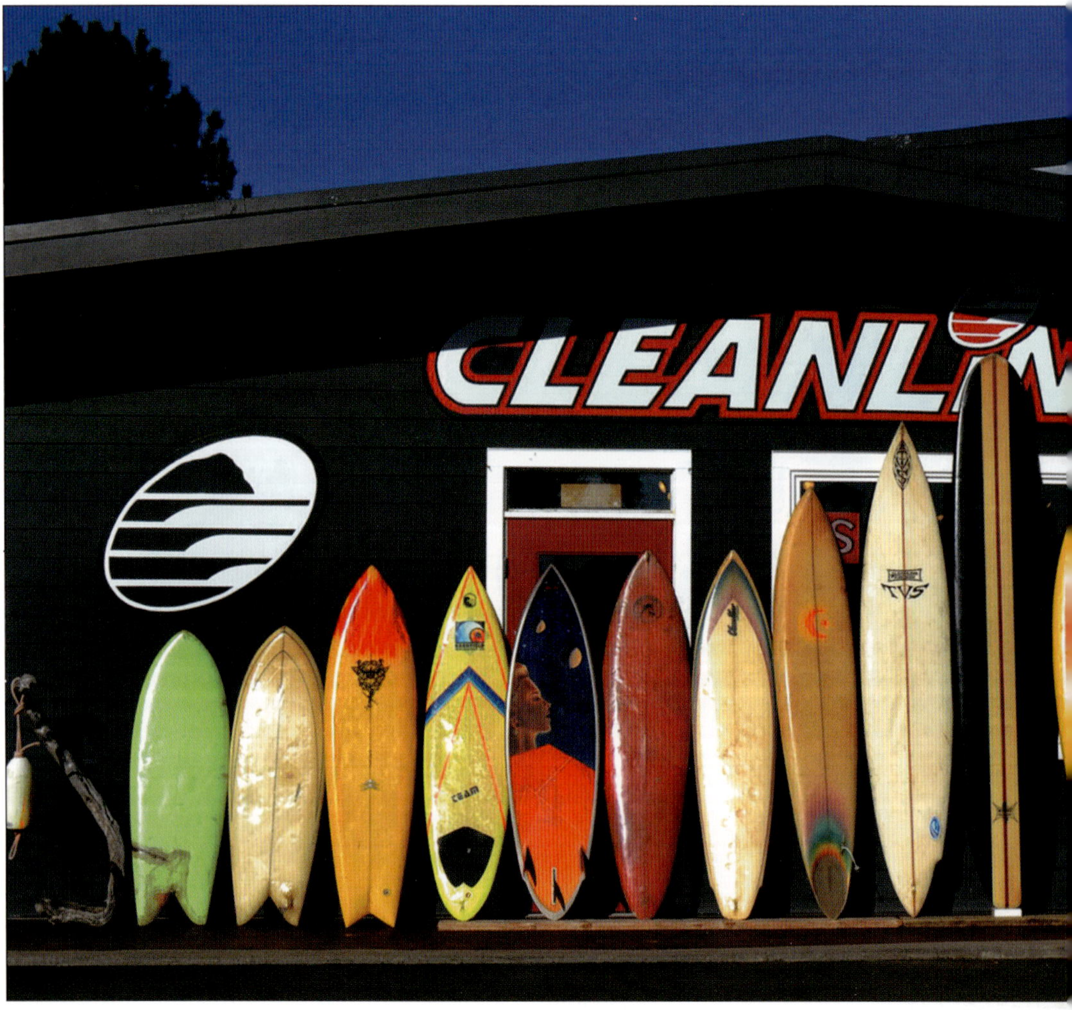

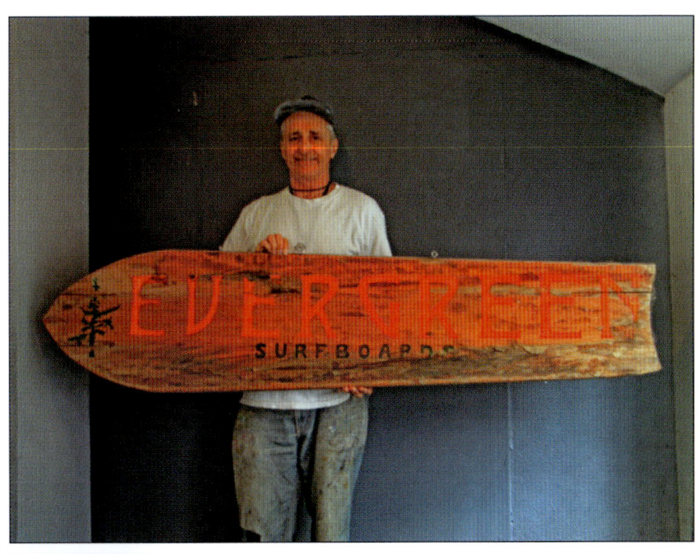

Lanny Shuler is pictured here in his Seaside shop, Shuler Surfboards, in March 2013. Shuler grew up in West Long Beach and recalls, "My dad used resin, fiberglass with his boat and I made skim boards out of his stuff. I was learning how to shape without knowing it, a natural transition back then. I met Art Spence in 1971 and together we formed a business making Evergreen surfboards." (Photograph by Scott Blackman.)

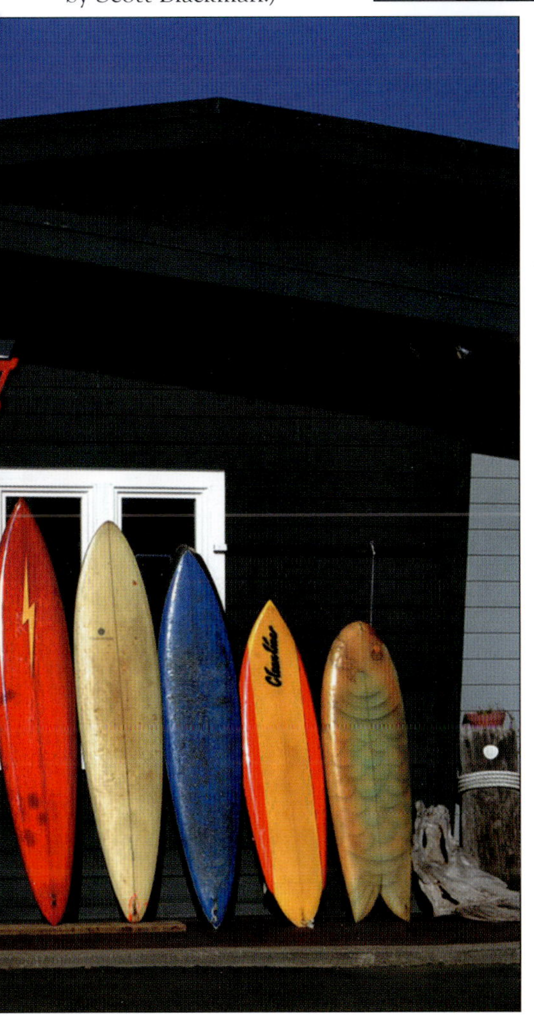

This is a display of historical surfing boards at Seaside's Cleanline Surf Shop. The boards are, from left to right, a Stevie Lis Fish owned by Al Ritter; a Steve Lis five-foot-three knee board with two fins owned by Lexie Hallahan; a six-foot-four twin-fin custom-built by Art Spence for Marc Ward; Josh Gizdavich's six-foot-four Team board custom-built by Bill Barnfield around 1976; custom-built Cleanline surfboard called *Lucy in the Sky with Diamonds*, shaped by Ron Chaloux and airbrushed by Allen Gibbons in 1980, restored by Tom Scott in 2012; late 1960s vintage Tillamook Head Fat Cat single fin with nose and tail leash loop, compliments Tommy Lewis; custom-built early 1980s Cleanline surfboard shaped by Ron Chaloux and airbrushed by Allen Gibbons, glassing by Sandy Barrett; seven-foot-six Free Spirit surfboard owned by Lexie Hallahan; nine-foot asymmetric Big Wave Gun built for Bruce Prator for riding Second Point by Tom Scott, mid-1980s; ten-foot-four Wardy custom-built for Needham Ward from the early to mid-1960s; eight-foot single fin Gun built by Art Spence around 1970; Josh Gizdavich's big surf Gun built by Bill Barnfield in the early 1980s; an early vintage Tillamook Head from the late 1960s; a seven-foot-ten Art Spence Xcalibur, called *Tinkertail*, owned by Lexie Hallahan; custom-built Cleanline for Josh Gizdavich by Ron Chaloux, 1981; classic twin-fin Fish built by Art Spence in the early 1980s, compliments of Andy Toothman. (Courtesy of Josh Gizdavich.)

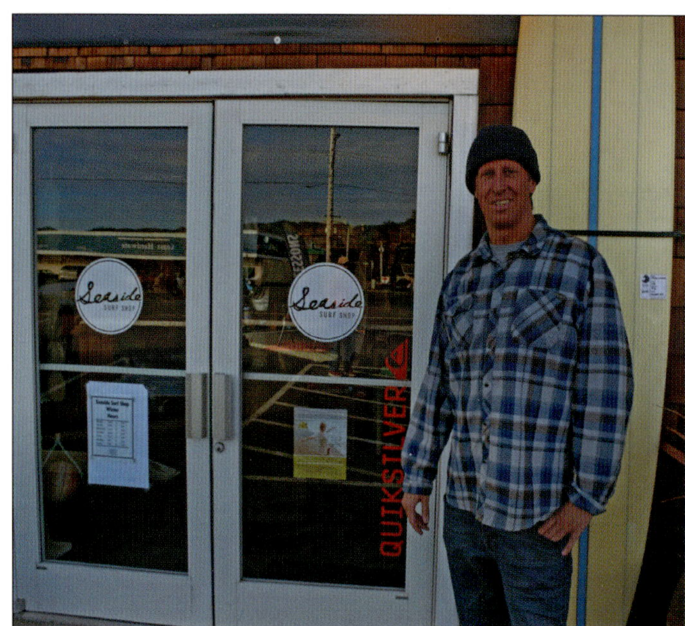

Dennis Smith, owner of Seaside Surf Shop, first surfed the Cove in 1983 at age 15. Two decades later, after working a while at Cleanline, Dennis and Sydney Nelson started Seaside Surf Shop in 2003. Nelson left in 2012. Smith explains, "We wanted it to be core but laid back. We wanted to make surfing more fun, because that's the whole point. We keep our community stoked, and they keep us stoked." (Photograph by Sandy Blackman.)

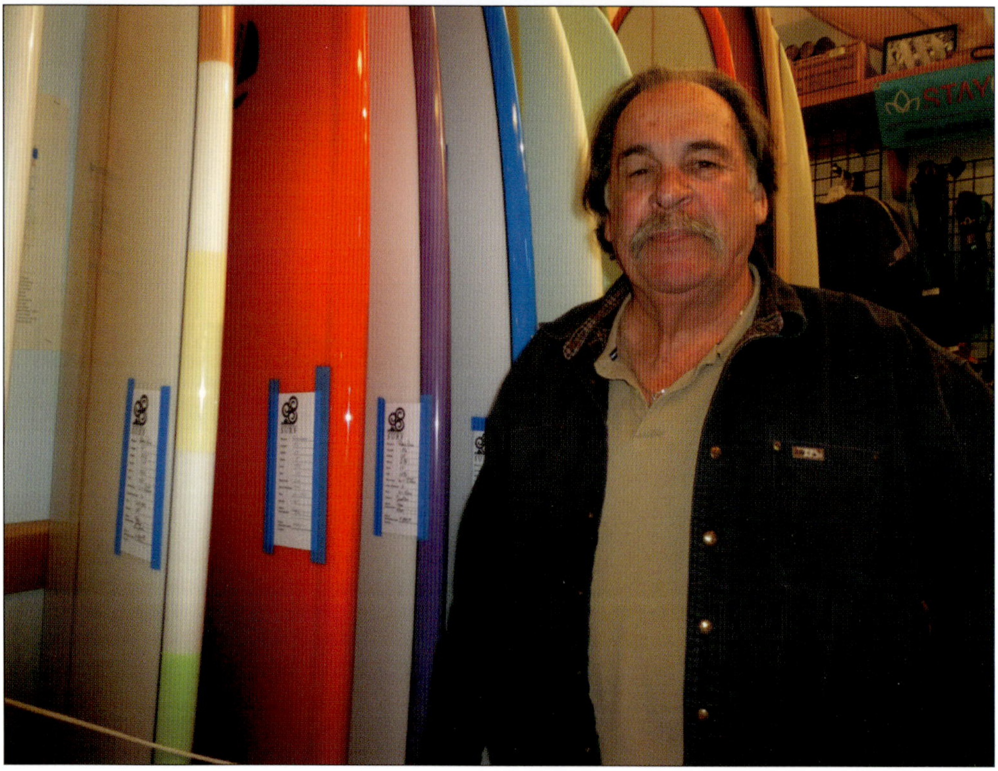

Mark MeKanas, owner of Cannon Beach Surf Shop, is pictured here in winter 2015. "I grew up in San Diego and started surfing in 1960," explains MeKanas. "Discovered Cannon Beach while vacationing here in 1981 and came here lots. Loved it and Indian Beach. We moved here and started selling boards and wetsuits in 1999. I have been in this spot since 2000 and built a new building onto the old building in 2008." (Photograph by Sandy Blackman.)

Josh Gizdavich poses with a Lightning Bolt surfboard outside Seaside Cleanline Surf Shop in 2015. Gisdavich celebrated 35 years in business in August 2015. When he opened in 1980, a newspaper quoted him: "Having a surf shop is a way to make surfing my whole life. Surfing's more than an obsession, more than addiction. It's a religion." Gizdavich believes the Point is one of the Northwest's finest gems. His brothers Needham and Mark Ward were Seaside surfers. (Photograph by Scott Blackman.)

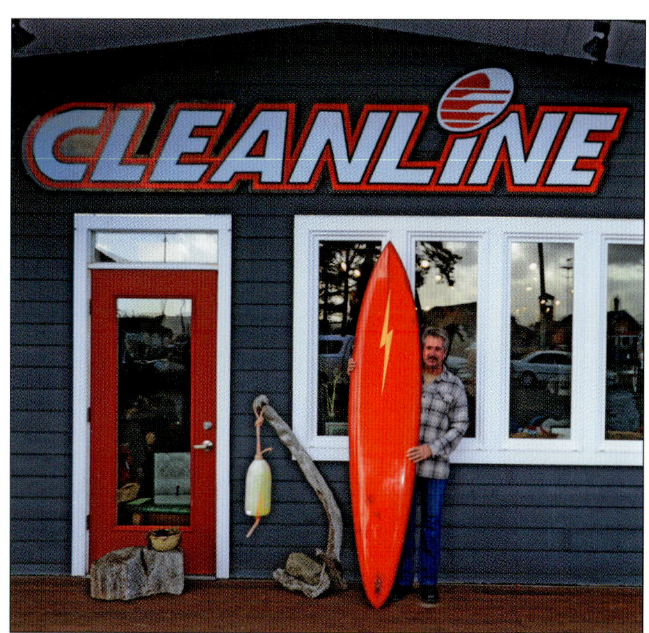

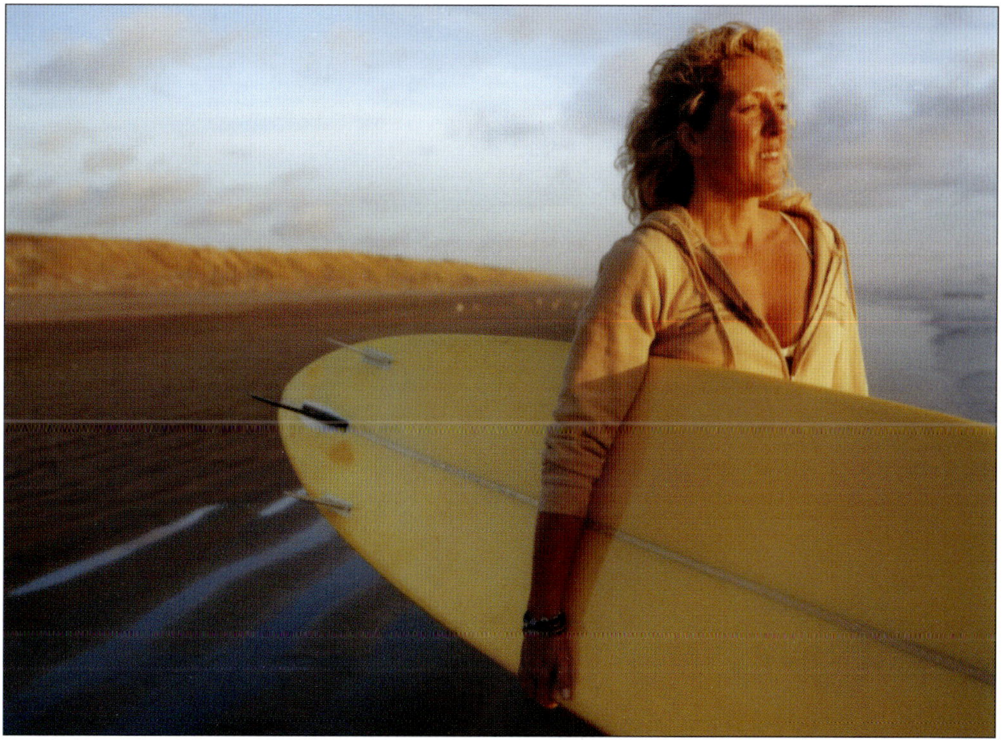

Lexie Hallahan is pictured at South Jetty Beach in 2006. Hallahan began surfing Oregon in 1989, the same year Cleanline's Josh Gizdavich asked her to work for him. "He wanted a woman presence," she recalls. "I was Cleanline Surf's general manager for 16 years." Inspired by an epiphany to create a vibrant women's surfing community here along the Oregon Coast, Hallahan began NW Women's Surf Camps in spring of 2005 and will celebrate the organization's 10th anniversary in 2015. (Courtesy of Lexie Hallahan.)

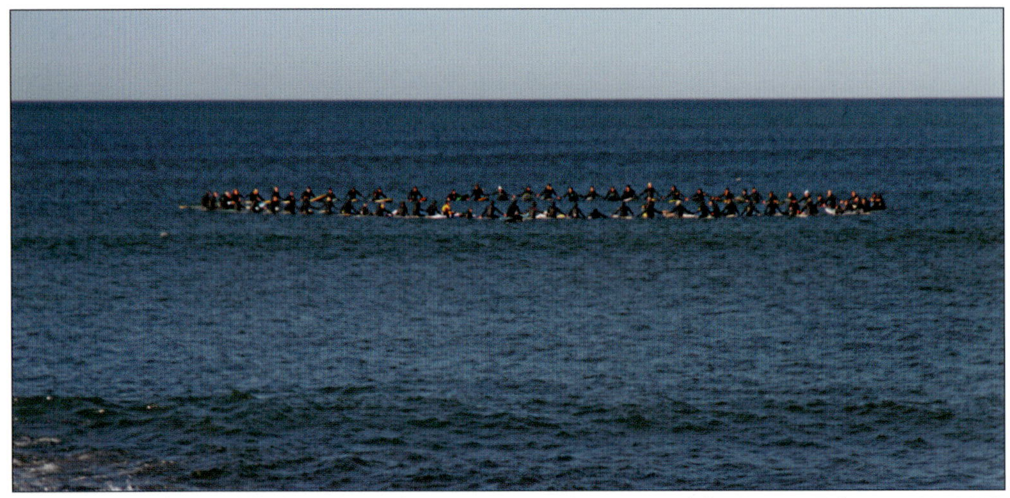

Nearly 100 surfers paddled out for Jack Brown's Seaside Cove Paddle Out on February 22, 2015. According to Lexie Hallahan, "Jack Brown was an extraordinary person, a gem! A great surfing buddy to us all over the nearly 45 years he surfed here along the North Oregon Coast. A mentor who lived his life simply, fully, with love and generosity. Jack was our hero! A man we all respected, loved and adored." (Photograph by Scott Blackman.)

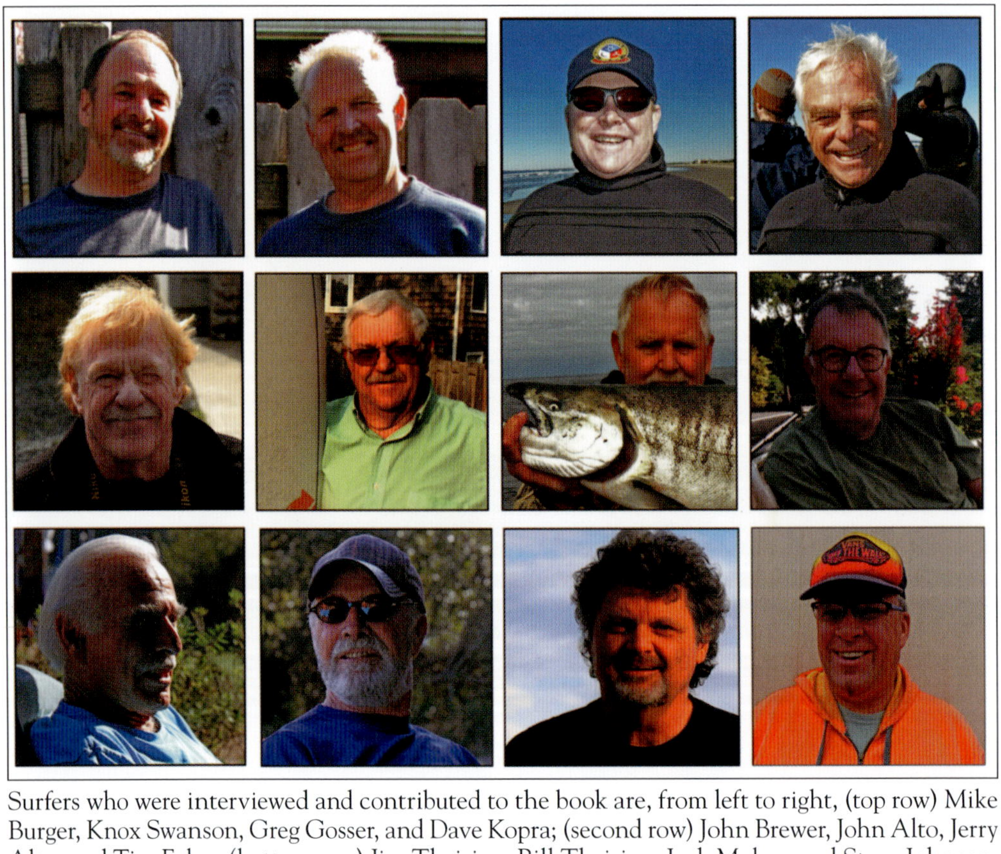

Surfers who were interviewed and contributed to the book are, from left to right, (top row) Mike Burger, Knox Swanson, Greg Gosser, and Dave Kopra; (second row) John Brewer, John Alto, Jerry Alto, and Tim Foley; (bottom row) Jim Theiring, Bill Theiring, Jack Molan, and Steve Johnson. (Authors' collection.)

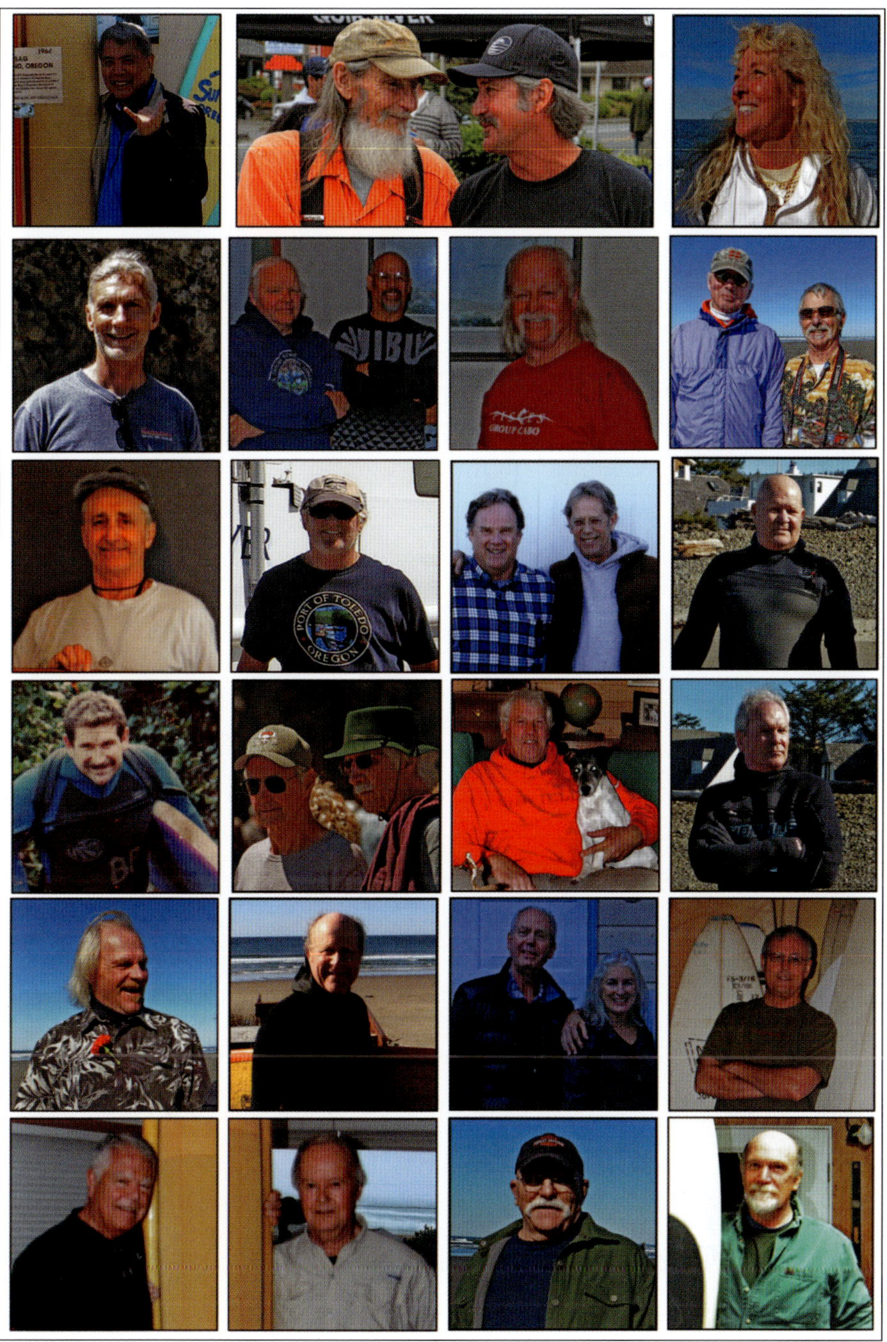

Surfers who were interviewed and contributed to this book are, from left to right, (top row) Jim Sagawa, Dana Williams, Josh Gizdavich, and Lexie Hallahan; (second row) Randy Barna, Max Justice, David Louis, Bill Smith, Peter Lindsey, and Dick Borovicka; (third row) Lanny Shuler, Perry Shoemake, Glenn Kellow, Jay Nichols, and Sandy Barrett; (fourth row) Bruce Prator, Peter de Turk, Dick Wald, Gary Hansen, and Mark Hansen; (fifth row) Dave Kron, Jeff Hull, David Matthews, Dellanne McGregor, and Dan Matthews; (bottom row) George Nelson, Tibby Utter, Dallas Cook, and Brand Dichter. (Authors' collection.)